Strandkanten

DEN TRIVELIGE DELEN AV LYSAKER

WILH. WILHELMSEN
1861 -1994

A Brief History
by Bård Kolltveit
Director, Norwegian Maritime Museum

and

A Fleet List
by Michael Crowdy
of the
World Ship Society

in cooperation with Hans Chr. Bangsmoen
and Per H. Kjærvik

Editor: Hans Chr. Bangsmoen
Vice President, Public Affairs
Wilh. Wilhelmsen

Published by World Ship Society, Kendal LA9 7LT, England
1994

CONTENTS

ISBN 0 905617 73 8

Published by the World Ship Society
28 Natland Road Kendal LA9 7LT England
1994

Printed by William Gibbons & Sons Ltd.,
Wolverhampton, England

FOREWORD BY WILHELM WILHELMSEN

WW is a company with outstanding tradition taking care of more than 132 years of transportation needs for our clients. Through all these years we have been one of the leading shipping companies in our country, thus also playing an important part in the national shipping history. Through four generations of family control we have succeeded to combine personal dedication and professional leadership. At heart of the business are the ships, altogether 394 that have been in our ownership. The wide variety, spanning sail, steamers and diesel vessels leave an endless keelwater of shipping history.

Our heritage carries with it an obligation to keep a complete update of all these ships. The vast variety in size and kind demonstrates the fact that WW have been involved in many different trades. Our core business has nearly always been the liner trades. Liners more than anything else have contributed to our international reputation. They have formed the backbone of our business and given us an understanding of international trade and culture that no other kind of shipping could have done.

Whilst our trading is truly international, our corporate headquarters remain in Oslo. This enables us to combine the finest of Norwegian tradition and knowhow with the international market place. Our continued aim is to be an international maritime organization owned and controlled from Norway.

An enthusiastic team headed by our Director for Information Hans Christian Bangsmoen has done a formidable job in piecing together all the information pertaining to the vessels. Present and future students of ship history will hopefully enjoy this complete record of our company fleet.

Oslo
December 1993

INTRODUCTION AND ACKNOWLEDGEMENTS

It was with great pleasure that, on behalf of the World Ship Society, I accepted Mr. Bangsmøen's invitation to publish this 1994 history of Wilh. Wilhelmsen Limited A/S.

His briefing was a very simple one: "A5 size, and let us make it as good as we can".

It is 33 years since the first W.S.S. history of the firm in 1961 and at that time the fleet had numbered 239 ships. By the time of the 1977 edition it had grown to 324 and the tally has now risen to 394.

Over the years new sources of information have become available and for this edition each ship's history has been re-researched and augmented, and for their help in this work I would like to record my thanks to Barbara Jones and Leslie Spurling of Lloyd's Register, Roy Fenton and Kevin O'Donoghue of the Society's Central Record, together with David Burrell, Rowan Hackman, Bill Schell, A. I. Tandberg, A. J. Tennent and the other correspondents who have provided me with information.

Mr. Bangsmøen has combed the Wilhelmsen photographic archives and photographs not otherwise acknowledged come from that source, as do those by J. Krayenbosch and the Norsk Sjøfartsmuseum. It has been very impressive to realise how extensive are the resources upon which I could call within the World Ship Society — negatives within the Society's own library (acknowledged as W.S.P.L.) and slide collection — and individual members. The aim has been to select the best photograph(s) of each ship and to show the various liveries and appearances. For their help in providing the feast of material I extend thanks to Rudiger von Ancken, Torsten Andreas, Keith Byass, Michael Cassar, Malcolm Cranfield, Alex Duncan, Malcolm Dippy, Ian J. Farquhar, David Finch, Jim Freeman (photographs by the last four named are taken in Australian waters), the proprietors of Fotoflite, Lord Greenway, Bill Harvey, Dietmar Hasenpusch, Fred Hawks, Joachim and Silke Pein, Jim Prentice, Graham Prosser, Table Bay Underway Shipping, Ken Turrell and Ulstein Vaerft and, particularly, my Society Photo Library colleagues Jim McFaul, Cliff Parsons and Tony Smith.

Finally, I would like to place on record what a pleasure it has been to work with my co-author Bard Kolltveit, and my mentor Hans Bangsmøen.

MICHAEL CROWDY

Kendal
December 1993

THE HISTORY OF THE FIRM
1861-1994

Prologue

For thirteen decades, Wilh. Wilhelmsen (WW) has influenced and reflected Norwegian shipping history in all its aspects — local, national and international.

Soon after it was established in 1861, WW had become one of Tønsberg's foremost shipping companies. Some decades later it had gained the position as Norway's largest shipowner, and prior to World War II it provided one of the most extensive networks of regular cargo services in the world.

The simple, yet unmistakeable, flag and funnel markings — respectively a blue ''W'' on a white rectangular flag, and two blue rings on a black funnel — and the almost universal ''T'' nomenclature were, and still are, recognised in any port. Like all companies with a long history, WW has created its own traditions and culture.

Family background

As indicated by its name, Wilh. Wilhelmsen began as a personal firm, and it is still strongly tied to the Wilhelmsen family. But whereas the chronicle of most family-founded Norwegian shipping companies opens with the sailor who, after a sea career from greenhorn to captain, settled ashore as a shipowner, the genesis and early history of WW is business all the way. There was no known grain of salt in the veins of the family fore-father Wilhelm Zachariassen Møller, who emigrated to Norway from North Germany in about 1700, except what he might have inhaled in the Vallø salt works near Tønsberg, where he found employment. His descendants continued to prosper ashore, and his grandson, Abraham Wilhelmsen, a successful tanner, was one of Tønsberg's most prominent citizens in the first half of the 19th century.

Norway's oldest existing town, Tønsberg dates back to the late 9th century A.D., at which time it was the major Viking trading centre in the Vestfold region. The famous Viking ships from Oseberg and Gokstad were discovered in this area. The trading links, taken together with the richness of the soil and the strategic location of the area — at the intersection between the North Sea and the Baltic — suggest a high social status for the local chiefs, and there is no doubt that the people of Tønsberg and Vestfold have been closely involved with the sea and sea trade for a millenium and more.

The debut of Norway in modern maritime history coincided with the transition from mercantilistic protectionism to liberalism and free trade. Once international cross-trade was open to any shipowner who could offer the cheapest transport between two countries, Norway was perfectly positioned to take advantage of the possibilities created by the vast, new export markets.

With some of Norway's wealthiest shipowners amongst its citizens, Tønsberg was right in the midst of these advances in Norwegian seafaring. Partnership in sailing vessels was also a common investment practice for people in other trades and businesses and the tanner Abraham Wilhelmsen had shares in several Tønsberg ships. He was, however, not directly involved in their management, except when he had to take over ships as securities for loans granted to shipowners.

Shipbroker and Shipowner

Abraham Wilhelmsen was, however, fully aware of the favourable prospects for Norwegian shipping. His son, Morten Wilhelm Wilhelmsen, born in 1839, was trained for a professional career related to the sea — but as a ship operator, not a sailor. After the best possible education in his native town, he went first to Oslo, and then to France, to qualify himself as a shipbroker. In 1861 he returned to Tønsberg from Honfleur on board the sailing vessel SOPHIE which was owned, although not managed, by his father. He was now ready to embark upon his chosen career as a shipbroker and shipowner.

At 22, Morten Wilhelm Wilhelmsen was still three years before his full legal age and he could therefore not establish a firm in his own name. A temporary partnership was accordingly arranged with Jens Wilhelm Balchen, of Tønsberg, but the name of the new firm was ''Wilh. Wilhelmsen'' from the very start. It was formally registered on the 1st October 1861, with brokering and ship chandlering as its declared purposes. The Balchen/Wilhelmsen partnership was dissolved when Wilh. Wilhelmsen (his first name Morten was no longer used) legally came of age in 1864. Within a short time he had become Tønsberg's leading broker in the Baltic — France — Spain timber trade. His business was not restricted to local vessels only, but extended also to ships from many other parts of Norway.

When the partnership with Balchen ended, Wilh. Wilhelmsen turned to shipowning as well as shipbroking. While records show that — like his father — he had part ownership in several vessels, including the eighty-year-old barque PETRUS, it is his purchase on 20th May 1865 of a two-sevenths share in the wooden barque MATHILDE of 337 net register, built at St. Malo in France in 1840, that marks the beginning of WW as a shipowning / ship management firm.

MATHILDE was acquired for 7,000 Norwegian speciedaler (Norwegian kroner (NOK) 28,000 in contemporary value). The brokering business continued, but shipowning became more and more important, and the WW sailing ship fleet increased steadily during the next two decades, with one ship added per year on average. Of the nineteen vessels, only three were newbuildings. The others were obtained second-hand, in Norway, or abroad. Some ships were sold, but several were wrecked — incidents all too common in the large, but ageing, fleet of Norwegian sailing ships.

In 1886, twenty-five years after the firm was founded, Wilh. Wilhelmsen was Tønsberg's largest shipowner, controlling 11 ships of 6,165 net register tons. The progress had been steady and deliberate, but also marked by the economic caution that characterized most Norwegian sailing ship owners. Although rich by Norwegian standards, their wealth was in fixed assets, namely the ships themselves, rather than in liquid capital, and money for risk-taking was not readily available in Norwegian financial circles at that time. However, it was fairly easy to obtain wooden sailing ships of well-proven design, built by Norwegian shipwrights from Norwegian timber. Second-hand square-riggers were also available abroad at modest prices.

BERNADOTTE, which joined the fleet in 1885 and was sold in 1898

Foreign shipowners, on the other hand, with better access to risk capital were now investing in more expensive, but also more profitable and evermore competitive, steamships.

Another retarding factor in Norway against the transition from sail to steam was the profound scepticism of sailors, ships' captains and ship owners, whose professional knowledge, experience and insight was inseparably associated with wind power and wooden hulls, not with steam and iron. So far, Norwegian steamships had been used solely on regular mail and passenger services, in order to stimulate domestic and short-sea trades, rather than as profit-makers in their own right. Steamships in general trade were regarded as too expensive and capital-demanding by investors in Norway. But the writing on the wall was becoming ever clearer: The age of sail was nearing its end.

Halfdan Wilhelmsen and the steamships

One person who read this message was Wilh. Wilhelmsen's eldest son, Halfdan, born in 1864. His exceptional business talent was evident from an early age. Having completed his commercial education in Norway with the highest marks, he then lived abroad for two years as a trainee with major shipbroking firms in Hamburg and London. He was convinced of the futility of the battle of the sailing vessels against the steamships and on his return to Tønsberg in 1886 he was determined to specialize as a steamship owner. His father, however, did not see eye to eye with him in this: The earlier success of the firm was due to the sailing ship. True enough, the world economy and the shipping market had weakened during the 1880s, and it was equally true that steamships gave the best profits. Nevertheless, the sailing ships would still yield a profit, even if a modest one, and a bird in the hand was worth two in the bush. His opinion was shared by most of his conservative fellow citizens.

But paternal warnings and local scepticism could not sway Halfdan Wilhelmsen's conviction and he concentrated his will-power and gifts of persuasion on his father and others in order to obtain financial support for the purchase of TALABOT, a steam freighter of 1,800 tons deadweight, built at Newcastle-upon-Tyne in 1881 and named after a French railway engineer. Halfdan Wilhelmsen needed NOK 210,000 to acquire the ship. Response remained slow for a considerable time, until one of the wealthier Tønsberg citizens at last listened to his ideas. This person was not his father, but another prominent shipowner, Gustav Conrad Hansen. Although a sailing ship owner, Hansen had shown ingenuity and a willingness to test new ideas when he converted the hold of his wooden barque LINDESNÆS to carry petroleum in bulk, thus producing the world's first real oil tanker. Now, Hansen signed up for NOK 20,000 in Wilhelmsen's steamship venture. This act of confidence tipped the scales, and before long all the necessary capital was secured: TALABOT was purchased by Wilhelmsen at the end of December 1887.

Those who placed confidence in Halfdan Wilhelmsen's steamship project had no reason to regret their decision. TALABOT showed a profit after one year of NOK 60,000, which exceeded all expectations. In fact, the results and prospects were so good that from their very first steamship purchase the letter "T" was to become synonymous with WW nomenclature. TALABOT was a trailblazer not only in the company's history, she is also recognised as one of the pioneer vessels in the transition from sail to steam in Eastern Norwegian shipping history: Halfdan Wilhelmsen had demonstrated that Norwegian shipowners were fully able to operate steamships at a profit. WW's second steamer, TRANSIT, of 2,000 tons deadweight, was ordered immediately and delivered in May 1889. No fewer than four steamships, of which three were newbuildings, joined the WW fleet that year, and the growth continued.

Halfdan Wilhelmsen was now a permanent member of the firm, and in 1890 he became a full partner, together with his father. Wilh. Wilhelmsen had by now reached his early sixties and the future WW strategy was now unquestionably in the hands of his son. The course was set, with "Full Steam Ahead", both literally and figuratively: W.W. was to be turned into a modern and forceful steamship company, not only by Norwegian, but also by international, standards.

The barque CHIPMAN, WW's last square-rigger, was acquired in 1890, at which time the fleet of Wilhelmsen sailing vessels stood at 13 units. A decade later, only one windjammer, the barque ENTERPRISE, flew the Wilhelmsen flag, and she was sold in 1902. Since 1861, Wilh. Wilhelmsen had managed 29 sailing vessels, and been owner/part owner of a total of 38. On the other hand, WW controlled no fewer than 22 steamships in 1900, and the number grew steadily. Most steamers were newbuildings.

The crew of the sailing vessel **JARLSBERG**, photographed at Cardiff in 1896

Timecharters and big freighters

In the 19th century steamships had primarily been associated with the extension of regular shipping lines but although Halfdan Wilhemsen studied the liner trade most carefully, and even as early as 1903 considered the possibility of a regular trans-Pacific cargo service between the United States West Coast and the Far East, he decided against this idea. He concentrated instead on the development of the tramp trade and timecharters.

The WW freighters were relatively large ships for the time, with an average capacity of 5,000-7,000 tons deadweight. After the initial practice of voyage-to-voyage chartering in the Baltic and North Sea area with the first WW steamers, the larger ships which joined the fleet from 1900 onwards were mainly employed on long timecharters, running between specific ports. Some of these freight contracts had a character which made them difficult to distinguish from regular liner cargo services. A good example is a charter contract with an American steamship company for the transportation of coal from Hampton Roads to Colon in Panama, in connection with the construction of the Panama Canal: four of WW's largest steamships were chartered for up to ten years on this trade. Others were employed for equally long periods in the sugar trade between Cuba and the United States.

During its first quarter century, from 1861 until 1886, WW had managed a total of 23 sailing vessels — an average of almost one additional ship a year. In the 24 years from 1887 to 1911, no less than 56 tramp steamers were added to the fleet, an average of more than two ships annually. Thirteen of these were not actually owned by WW, but by the Danish and Scottish shipowners A. N. Hansen & Co. and Macbeth & Gray. The main reasons for the switch to Norwegian registry and management were that the Plimsoll load line had not yet become compulsory for Norwegian ships, and that a Norwegian crew was synonymous with high skills and relatively low wages. The "foreign" steamers were registered in Norway and formally owned by companies in which WW was a shareholder and manager. The first of these vessels, ST ANDREWS (I), was delivered in 1891 and the thirteenth and last, ST. ANDREWS (II), entered service in 1906 and was sold in 1920.

ST. ANDREWS of 1891   *Norsk Sjøfartsmuseum*

In 1902, the company's administration was moved from Nøtterøy, primarily for tax reasons. In that same year, Halfdan Wilhelmsen's younger brother, Wilhelm Wilhelmsen, began his career at the office, becoming a partner in 1904. Born in 1872, he was the first member of the Wilhelmsen family to have had a sea career, from deck-boy to master. He was always known as "Captain Wilhelmsen" partly as a proud reference to his professional background, and partly to avoid confusion with his name-sake father. Wilh. Wilhemsen senior passed away in 1910. At the time of his death, the WW fleet of steamships was Norway's largest, totalling 160,347 tons deadweight capacity.

WW's first funnel symbol was a rectangle on a black funnel with a white diagonal line on the rectangle separating a light blue upper half from a darker blue lower half. In 1902 the present WW colours were introduced: Two pale blue bands, set close together, on a black funnel. Until the early 1970s another feature would be equally readily associated with the company — the white "waist line" encircling the black hull.

The halcyon days of WW as a tramp shipping company were the decades immediately before and after the turn of the century. In 1911, at its fiftieth anniversary, WW took delivery of two steamships as fitting symbols of a half-century of progress: A nine-year timecharter with an option for a further ten years had been concluded in 1910 with Nova Scotia Coal Company, New Glasgow, for the transportation of ore from Wabana, Newfoundland, to Rotterdam and two ore carriers were ordered in Sunderland for this contract. Of 13,000 tons deadweight capacity each, TELLUS and THEMIS were the world's largest dry cargo ships when delivered.

WW and the Scandinavian overseas liner trade

Some years earlier WW had co-operated with the Oslo-based shipowners and brokers Fearnley & Eger (F & E), to obtain a freight contract from North Norway to the Continent. In addition to a tramp trade with sailing vessels and steamships, F & E had run a regular service between eastern Norway and Bordeaux since the 1870s. It was the first Norwegian shipping line to reach beyond the North Sea. The creation of overseas shipping lines, based on each nation's exports and imports, was a dominant feature in most Western sea-trade before World War I, but whilst tramp shipping was entirely based on international economic liberalism, many nations protected their own regular liner services by government subsidies in various forms in order to ensure control of their imports and exports. ''Trade will follow the flag'' was the motto, and like the colonial empires before them, every industrial nation, large and small, regarded the transportation of merchandise in vessels of its own registry as a stimulant to foreign trade. Subsidies would range from downright financial support to the shipping line to less obvious methods such as generous compensation for the carriage of mail or the transportation of administrative and military personnel, etc.

The fledgling Norwegian industry needed to broaden its foreign markets, and a network of national shipping lines was seen as being necessary in order to obtain a commercial foothold abroad. But state support to the shipping industry would have been completely against the ''free trade'' principle in Norway's economic policy, a principle which was fully shared by most Norwegian shipowners. This conflict between liberalistic principles and the constant shortage of venture capital in Norway gave Norwegian trans-ocean lines a belated start compared to other maritime nations in Europe. Helped by a more advanced industrial base, and a more developed monetary economy, Swedish and Danish shipowners had been active earlier than their Norwegian counterparts in establishing and extending overseas shipping lines. By 1910, the Swedish Rederi AB Transatlantic and the Danish East Asiatic Company (EAC) ran regular services to South Africa and Australia and to the Far East respectively.

Now that the time seemed ripe for the establishment of Norwegian liner services, it was natural for WW and F & E to discuss the joint operation of such services. Fearnley & Eger had operated the Bordeaux service for three decades and were also the Norwegian agents for the Swedish line to South Africa and Australia. WW was not only their business associate in the North Norway-Continent ore trade, it was also Norway's largest shipowning company. The impetus for the discussions was provided by Transatlantic's need for more tonnage to fight off German competition in the Australian trade, and the suggestion of co-operation by the two Norwegian companies was well received by the Swedish company. On Christmas Eve in 1910 WW's THYRA, of 6,200 tons deadweight, left Norway via Gothenburg fully loaded for South Africa and Australia.

The formal agreement between Transatlantic, EAC, WW and F & E was signed on the 23rd January 1911, and under it the Norwegians became entitled to enter the Australian service with three ships and the South African with two. Three purpose-built steamers were ordered for the Australian service, each of about 8,500 tons deadweight and with a speed of 11 knots. A new company was established by WW and F & E in 1911 — ''The Norwegian Africa and Australia Line'' (NAAL). WW was responsible for the maritime management and for homeward sailings and F & E became general agents for the line in Norway, responsible for all outward loading. The dominant outward cargo was lumber, augmented by cement, steel rails, carbide, etc. Homeward sailings were based on whatever fixtures were available in the open market, for example coal from South Africa to India, where a bulk cargo of grain or ore to the U.K./Continent could be obtained. Since NAAL was a joint operation, the "T" nomenclature was discontinued in favour of the names of Norwegian rivers: the s.s. ATNA, of 8,520 deadweight, was handed over in August 1911, followed by TYSLA and RENA in October and November. NAAL also had its own funnel emblem — a combination of WW's two blue bands and F & E's Maltese Cross.

The Scandinavian co-operation gave NAAL a flying start and the combined export volume of the three Scandinavian countries provided a sufficient freight basis for a profitable operation. WW and F & E did, in fact, apply for a subsidy from the Norwegian government but the application was withdrawn when the first voyage showed promising results. 1912, the first full year of operation, gave NAAL's shareholders a six per cent dividend. Extensions of NAAL's services were soon to follow and India, the Straits, China and Japan were included in the sailing lists in 1913 and 1914. An extension of the Australia line to Indonesia (Java) was established in 1915.

Equally important to the success was the fact that the German lines were forced to realise the competitive strength of the concerted Scandinavian companies and accept their membership of the Australian freight conference Hitherto, the Germans had regarded Scandinavia as part of their sphere of interest in Europe, but henceforth they had to limit their Scandinavian sailings to one every sixth week; for their part, the Scandinavian lines were not permitted to load in Continental ports.

Whereas NAAL could stand on its own financial legs, a considerable state subsidy had been needed to launch Norway's first transatlantic shipping line, the Norway-Mexico Gulf Line (NMGL), founded in 1908 by the shipowner G. M. Bryde. Despite the generous subvention, the freight volume between Norway and the Gulf was too small to sustain the profitable operation of NMGL's two 5,800 ton deadweight purpose-built steamers, TEXAS and NORUEGA. Accordingly, an agreement was made in 1912 with the Swedish shipowner Dan Broström, and TEXAS was acquired by Broström's newly-established Swedish American Mexico Line when Bryde took delivery of his third ship, MEXICANO. The agreement gave NMGL full access to the Swedish export and import market and revenues increased, but NMGL was still in need of investment capital for further tonnage expansion.

Bryde approached Halfdan Wilhelmsen as a possible co-investor, but during the negotiations a full take-over by WW and F & E became an increasingly realistic alternative. In May 1913 agreement was reached, whereby the two companies would provide the necessary capital infusion in to NMGL, while Bryde would transfer sufficient shares to give them a controlling interest. The actual take-over was concluded on 1st January 1914. At the outbreak of World War I, WW and F & E were thus operating a Norwegian network of overseas liner services which extended from Mexico in the west to Japan in the east and from Scandinavia in the north to Australia in the south.

Pioneers in the tanker trade
It must be remembered, however, that WW was at that time as much a tramp ship owner as a liner operator. Even more importantly, the company was to play a leading, if brief, role in the pioneering years of the Norwegian tanker trade. In 1912 Halfdan Wilhelmsen made a bold decision to combine newbuildings / contracts with the still embryonic, but growing, demand for the transportation of oil from America to Europe. A/S Tankfart I was founded, followed by A/S Tankfart II and III in 1913, with a total share capital of about 8 million NOK. Four 10,000 ton deadweight steam tankers were ordered in the U.K. for delivery in 1913-1914. The average cost was in the region of £100,000, about twice the cost of a dry cargo vessel of equal size. The tanker

14

investment was, indeed, staggering by Norwegian standards of the time. However, all four of the tankers were prudently secured on 10-year timecharters to American oil companies, and new orders followed. The first tanker, SAN JOAQUIN, of 10,360 tons deadweight, was handed over in Sunderland in December 1913. By 1918, WW had taken delivery of no less than ten oil carriers, representing 92% of Norway's entire tanker fleet at the end of World War I.

SAN JOAQUIN, the first Wilhelmsen tanker

WW and World War I

At the outbreak of hostilities in 1914, WW's tramps and tankers had been fixed on timecharters of between four and ten years. They could not instantly profit from the steep rate increases in the spot market, although some contracts were renegotiated after a relatively short time, but they were hit in full by the rising costs. In addition to the oil carriers, WW had placed orders for five dry cargo vessels with British yards by the end of 1914. Tankers and freighters alike were all requisitioned by the British Government on completion and were placed under the registry and management of British shipping companies for the duration of the war.

The liner trade, on the other hand, was to benefit immediately from the war, partly because of the sudden disappearance from the seas of all the German lines, and partly because of the redeployment of Allied liner tonnage for the war effort. The demand for space on all remaining (neutral) lines grew enormously and whatever tonnage was available was chartered in. The war also gave Wilh. Wilhelmsen its first access to the international cross-trade liner market. The forced absence of British lines from the trade between the still neutral United States of America and South America opened this market to other neutral shipowners, and WW seized the opportunity and established Wilhelmsen Steamship Lines in November 1916, offering regular sailings between the United States East Coast and Brazil / River Plate. After a break caused by the entry into the war of the United States, the line was reopened in August 1918.

But war profits had their price. The first Norwegian shipping casualty of World War I was a WW ship—TYSLA, which was mined on the 7th August 1914 and three of her crew were killed. A total of six WW tramp ships, five cargo liners and one oil tanker became war losses. But the WW fleet, reckoned in terms of tonnage, was nevertheless larger at the end of the war than it had been at the beginning—41 vessels totalling 298,974 tons deadweight, as against 43 ships of 285,044 deadweight in 1914. The composition of the fleet in 1918 also reflected new trends both in Norwegian and WW shipping policy: the number of tramp steamers had been halved, while the liner and tanker fleet had practically been doubled.

The American-built **BESSA** in Australian waters   *Ian J. Farquhar*

During the war, Oslo had consolidated its position as Scandinavia's maritime metropolis: new shipping and shipbroking companies were established, and many shipowners from smaller coastal towns and communities in Eastern Norway now found it more practical and convenient to re-locate their headquarters in the capital city. Thus, WW transferred the administrative headquarters from Ørsnæs to Oslo in 1917, although a branch office was still retained in Ørsnæs, and Tønsberg continued as the port of registry for the company's ever-growing fleet. The close links with Vestfold county were also evident in the recruitment of WW's sea-going personnel. Company pride and loyalty were very strong, even if WW had gained a reputation for demanding full yield for wages earned. The lampoon "WW — black and blue, nothing to eat and plenty to do" was probably quoted more by people outside the company than by those inside, although no one could blame a hard-working WW seaman or oiler who muttered it between clenched teeth while working under the watchful eye (but out of hearing range) of a mate or engineer. The spotless "Black Tie" appearance of a Wilhelmsen ship did not come of itself.

Halfdan Wilhelmsen had good reason to be satisfied with his achievements at the beginning of the 1920s. Despite all setbacks, the company had emerged from the war with a stronger fleet than in 1914. Profits from war freights, and war loss insurance payments, were wisely ploughed into reserve

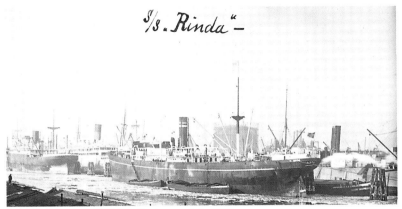

The British war-built **RINDA** at Hamburg early in 1927

16

funds rather than expensive newbuilding contracts in a rising market, or excessive share dividends. WW thus came financially unscathed through the world depression of the early 1920s. Many over-expansive and over-optimistic shipowners had continued to order new ships at ever higher prices during the immediate post-war boom, with delivery four or even five years ahead. When they received these modern but expensive, and idle, ships from the equally debt-ridden shipyards—who were pressing for payment in order to stave off banks and other financial institutions in the same desperate situation—economic disaster was inevitable.

By adhering to their declared principle of never running into debt and always having cash ready to pay for new ships, WW, in contrast, could take full advantage of this situation. New ships and newbuilding contracts were obtainable at rock-bottom prices, leaving the company with no debt and a first-class, highly competitive fleet when the shipping market picked up later in the decade.

WW and the inter-war years: "For Speed and Service"
WW assumed full control over NAAL and NMGL in 1920, when Fearnley and Eger were bought out. The existing liners retained their original names, but they were all repainted in full WW livery. From now on, the trade name "Wilhelmsen Lines" replaced the earlier individual line names, and new additions to the liner fleet were named in accordance with the company's established "T" nomenclature.

MIRLO   *Norsk Sjøfartsmuseum*

MIRLO, of 1922, was the eleventh WW oil tanker delivered in a decade. It was also the last to enter the fleet for almost three decades. The post-war depression and an anticipated over-tonnaged market resulting from the many tankers built and ordered by the oil companies themselves in the preceding decade, made this change in policy seem logical at the time. Whether, with the benefit of hindsight, everyone would subscribe to its wisdom is another question. After World War I WW also decided upon another deliberate strategic change, namely to reduce their engagement in tramp operations to an absolute minimum. The complete merger of NMGL's assets into NAAL in 1927 is another indication of WW's deliberate plan: to be in the top league of the world's liner operators, at the expense of all other previous activities—tramp as well as tanker operation.

The early 1920s were difficult years for shipping, industry and the financial market. Although WW was less affected that most others, steady leadership was essential. Halfdan Wilhelmsen passed away after a brief illness in 1923, only 59 years old. It was a bad shock, but the tiller remained in another firm hand — that of his younger brother and co-partner since 1904, Captain Wilhelm Wilhelmsen. Kaare Schøning, Attorney at the Supreme Court of Appeal, was made a partner in 1927. When Halfdan Wilhelmsen's son Willie decided not to join the family firm, Niels Werring, married to Halfdan's daughter Else, took over the interests of his late father-in-law and joined the firm as a partner in 1930. The Captain's son, Tom Wilhelmsen joined the family firm as a partner in 1938.

The noticeable trend during Halfdan Wilhelmsen's final years as senior partner, further to reduce the firm's involvement in tramp shipping, was vigorously pursued by his brother. Captain Wilhelm Wilhelmsen had one declared aim: to cultivate WW into being one of the largest and most prestigious operators of cargo lines in the world. Whereas tramp and tanker operations might yield high profits during booms, such trades were also more exposed in periods of depression. Cargo lines, by contrast, were less affected by variations in the world economy. Although they could not take full advantage of hectic boom periods, they could navigate with greater steadiness in times of depression.

The development of WW to near-perfection as a liner company under its world-renowned motto ''For Speed and Safety'' was, in the Captain's opinion, the safest and most beneficial policy for each and everyone in the long run. With his seafaring background, there is good reason to add an element of personal pride and ambition: ''Style and elegance'' is more associated with cargo lines than with any other sector of overseas freighter trade.

As previously stated, WW was financially well-positioned in the 1920s to realise Captain Wilhelmsen's vision of a highly specialised, global shipping line in the international top class. Shipyards were pining for new contracts. Scandinavian liner operators were also able to gain a competitive advantage over shipping lines in other countries by a deliberate commitment to diesel propulsion. Although more complicated than a steam engine, the diesel motor was superior in fuel consumption and economy of space. Motor ships had more remunerative cubic capacity, and could cover longer distances without refuelling, than steamships of similar dimensions.

WW pursued the motor ship policy deliberately and vigorously. The last new-built steam freighter, TANA, was delivered in 1921, and by then the company's first motor ship, AMERICA, had already been completed by Akers Mek. Verksted, Oslo, for the Mexico Gulf service. No fewer than eleven diesel-powered cargo liners were added to the fleet in the next four years, from Danish and German yards. Except for their machinery, however, these vessels were basically replicas of the cargo liners delivered prior to 1914: 6,000-7,000 tons deadweight capacity, and 10-12 knots speed.

It will be remembered that the pre-1914 Scandinavian lines were primarily based on the Scandinavian export trade. Return voyages were frequently arranged as spot fixtures, because long-term homeward freight contracts for basic cargoes to Scandinavia were hard to obtain. There existed, however, a possibility for profitable voyages from Australia to Europe, provided that quick passages could be guaranteed, namely, the valuable and prestigious wool trade. WW seized the opportunity, and in 1925-26 the company took

The steamship **TANA** at Hamburg in 1921 *Ambrose Greenway collection*

delivery of a series of 9,500 tons deadweight motor liners with more powerful machinery and higher speed—13 knots: TOURCOING, TOURAINE and TRIANON. The French names were directly related to the Australian wool trade, which entailed considerable shipments to France. On her maiden voyage home in 1925, TOURCOING completed the voyage Sydney—Dunkirk in 39 days. She was hailed as the year's winner of the wool race, but was beaten successively in the following years—by other WW liners.

The "wool-racer" **TOURCOING** *Ian J. Farquhar*

19

WW's cross-trade liner operation outside Scandinavia began when Wilhelmsen Steamship Lines started sailings between the United States and Brazil / River Plate in 1917. Resumed in 1918, when requisitioned ships were returned to WW, the line met heavy competition when the pre-war lines returned to the trade, but these challenges were overcome and new WW lines were added. For a period the line was extended into a U.S.—South America—Northern Europe triangular service, but when Argentina's meat exports declined, the sailings to Europe were abandoned in 1929. The Wilhelmsen Steamship Lines service between New York and South America continued to operate until 1947.

Halfdan Wilhelmsen had contemplated a trans-Pacific cargo service between the U.S. West Coast and the Far East as early as the turn of the century, but at that time the unreliable cargo supplies and the risk of competition from the larger, established American and Japanese liner companies had made him give up the idea. The United States—Far East service became a reality, however, in November 1927. An agreement was made with Barber Steamship Company, of New York, for WW to provide tonnage for Barber's regular service between the New York area and the Far East, in co-operation with the Liverpool firm, James Chambers & Company.

TAI PING YANG at No. 12 Pyrmont, Sydney, N.S.W., 3.7.1954   *David Finch*

To ensure a fortnightly service, each company was to have five ships available. The sailings began in January 1928 with existing tonnage, but within two years five new-built WW vessels had entered the Barber service, as part of a vast new building programme between 1929 and 1930, comprising ten almost identical motor liners. Four were built by Deutsche Werke in Kiel, another four by Kockums Mek. Verkstad in Malmö and two units by Burmeister & Wain in Copenhagen. Of similar hull dimensions and with a speed of 14.5 knots, their carrying capacity would range between 9,800 and 12,400 tons deadweight, depending on open/closed shelterdeck arrangement. The vessels were specially adapted for transportation of vegetable oil and reefer cargo. Five of the ships were given Chinese names, beginning with the prefix "Tai". The first in the series, TAI YANG, was delivered from Deutsche Werke in March 1929, while TROJA, the tenth and final unit, was handed over from Burmeister & Wain in November 1930.

When TAI YANG entered service in 1929, regular sailings from the Far East to New York were also established, under the trade name Barber-Wilhelmsen Line. The ships sported Barber's funnel emblem on the outward, and the blue WW rings on the homeward leg of what was virtually a round-the-world service.

TROJA

Despite their imposing appearance, the Wilhelmsen liners of the 1920s were characterised by a rather boxy, vertical exterior. A transition to a more streamlined design became apparent in the WW fleet during the 1930s. It began in 1933 with the Dutch-built "wool racers" TRICOLOR and TARN, of 10,000 tons deadweight, and a 16.5 knot service speed. Their slanting prow, sharper hull lines and rounded bridge front made them prototypes for the next two decades. The "split superstructure" profile, with a cargo hatch situated between the bridge and the machinery deckhouse, was a common

TARN   *J. Y. Freeman*

21

feature of most dry-cargo ships of the first half of the 20th century. But many would also regard this as a "classic Wilhelmsen liner" feature, as inseparable from a WW ship as the white line, the blue rings and the "T" name. It is probably true that no other major shipping line used this deckhouse arrangement so consistently and for such a long time. The last "split superstructure" WW liner was delivered as late as 1954.

Between 1920 and 1940 WW took delivery of no less than 59 newly-built cargo liners, representing a total investment of 204 million pre-war Norwegian kroner — the equivalent of about £10 million. This tremendous investment was achieved without any debt whatsoever being incurred. Every penny was fully financed and paid for by the owner. WW had thus further consolidated its position throughout the 20th century as Norway's largest shipping company. But the composition of the fleet was very different from that of other major shipowners. Although there were other substantial liner operators, the diesel-powered tanker dominated the total picture of Norway's merchant fleet at the outbreak of World War II. Apart from the ships owned by the oil companies themselves, the Norwegian tanker fleet was the world's largest and most modern. With only one steam powered oil tanker, and that 18 years old, WW was conspicuously atypical in this picture. Captain Wilhelmsen's strict and undeviating cargo liner policy had seen the company well and safely through the tumultuous inter-war years, including the depression after the Wall Street crash in 1929. It must be mentioned, however, that in 1933, no fewer than 15 Wilhelmsen ships were lying idle in Oslo's roadstead. Five of these were oil tankers.

Still, it was no great secret that not everyone in the WW management agreed with the Captain's policy of putting all eggs in one basket. Niels Werring had been very vocal in his arguments for a greater commitment to the oil trade, not least after the recovery of the tanker market from the mid 1930s. As senior partner, however, Captain Wilhelmsen had the last word, and he was adamant about concentrating entirely on the liner business. This was a trade the company knew.

WW, World War II and the post-war years

Twenty-six of WW's 54 ships were lost, and 52 WW sailors gave their lives, during World War II. 44 WW vessels served the Allied cause under the auspices of the exiled Norwegian government through Nortraship, with headquarters in London and New York. The most modern cargo liners continued on regular services, whilst the older ships were chartered to the

The sunken remains of **TALABOT** at Malta, 14.10.1946   *Michael Cassar*

22

British Ministry of War Transport. Of the ten ships trapped in German-controlled waters in 1940, four were requisitioned as German naval auxiliary cruisers, while three were chartered to the Norwegian Shipping Directorate to bring supplies from the Continent to Norway.

WW's paramount task at the end of the war in 1945 was to rebuild and consolidate the pre-war liner services and to fill the gap caused by the forced withdrawal from the scene of German and Japanese lines. WW also opened new liner services in 1946-47: New York—West Africa, Europe—New Zealand, and Europe—Iranian Gulf. The West Africa line was a result of co-operation between Barber, WW, Fearnley & Eger and A.F. Klaveness. After the WW / F & E liner partnership ended in 1920, Fearnley & Eger and A.F. Klaveness had developed a close co-operation in liner service between the United States and the Far East. After the war, an increasingly close contact was developed between WW, F & E and Klaveness. Thus the United States—Far East service of Barber Lines was, from 1948, maintained by 12 sailings per year by WW, and 12 sailings made jointly by Fearnley & Eger and A.F. Klaveness.

An ambitious post-war newbuilding programme was put into effect immediately. Already by 1946, 18 motor liners had been ordered, and the first newbuilding—TALABOT (III)—was handed over in November that same year. This order had been placed during the war, officially for the account

The new **TALABOT** on trials in 11.1946. Note the Swedish ensign and builders' houseflag

of Broström, hence the early delivery. It says a lot about the deep mutual trust, understanding and cooperation between the Scandinavian liner operators, that the arrangement for this order in Sweden was based entirely upon an oral agreement between Captain Wilhelmsen and Dan-Axel Broström. Although she was basically a repetition of her immediate pre-war sisters, TALABOT cost nearly three times as much—NOK 9.25 million, against 3.5 million. In the fifteen years from 1946 to 1961, when WW celebrated its 100th anniversary, a total of 52 cargo liners joined the fleet. With only a few exceptions all were newbuildings.

23

The newly-built **TRITON** loading chrome ore at Masinloc, Philippine Islands, 22.9.1948

In 1961 WW owned 72 ships totalling 846,000 tons deadweight. The post-war newbuilding programme had so far represented an investment of 1.14 billion NOK, or about £55 million. The cargo liner fleet counted 63 vessels of 626,000 deadweight — a clear indication that WW had regained its position as one of the world's foremost cargo line operators. More interesting, though, is the fact that the fleet also included nine tankers totalling 217,000 deadweight. Niels Werring's persistent arguments had won through at last. Captain Wilhelmsen had also accepted that cash payment in full for newbuildings was irrevocably a feature of the past. Financing had to be obtained from external sources, and there was no doubt that the current tanker rates would secure a far quicker repayment of a loan on an oil tanker than on a cargo liner.

A typical break-bulk cargo being loaded

24

TARTAR   *Fotoflite incorporating Skyfotos*

TARTAR, the first WW oil tanker for almost three decades, was ordered in 1948 and delivered in 1951. She was fixed for five years to a Panamanian oil company, at a rate which enabled the investment to be redeemed in just three years and a half. A second tanker, TUAREG, of 1953, was also secured on a five-year timecharter. Of just over 16,000 tons deadweight capacity, these modest-sized tankers were joined by gradually larger additions. TOSCANA, delivered in 1961, measured 38,450 tons deadweight. In 1956-57, after the first Suez crisis, the seven WW tankers showed a bigger profit than the fifty-two cargo liners combined.

TOSCANA when she had an orange hull

Captain Wilh. Wilhelmsen died in 1955, at the age of 83, having been a member of the firm for 51 years, 32 as its senior partner. Kaare Schøning retired in 1957 after 30 years as partner. Niels Werring jr, son of Werring senior, became a partner in 1958, whilst Tom Wilhelmsen's son, Wilhelm Wilhelmsen, became a partner in 1963.

TROUBADOUR at Hamburg

"Never change a winning concept". Apart from increased speed and certain technical improvements, cargo liners in general, and WW liners in particular, had followed the same basic general arrangement since the inter-war period. The first visual evidence of change was the abandoning of the "split superstructure" in favour of a compact midship deckhouse from 1954 onwards, initiated by the m.v. TROUBADOUR. In 1957, TEMERAIRE was delivered, the first of seven exceptionally handsome 10,000 deadweight, 18 knot, cargo liners for the United States—Far East service, built by Deutsche

The Deutsche Werft-built **TAI PING** at New York

Werft and Charles Connell. However, despite their elegant appearance and high speed, they were still representatives of the past rather than the future. Loading gear was traditional, and the machinery still occupied the most remunerative cubic space on board.

Flexibility and joint operations

A more radical step was taken with the delivery of TRICOLOR (V) in January 1960 — the first WW cargo liner in a series of six with machinery and accommodation situated right aft, and with deck cranes in addition to the conventional derricks for more efficient cargo handling. Improved efficiency was sought, and obtained, through higher speed and shortened stays in port.

TØNSBERG, the third of the "Tricolor" class   *W.S.P.L.*

During the latter part of the 1960s a close co-operation was established between WW and its Swedish liner consorts, Transatlantic and Broström, for the construction of still more advanced ships for the Australian and Far Eastern trade. The so-called "Scandia" ships were the outcome: "Open ships", with twin hatches and deck cranes, and with a service speed of 19 knots. A dozen Scandia ships were delivered from Swedish yards, four of which were for WW. The first, TORRENS (II), was completed in 1967.

TORRENS   *W.S.P.L slide collection*

27

The "Scandia" ship **TAIMYR** at Hong Kong

Furthermore, four slightly larger and faster Scandia ship versions, headed by TALABOT (IV), were built in Japan that same year. These four 15,600 tons deadweight, 21.5 knot racehorses represented the ultimate in conventional cargo liner design by WW. TAIMYR, of 1968, completed the quartet and was also the last cargo liner to enter service in the familiar "black tie" livery of the Wilh. Wilhelmsen fleet. From now on, new colours would characterize the Wilh. Wilhelmsen fleet, whether dry cargo, tank or anything else. And although a series of six Japanese-built, 21,000 deadweight multi-purpose carriers were added to the fleet in 1977, it is fitting to close the era of the speedy, elegant and sophisticated, yet conventional, cargo liner in the Wilhelmsen fleet with these four thorough-breds.

The growing Scandinavian / European liner co-operation was also demonstrated in an even more concerted marketing of the Scandinavian — Far East services. Begun in 1966 by WW and Broström's Swedish East Asiatic Company as Seaco-Wilhelmsen Line, the co-operation was extended to include the Danish East Asiatic Company in 1969 under the joint banner of "Scanservice", which was further expanded into "Scandutch" when Dutch and French operators became partners in 1972 and 1973. A common houseflag was introduced, but each partner retained its individual funnel symbol.

A major event in the ScanDutch co-operation was the introduction of fast, purpose-built container vessels. This resulted in the building of the largest and most sophisticated WW vessel so far. In November 1972, the m.v. TOYAMA was completed, one of the world's largest and fastest pure container carriers at that time, with a capacity for 2,200 standard containers and a service speed of 27.7 knots. Her maximum speed, in excess of 30 knots, placed the TOYAMA in the Blue Riband category. Although lengthened in 1984 to increase her container capacity, she nevertheless remained a lonely bird in the WW family.

During the last two decades, WW's engagement in overseas liner services has been dominated by the commitment to combined container / ro-ro operation. Today's WW cargo liners are characterized by the angled stern door / loading ramp which makes them independent of ferry slips for loading and discharge. The ro-ro concept was developed jointly by WW, Transatlantic

28

The container ship **TOYAMA** alongside a container berth

and EAC in the Australian trade. Five ro-ro sister ships, with a service speed of 21.5 knots and with capacity for more than 1,300 standard containers, or any kind of unitized cargo, entered service between 1972 and 1973. Three were built for WW, and the first, TRICOLOR (VI) was handed over in 1972. Sporting an orange-red hull and discarding individual funnel symbols for a diagonal in the same colour on a white funnel, the new service was marketed as "ScanAustral" and later as "ScanCarriers".

The ro-ro **TRICOLOR** in ScanAustral livery at Sydney, 19.3.1977   *J. Y. Freeman*

Ever closer co-operation had also characterized the United States—Far East services. In 1969, Wilh. Wilhelmsen, Fearnley & Eger and A.F. Klaveness came together and established Barber Lines A/S, which co-ordinated their previously individual services from the United States to the Far East, as well as to West Africa. Exterior beauty and company individualism were sacrificed for easier maintenance and a new, common image. The former grey and black hulls and white upperworks gave way to orange and pale green, and two vertical orange stripes replaced each company's emblem on the funnels. For

TENNESSEE in the new livery   *Michael Cassar*

a period, orange and green was universal on the entire WW fleet, until white deckhouses were reinstated.

In 1975, Fearnley & Eger and A.F. Klaveness decided to abandon the liner trade altogether. WW acquired their interests and thus assumed full ownership of Barber Lines A/S. In that same year a co-operation was established with the Blue Funnel Line in Liverpool and Broström's Swedish East Asiatic Company for a new liner pool, named Barber Blue Sea Line. So far, these services had been performed by conventional cargo liners, somewhat rebuilt to accommodate unit loads and containers in limited quantities. New, cellular, midship sections had been added, and side doors

TIRRANNA, one of the rebuilt cargo liners   *W.S.P.L.*

BARBER TOBA leaving Hamburg, 27.2.1988   *Joachim Pein*

and flush 'tweendeck hatches had been introduced to facilitate forklift and wheeled cargo handling on board. The success of the multi-purpose ro-ro ships in the Australian / New Zealand trade had paved the way for similar flexible ships for the United States—Far East trade as well, in face of the growing competition from operators of pure container vessels. Five ro-ro / container vessels, the world's largest of their kind till then, were ordered in Japan and Norway. BARBER TOBA entered service in early 1979. Two even bigger units, BARBER TAMPA and BARBER TEXAS, were added to Barber Blue Sea in 1984.

Cargo being loaded aboard **TAMPA** shortly after she had been renamed in 1989

31

The Mexico Gulf Line had been discontinued since 1971, together with the service to Indonesia. A foothold in the Latin American liner trade was regained temporarily by WW in 1980, with the purchase of the remaining Norwegian interests in the Norwegian South American Line (SAL), serving Scandinavia—Brazil—River Plate jointly with the Swedish Johnson Line. It was the final WW service operated solely by conventional cargo liners, and the Mitsui-built TAIKO thus ended the long line of WW cargo liners which had called regularly at Oslo. The other services turned round in Gothenburg or in Continental ports. Ro-ro vessels were introduced to SAL in 1985 when the Johnson Line and WW pooled their interests with Danish and Finnish partners to establish RoSa Line. All existing conventional tonnage was replaced by two new-built ro-ro ships, of which ROSA TUCANO was owned by WW.

TURCOMAN of 1954 at the Shell Terminal, Gore Bay, Sydney, 4.5.1957   *David Finch*

As previously noted, WW re-entered the tanker trade in 1951. During the next 26 years twenty-five ever-larger oil carriers were added to the company's fleet. The climax was reached with the 380,000 tons deadweight Nippon Kokan-built TITUS in 1976. She was, in fact, the first of three ships ordered, but after the collapse of the tanker market in 1973, the second and third orders were re-negotiated, and orders were placed with the builders for two 70,600 tons deadweight bulk carriers and six 21,000 tons deadweight multi-purpose carriers. All of these ships were delivered in 1977, with TSU being the first of the multi-purpose carriers.

Whilst oil transportation had thus been an increasingly vital sector of WW's sphere of activities from the 1950s onwards, involvement in the general tramp and bulk trade had remained modest. The first WW bulk carrier since World War I, TEMPLAR, of 18,700 tons deadweight, was delivered in 1962, followed by TROJA of similar capacity in the following year. Two 56,000 tons

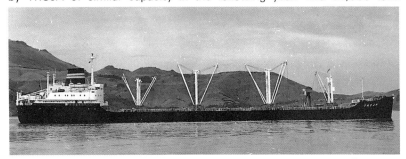

TROJA of 1963   *Alex Duncan*

deadweight bulk carriers, TONGA and TANABATA, were delivered in 1968. In 1970, a Canadian—Norwegian joint venture, registered in Bermuda as Open Bulk Carriers, was established on a 50 / 50 basis between Leitch Transport, Toronto, and WW. Marketed as "Troll Carriers", it specialized in bulk, car and paper transportation. One of the ships, TROLL FOREST, was built for WW's own account. In addition to these ships, five combined oil-ore and oil-bulk-ore carriers, ranging in size from the 90,000 tons deadweight TEHERAN (II) to the 215,000 ton TARTAR (III) were delivered to WW between 1968 and 1972.

TARTAR (III)

The late 1970s and early 1980s were a period of almost constant depression in most shipping markets, particularly tank and bulk. WW decided once again to reduce their involvement in these sectors. The company's second epoch in the tanker trade ended with the sale of the turbine tanker TIGRE in 1984, and in the following year WW's last two conventional Panamax bulk carriers left the fleet as well.

In contrast to this general bleak picture, one sector showed healthy growth and expansion, namely the transportation of factory-new automobiles. WW entered into car transportation as operator of the 1983-built car carrier TAKAYAMA, owned by a Bermuda subsidiary, and in 1984 a joint operation was established with Øivind Lorentzen A/S, a prominent operator in car transportation. WW acquired a 20% ownership share in Lorentzen and had for a period a 50% ownership in the car transportation pool, which was marketed as NOSAC (Norwegian Specialized Auto Carriers). Between 1985 and 1987 four purpose-built car carriers entered NOSAC on behalf of WW, four of them on bareboat charter with a purchase option. Lorentzen's ownership share in NOSAC was sold to Den norske Amerikalinje in 1987.

WW and the offshore industry
WW's boldest and biggest step into new activities during the 1970s was unquestionably their involvement in the offshore oil industry. This included drilling operations as well as supply services. Wilhelmsen Offshore Services

(WOS) was established as an independent partnership, owned by Skips-A/S Tudor (Wilhelm Wilhelmsen) with 50% and by the brokering firm R.S. Platou and the insurance company Storebrand with 25% each.

In September 1972 WW took delivery of its smallest fleet unit since the purchase of the tiny m.v. TRANSIT in 1925—to wit, the 498 tons gross TENDER TROUT. At the time of completion, she was indeed an odd-looking vessel in Norway's merchant fleet—a hybrid between a tug and a floating lorry. She was built for WOS in Houston, Texas, as a combined tug and supply

TENDER TROUT   *Ken Turrell*

ship for offshore drilling rigs. The offshore supply fleet increased rapidly and during the next fifteen years over thirty pipe carrying / supply / fire-fighting / anchor handling / diving support / rescue vessels were operated by WOS.

It was, however, the commitment to the offshore drilling industry that really dominated WW during the decade between the mid 1970s and the mid 1980s, for better or for worse. The company's first financial involvement in a drilling rig was through an ownership share in ODIN DRILL, completed in 1974 for North Sea operations. WW now decided to go heavily into the

The Anchor-handling tug **TENDER PULL**

34

oil rig sector, and in 1974 no less than three platforms of the Aker H3 semi-submersible type were ordered, with more to follow. TREASURE HUNTER was handed over by the Aker Group in December 1975, with a price tag of more than 200 million Norwegian kroner. Then came TREASURE SEEKER, TREASURE FINDER, TREASURE SWAN, TREASURE SCOUT and TREASURE SAGA. TREASURE SUPPORTER was bareboat chartered. The final addition, POLAR PIONEER, completed in 1985, is purpose-built for operation under severe weather conditions in Arctic waters.

The Semi-submersible Drilling Rig **TREASURE SCOUT**

Rough weather and restructuring

Tom Wilhelmsen passed away in 1978, and Niels Werring senior died in 1990. Their sons, Wilhelm Wilhelmsen and Niels Werring jr now represent the family interests in WW. Since 1973 an appointed Chief Executive Officer has been in managerial charge: Leif Terje Løddesøl has been the CEO since 1973, except for a period between 1979 and 1988, when Ivar Løvald was in office.

In 1981 the seven individual shipowning companies managed by the personal firm Wilh. Wilhelmsen were merged into one company, which in 1984 also took over the management responsibilities. In the following year, 1985, the share capital was expanded by public subscription, which increased the non-family controlled amount of shares from less than 10% to more than 30%. The firm was restyled Wilh. Wilhelmsen Limited A/S.

As mentioned earlier, it was the great commitment to large-scale Roll on-Roll off liner shipping and the offshore oil industry that characterized above all the strategy of WW during the 1970s and early 1980s. The stakes were high, but so were the yields, in contrast to most other maritime sectors in this period. At the middle of the 1970s, WW had based an increasing part of its liner services on the booming economic development in the Middle East. This area had, in fact, become a major hub in the network of scheduled services where WW was involved. Based upon glorious financial results and rosy prospects in the Mid-East trade, as opposed to an otherwise depressed shipping market, WW invested heavily in modern, but expensive Ro-Ro tonnage during this period. However, the outbreak of the Iran-Iraq war in 1979 led to a total collapse in the trade to the Middle East, seriously affecting the profitability of the Ro-Ro fleet. At this time, however, WW was able to compensate for the setbacks in the liner trade, with healthy results in the North Sea offshore industry. In 1985 64% of WW's total operating results came from the offshore activities, and the strong and deliberate commitment was based on the assumption that this sector would continue to grow. By the mid 1980s, however, the depression also hit the offshore sector. When the oil rigs, expensive and heavily mortgaged, were redelivered from their existing charters, they found no profitable employment. From lifebuoys they turned into millstones, seriously threatening WW's financial strength.

The management acted quickly to avert the impending crisis. Banks and other financing institutions were contacted, and by mid-1986 most of WW's loans had been re-arranged. WW obtained a 30-month moratorium on the payment of instalments on 60% of the total debt, while interest would be paid in full. It was inevitable that several units in the large and still modern fleet of Ro-ro vessels would have to be sold, partly to adjust the liner capacity to market requirements, and partly to help debt repayment. WW's partnership in the NOSAC car pool was reduced from 50% to 30% by a 20% sale to Den norske Amerikalinje.

By this time, a very large part of the WW fleet had been transferred from Norwegian to Liberian registry in order to stay competitive in the depressed international freight market. When the Norwegian International Ship Register (NIS) was introduced in 1987, allowing non-Norwegian crew with local wage agreements on Norwegian-flag ships, the WW fleet was transferred back to Norwegian registry, home-ported in Tønsberg.

WW was able to meet the financial requirements of the 1988 agreement, but operating results were still unsatisfactory. The administration worked very hard on a restructuring of the entire company in order to face future challenges and during 1988 the various activities of Wilh. Wilhelmsen Limited A/S were grouped into the following sub-divisions:

Wilhelmsen Lines A/S (liner services)
Wilship (other shipping activities)
Wilrig A/S (offshore engagements)
Barber International A/S (ship management and marine consultancy)
Barwil Agencies A/S (shipping agencies outside Norway)
Wilh. Wilhelmsen Services A/S (agencies / transportation in Norway)

WW in the 1990s

In 1989 the re-structuring began to show results. The situation was also much helped by a general turn for the better in the international shipping market. Wilhelmsen Lines A/S took over all the assets in Barber Blue Sea (WWL 52%) and ScanCarriers (WWL 53%) from the other partners, Ocean Transport & Trading (Blue Funnel), Transatlantic and EAC. WW now had a 55% ownership share in Wilhelmsen Lines, the remaining 45% being held by a Finnish investor consortium (Hollming Ltd., TR Shipping KB and OY BS

Finance). The two Blue Funnel vessels were transferred to a Swedish-registered Wilhelmsen Lines subsidiary. When the various services (ScanCarriers, Barber Blue Sea and Open Bulk Carriers) had been incorporated into one round-the-world ro-ro liner service, employing nine of the world's largest purpose-built Ro-ro vessels, Wilhelmsen Lines had regained its historical position as one of the world's leading operators of regular overseas services.

Wilh. Wilhelmsen Services A/S was sold during 1989 to its management and its agency activities and terminal operations in Norway were transferred to Barwil Agencies A/S. It was no longer now in WW's operation strategy

ROSA TUCANO leaving Santos, Brazil, 14.6.1989 *Torsten Andreas*

to be a minor part of any ''joint operating company''. Therefore, in 1989 it was decided to withdraw from RoSa Line between Scandinavia and Brazil / River Plate. The ScanDutch container service between Europe and the Far East had also been kept outside Wilhelmsen Lines and in 1989 it was decided to withdraw from the ScanDutch pool by 1992. TOYAMA, the only fully-fledged Norwegian container vessel and probably the fastest unit ever in Norway's ocean-going merchant fleet, was sold in 1991. Thus WW's seventy-year involvement in the Europe—Far East liner trade, once a corner-stone in the company's activities, came to an end

It was a terrible shock to all WW employees and a blow to the promising development of Wilhelmsen Lines when fifty employees, amongst them half of Wilhelmsen Lines' office staff in Oslo, lost their lives when a chartered aircraft crashed on 8th September 1989. They were en route from Oslo to Hamburg to attend the handing-over ceremony for a new addition to the Ro-ro fleet. With whole-hearted assistance from each and every member of the WW organisation it was possible to continue operations through the initial, paralyzing period and to rebuild Wilhelmsen Lines' administrative organisation with a relatively short time.

The collapse in oil drilling activities in 1986 almost coincided with the first signs of an upturn in the long-depressed tank and bulk market. Acting accordingly, WW had already made an agreement in 1985 with Brazilian interests for a joint venture, based on the ordering of two of the world's largest oil / ore carriers. Delivered in 1986 and 1987 respectively, the 310,000 tons deadweight DOCEFJORD and TIJUCA were each secured on a 15-year charter for the transportation of ore from Brazil to Japan, combined with a contract for crude oil transportation from the Middle East to Brazil. In some respects the Brazilian contract can be seen as a contemporary parallel to the building of the two 13,000 tons deadweight ore carriers TELLUS and THEMIS 75 years earlier. They were at that time the world's biggest of their kind, and they were ordered on the basis of a long-term freight charter.

WW has faith in newly-built crude carriers as profitable replacements when today's ageing fleet is ripe for retirement and scrapping, and two 300,000 tons deadweight tankers were ordered in Japan for delivery in 1993. In 1990

TARTAR, the first of the 300,000 ton tankers, delivered in 1.1993

WW also became involved in a highly specialized tanker trade, with the take-over of Bj. Ruud-Pedersen A/S. This Oslo-based shipping company owned three chemical tankers specially equipped for the transportation in bulk of anti-knock compound and caustic soda liquors. Thus WW has entered upon its third period in oil and ore transportation.

During the summer of 1993 WW announced that an order had been placed in Japan for a 5,800 unit PCC (pure car carrier), to be delivered for the Nosac service in late 1994 and to be named NOSAC TANABATA.

Wilrig A/S has been very active since it took over WW's offshore engagements in 1989, but with further capitalisation the WW ownership share in drilling rigs / floatels has been reduced to about 20%. The only oil rig in which WW has direct ownership interests today is the POLAR PIONEER, in which they have a 47.5% share, and which is operated by Norsk Hydro as their basic rig for drilling operations in Norwegian waters.

Two WW success stories in recent years have been the development of the agency chain Barwil Agencies A/S, and the maritime management / consultancy company Barber International A/S.

Barwil Agencies is one of the world's leading ship agency companies, a re-structured offspring of WW's vast network of agencies from the halcyon days of world-wide liner trades. Today Barwil has more than 80 offices in Europe, the Middle East, Africa, South-East Asia, the Far East, Australia, Panama and North America, representing a large number of liner services and tank/tramp/gas operators world-wide. Barwil is also responsible for the operation of a large number of small service vessels in the Middle East and South-East Asia.

Barber International is equally strongly positioned in ship management, with offices in Oslo, Bombay, Dubai, Hong Kong, London and New Orleans. In November 1993 the company was responsible for a total of 170 ships of over 14 million tons deadweight capacity, employing 5,000 ship-board personnel. The fleet of managed ships was grouped as follows:

39 bulk carriers
19 container / ro-ro / multi-purpose ships
1 reefer ship
19 car carriers
56 oil tankers
7 oil / ore / bulk vessels
6 livestock carriers
2 supply / anchor handling vessels
21 seismic vessels

Epilogue

There is — in every respect — a vast distance between the brokering / ship chandlering partnership established by Morten Wilhelm Wilhelmsen and Jens Wilhelm Balchen in 1861 and the shipping concern Wilh. Wilhelmsen Limited A/S of 1994. But throughout these 133 years, WW, in its various forms, has constantly been conspicuously present in the overall picture of maritime Norway and today it maintains this prominent position, engaged in liner operation, oil and ore transportation, offshore activities, ship management and international agency services.

WW Towards 2000

OBJECTIVES: The WW Group's area of business is international maritime activities with a central base in Norway. Our objective for the year 2000 is to be clearly positioned as one of Norway's leading shipping groups, and with such importance and strength that we also carry weight internationally. We will be a group organisation, with broad expertise and with emphasis on industrial shipping and related services.

Profitability, financial strength and good liquidity are fundamental to all our activities.

THE PEOPLE

Wilhelm   WILHELMSEN

1839 - 1910

Founder of the   WILH. WILHELMSEN

HALFDAN WILHELMSEN

CAPTAIN WILH. WILHELMSEN

NIELS WERRING

TOM WILHELMSEN

NIELS WERRING JR.

WILHELM WILHELMSEN

LEIF T. LØDDESØL
Managing Director 1973-1979
President and Group Chief Executive 1988-

IVAR LØVALD
Managing Director 1979-1988

THE SHIPS

1. **MATHILDE** of 1865, the first ship in the fleet

161. **TROJA** of 1930

176. TORRENS in 5.1959   *J. Y. Freeman*

193. TALLEYRAND at Rotterdam, 29.5.1971   *W.S.P.L. slide collection*

212. TIBER at Rotterdam, 13.9.1975   *W.S.P.L. slide collection*

234. TØNSBERG at Gothenburg, 6.10.1974

Ambrose Greenway

272. TYR at Rotterdam, 27.6.1976

W.S.P.L. slide collection

275. TAIMYR in her new colours at Rotterdam, 21.6.1979

W.S.P.L. slide collection

292. **TOYAMA** in the Strait of Malacca   W.S.P.L.

295. **TARAGO** in ScanCarriers livery   W.S.P.L. slide collection

330. **TOBA**   J. Krayenbosch

347. TROLL MAPLE with pale green upperworks   *Fotoflite incorporating Skyfotos*

363. TEXAS in Barber Blue Sea Livery   *J. Krayenbosch*

372. NOSAC TANCRED   *J. Krayenbosch*

382. TORRENS

J. Krayenbosch

368. POLAR PIONEER

One of the "**TENDER**" Supply Ships in rough seas

371. DOCEFJORD

380. TAPIOLA at the ro-ro berth at Sydney, 9.9.1993   *Michael Crowdy*

393. TARIM, the latest ship in the fleet

56

THE FLEET

FLEET LIST NOTES

In the Fleet List the number preceding the name is the ship's chronological number in the Wilhelmsen fleet.

If more than one ship of a certain name has featured in the fleet "I", "II", etc. follows the name to indicate whether she is the first, second, etc. to bear that name. The dates following the name are those of entering and leaving the fleet.

Dimensions are length x beam x depth, in feet and tenths up to ship number 177, and in metres thereafter. Up to ship number 177 the length is at main deck level, thereafter it is at upper deck level, the overall length (including bulbous bow where fitted) being given in brackets. The ship's draught is also given.

Oil engines are Two or Four stroke cycle (2 S.C. or 4 S.C.) single acting (S.A.) or double acting (D.A.) and the indicated horse (i.h.p.) or brake horse power (b.h.p.) is given. For steam ships the indicated horse power (i.h.p.) or the shaft horse power (s.h.p.) is shown.

Where the ship is known to have carried passengers, the number accommodated is given.

Similarly, details of refrigerated cargo space are given where the ship is known to have been so equipped.

Where a ship is "completed", she is completed for Wilh. Wilhelmsen unless otherwise stated and the date is that of delivery to the firm. Where a ship is "bought", the date of purchase is the date when the ship was taken over, and where a ship is "sold", the date (unless otherwise stated) is that of delivery to the new owners.

Where "price paid" is mentioned, it is always the price paid (in Norwegian Speciedaler or kroner (NOK or kr.), Swedish kroner (SEK), or United States dollars ($)) when purchased by Wilh. Wilhelmsen.

Ships' histories are corrected to November 1993.

FLEET LIST

The following ships were managed and partly owned by Wilh. Wilhelmsen, but were not registered in the name of the firm.

PETRUS (1864-1878)	Ship	1/4 share
TALISMAN (1869-1891)	Ship	1/32 share
NIDAROS (1871-1891)	Ship	1/5 share
FREY (1872-1889)	Ship	1/4 share
CONDOR (1875-1890)	Barque	1/8 share
ALCYON (1878-1886)	Ship	1/16 share
FRITHJOF (1879-1879)	Brig	3/20 share
FØYENLAND (1883-1891)	Ship	1/4 share
CAMILLA (1886-1887)	Brig	1/2 share

MATHILDE

1. MATHILDE (1865-1880) Barque
Tonnages: 337 net, 504 deadweight.
Length 106.0 feet, beam 27.3 feet, depth 16.0 feet.
1840: Built at St. Malo, France. History prior to purchase not recorded.
20.5.1865: Purchased by Wilh. Wilhelmsen for 7,000.00 Speciedaler. *1880:*
Sold to Brødrene Thorkildsen, Tvedestrand. *1882:* Omitted from the ''Bureau
Veritas'' Register and subsequent history not recorded.

2. AKSEL (1866-1872) Ship
Tonnages: 502 net, 753 deadweight.
1854: Built at Plymouth, Canada. History prior to purchase not recorded.
1866: Purchased by Wilh. Wilhelmsen. *13.11.1872:* Wrecked at Kiøgebukt,
Sjælland, Denmark.

3. IDA (1869-1879) Brig
Tonnages: 298 net, 448 deadweight.
Dimensions: 114.6 x 26.7 x 14.6 feet.
1864: Built at Buctouche, N.B., Canada. Early owners not recorded but in
1865 owned by W.B. Wallø, Tønsberg. *1.9.1869:* Purchased by Wilh.
Wilhelmsen. Price paid 6,500.00 Speciedaler. *1879:* Sold to H.O. Hansen,
Skien. *1889:* Sold to Nicolai Friis, Porsgrunn. *20.10.1890:* Wrecked near
Richibucto, N.B., while on passage to that port from Rochefort.

4. FIN (1873-1887) Barque
Tonnages: 491 net, 686 deadweight.
Dimensions: 122.0 x 29.2 x 19.3 feet.
7.1848: Launched by G.W. & W.J. Hall, Sunderland, England, as BRITISH EMPIRE for Hall & Co., London. *1862:* Sold to J. Temperley, J.C. Cooper & others, London. *1863:* Sold to J. Bulley, Dartmouth. *1865:* Sold to Ashford Junior, Dartmouth. *1871:* Sold to J. Hore, Exeter. *31.12.1873:* Purchased by Wilh. Wilhelmsen and renamed FIN. Price paid 16,291.95 Speciedaler. *1887:* Condemned at St. John, N.B., due to ice damage.

5. HAABET (1874-1891) Ship
Tonnages: 431 gross, 417 net, 627 deadweight.
Dimensions: 117.5 x 29.1 x 18.5 feet.
1851: Built at Newcastle, England. Early owners not recorded, but in *1862* owned by A. Tollefsen, Tønsberg. *10.2.1874:* Purchased by Wilh. Wilhelmsen. *1891:* Sold to C.N. Nielsen, Brevik. *1894:* Condemned and dismantled after stranding damage sustained near Farsund.

6. SNEFRID (1874-1875) Barque
Tonnages: 550 net, 824 deadweight.
Dimensions: 123.0 x 30.3 x 19.7 feet.
1853: Built at Fiume, Austria. Early owners not recorded, but in *6.1873* bought by O. Eliassen, Drammen. *1874:* Purchased by Wilh. Wilhelmsen. *1875:* Wrecked at Santo Domingo, Dominican Republic.

7. NORA (1876-1878) Barque
Tonnages: 567 net, 850 deadweight.
Dimensions: 132.0 x 30.0 x 17.9 feet.
1869: Built at Hopewell, N.B., Canada. Early owners not recorded. *1.6.1876:* Purchased by Wilh. Wilhelmsen. Price paid 19,200.00 Speciedaler. *1878:* Wrecked at Lemon Sand while carrying a cargo of ice.

8. THETIS (1876-1882) Brig
Tonnages: 197 gross, 190 net, 285 deadweight.
Dimensions: 83.1 x 25.5 x 14.1 feet.
1847: Built at Kragerø as THETIS for P. Rømer, Kragerø. *1862:* Sold to P.A. Petersen, Kragerø and by *1864* owned by M. & M. Sundene, Tønsberg. *1867:* M. Sundene, Tønsberg, became owner. *14.12.1876:* Purchased by Wilh. Wilhelmsen. Price paid 2,466.00 Speciedaler. *1882:* Sold to Chr. Christoffersen, Nøtterøy. *1886:* Sold to M. Corneliussen, Lillesand. *1894:* Sold to H. Isaksen, Porsgrunn. *1898:* Sold to M. Hansen, Porsgrunn, and later to N. Danielsen, Risør. *23.11.1898:* Sank in harbour at Methil, Fife, while loading. Condemned and dismantled.

9. HERMES (1877-1886) Brig
Tonnages: 259 net, 390 deadweight.
Dimensions: 113.4 x 27.6 x 12.3 feet.
10.9.1877: Delivered by builders at Skuggevik, near Tvedestrand. Price paid 50,200.00 kr. *1886:* Sold to A. Olsen, Drøbak. *26.4.1889:* Lost in the ice near Carlso when bound for Gustafsborg.

10. FOLDIN (I) (1878-1886) Brig
Tonnages: 279 net, 418 deadweight.
Dimensions: 118.0 x 28.8 x 17.5 feet.
1.5.1878: Delivered by Jærc Skipsbyggeri, Porsgrunn. Price paid 54,011.39 kr. *1.2.1886:* Wrecked off Coatzacoalcos while bound from Minatitlan, Mexico, for orders.

11. HELIOS (1879-1890) Schooner
Tonnages: 282 gross, 264 net, 405 deadweight.
Dimensions: 119.5 x 28.0 x 11.9 feet.
1.4.1879: Delivered by Tvedestrands Varv, Tvedestrand. Price paid 50,000.00 kr. *1890:* Sold to P.A. Grøn, Sandefjord. *1904:* Sold to E.W. Tillberg, Sweden. *1912:* Sold to K.A. Rosenberg, Finland. *1926:* Broken up.

12. T.H. ASCHEHOUG (1880-1881) Barque
Tonnage: 745 deadweight.
1868: Built at St. Malo, France. Early owners not recorded. *4.1880:* Purchased by Wilh. Wilhelmsen. Price paid 42,879.00 kr. *1881:* Wrecked.

13. ZIPPORA (1881-1890) Brig
Tonnages: 267 gross, 256 net, 372 deadweight.
Dimensions: 112.9 x 26.3 x 12.9 feet.
1863: Built at Prince Edward Island, Canada. Early owners not recorded, but in *12.1870* bought by T. Govertsen and others, Lillesand and renamed ZIPPORA. *1873:* Sold to H. & W. Helgesen, Tønsberg. *1877:* Transferred to W. Helgesen, Tønsberg. *6.1.1881:* Purchased by Wilh. Wilhelmsen. Price paid 11,121.98 kr. *1890:* Sold to C.N. Christensen, Tønsberg. *1897:* Sold to S. Chr. Foyn, Tønsberg. *20.10.1898:* Wrecked near Peterhead while on passage from Newhaven to Tønsberg.

14. TEMPLAR (I) (1882-1887) Barque
Tonnages: 778 net, 1,167 deadweight.
Dimensions: 162.6 x 33.8 x 20.4 feet.
12.1871: Launched at Brookville, N.S., Canada, as TEMPLAR for Abel C. Robbins and others, Yarmouth, N.S. *31.7.1882:* Purchased by Wilh. Wilhelmsen. Price paid 48,000.00 kr. *9.5.1887:* Beached in Gibraltar harbour after stranding while on passage from Cette to Santos and condemned.

15. AMERIKA (I) (1882-1890) Barque
Tonnages: 459 gross, 436 net, 655 deadweight.
Dimensions: 130.5 x 29.0 x 15.8 feet.
1860: Built by Gebrüder Gross, Bremen, Germany, as ADMIRAL BRAMMY, but early owners not recorded. *14.9.1882:* Purchased by Wilh. Wilhelmsen. Price paid 24,076.00 kr. *1890:* Sold to H. Mathisen, Fredrikstad. *1894:* Sold to Actieselskabet ''Amerika'' (L. Schübeler, manager), Fredrikstad. *1.1900:* Broken up.

16. CHRISTINA (1883-1885) Barque
Tonnages: 358 net, 349 deadweight.
Dimensions: 100.9 x 27.8 x 18.8 feet.
Early history not recorded but in *1848* bought by Mrs. M.S. Bull, Tønsberg, and in *1849* rebuilt at Tønsberg. *1871:* Sold to Samuel Harris, Tønsberg. *1877:* Sold to I.H. Christiansen, Tønsberg. *24.2.1883:* Purchased by Wilh. Wilhelmsen. Price paid 5,100.00 kr. *1885:* Sold back to I.H. Christiansen, Tønsberg. *1889:* Converted into a lighter.

17. JARLSBERG (1883-1898) Ship
Tonnages: 1,265 gross, 1,142 net, 1,713 deadweight.
Dimensions: 190.0 x 36.0 x 23.7 feet.
Captain W. Wilhelmsen signed on as an apprentice aboard this ship.
5.1870: Launched by C. Cox, Maitland, N.S., Canada, as ALGONQUIN for Chas. Cox and others, Halifax, N.S. *24.2.1872:* Majority owner became T.C. Jones, Liverpool. *4.11.1872:* All 64 shares acquired by Israel Shear Lawson, St. John, N.B. *7.4.1883:* Purchased by Wilh. Wilhelmsen and renamed JARLSBERG. Price paid 92,500.00 kr. *1898:* Sold to Joh. Wallenstein, Germany and renamed ELBE. *1903:* Sold to J.J. Wegener, Netherlands. *1904:* Broken up at Swinemünde, Germany.

18. NYSTAD (1885-1891) Barque
Tonnages: 473 gross, 456 net, 684 deadweight.
Dimensions: 142.7 x 30.3 x 16.5 feet.
1865: Built by P.H. Kjaldstrøm, Nystad, Finland. Early owners not recorded, but in *12.1873* bought by W.F. Schlytter, Kragerø. *1882:* Sold to L.O. Røed, Hvitsten. *7.4.1885:* Purchased by Wilh. Wilhelmsen. Price paid 15,000.00 kr. *25.10.1891:* Went ashore at Metis while on passage from Quebec and condemned the following month.

19. BERNADOTTE (1885-1898) Ship
Tonnages: 1,452 gross, 1,404 net, 2,101 deadweight.
Dimensions: 207.4 x 39.1 x 23.8 feet.
1873: Delivered by Nevins, Fraser & Co., St. John, N.B., Canada, as BREADALBANE for W.R. Wright & Co., Liverpool. *1879:* Sold to Gillison & Chadwick, Liverpool. *1885:* Purchased by Wilh. Wilhelmsen and renamed BERNADOTTE. *1898:* Sold to A.T. Rosasco, Italy. *28.2.1899:* Abandoned by her crew in a waterlogged condition in the North Atlantic while on passage from Pensacola to Venice.

20. TREPORT (1886-1888) Brig
Tonnages: 312 gross, 297 net, 447 deadweight.
Dimensions: 106.8 x 27.5 x 16.5 feet.
1862: Built at Genoa, Italy. Early owners not recorded, but by *1874* owned at le Havre, France. *5.5.1874:* Bought by Johannes Bigum, Hvaler and registered at Fredrikshald. *9.4.1879:* Sold to M.E. & O.E. Haraldsen, Tønsberg. *4.3.1886:* Purchased by Wilh. Wilhelmsen. Price paid 3,803.00 kr. *1888:* Sold to N. Christensen Solberg, Horten. *1894:* Sold to Jørgen Andersen, Sandefjord. *23.4.1894:* Wrecked at St. Valery while on passage from Swansea to Sundsvall with a cargo of coal.

21. HAABETS ANKER (1886-1887) Barque
Tonnages: 304 net, 308 deadweight.
Dimensions: 91.6 x 27.5 x 17.3 feet.
1847: Built at Tønsberg for O. Andersen, Tønsberg. In *1864* owned by M. Kaas, Tønsberg. *1885:* Bought by D. Hesby, Tønsberg. *7.4.1886:* Purchased by Wilh. Wilhelmsen. Price paid 2,550.00 kr. *1887:* Converted into a lighter.

22. ALABAMA (1886-1888) Ship
Tonnages: 285 net, 427 deadweight.
Dimensions: 94.0 x 24.6 x 15.5 feet.
1821: Built in Nova Scotia, Canada. Early owners not recorded, but by *1864* owned by N.M. Gram, Drammen. *1877:* Sold to E. Haraldsen, Tønsberg. *1883:* Sold to O.E. Haraldsen, Tønsberg. *24.4.1886:* Purchased by Wilh. Wilhelmsen. Price paid 21,260.00 kr. *1888:* Sold to C.C. Sørensen, Tønsberg. *7.11.1888:* Wrecked near Yarmouth while on passage from Helsingfors to Ghent.

23. CALEDONIA (1886-1886) Brig
Tonnages: 318 gross, 305 net.
Dimensions: 105.7 x 28.9 x 15.8 feet.
1850: Built at Brahestad, Finland. Early history not recorded but in *1866* owned by I. Aslagen, Tvedestrand. *1869:* Sold to E. Aslagen & Co., Porsgrund. *1871:* Sold to H. Iversen, Soon. *1873:* Sold to O. Siewers and others, Soon. *1874:* Sold to N.H. Steen, Moss. *1875:* Sold to N.H. Munthe Kaas and others, Tønsberg. *1886:* Purchased by Wilh. Wilhelmsen. *1886:* Sold to H.C. Eriksen, Frederikstad. *1889:* Management assumed by L. Schübeler. *12.4.1895:* Abandoned in the North Sea during a voyage from Christiania (Oslo) to Troon with pit props. Taken in tow and brought in to Grangemouth but condemned.

ENTERPRISE

24. ENTERPRISE (1887-1902) Barque
Tonnages: 1,515 gross, 1,461 net, 2,141 deadweight.
Dimensions: 210.0 x 40.8 x 24.8 feet.
1875: Completed by Lane & Co., Quebec, Canada, as ENTERPRISE for John Lane, Quebec. *1877:* Sold to Arvon Shipping Co. Ltd., Caernarvon, Wales. *3.10.1887:* Purchased by Wilh. Wilhelmsen. Price paid 66,000.00 kr. *1902:* Sold to B. Mortensen, Arendal. *1904:* Sold to H.A. Henrichsen, Arendal. *7.4.1906:* Arrived at Fayal, Azores, leaking badly during a voyage from Mobile to Liverpool. *5.1906:* Condemned.

25. CHAPMAN (1887-1891) Ship

Tonnages: 441 gross, 425 net, 637 deadweight.
Dimensions: 143.0 x 30.9 x 15.9 feet.
1856: Built by Fredell, Westervik, Sweden. Early owners not recorded, but *12.1865* bought by G.C. Hansen, Tønsberg. *27.2.1875:* Sold to A.C. Jacobsen, Tønsberg, for 10,000.00 Speciedaler, 1/20th share being held by Wilh. Wilhelmsen until *1887* when she was purchased completely by Wilh. Wilhelmsen. *1891:* Sold to Henrik Svendsen, Drøbak. *1895:* Sold to C.H. Wilhelmsen, Drøbak. *1899:* Broken up at Copenhagen.

TALABOT   *Norsk Sjøfartsmuseum*

26. TALABOT (I) (1887-1905)

Tonnages: 1,298 gross, 804 net, 1,800 deadweight.
Dimensions: 245.6 x 33.3 x 16.5 feet.
Machinery: 2-cylinder compound steam engines of 770 i.h.p. made by R. & W. Hawthorn, Newcastle. Service speed 9 knots.
The first steamship in the fleet. Iron hull.
14.5.1881: Launched by Schlesinger, Davis & Co., Newcastle (Yard No. 116) as TALABOT for J. Mesnier, France. *1885:* Sold to Moss Steamship Co. Ltd., Liverpool. *1887:* Purchased by Wilh. Wilhelmsen. Price paid 196,990.11 kr. *20.12.1887:* Taken over at Sharpness, England. *1905:* Sold to Acties. Talabot's Rederi (Nilssen and Bjønness, managers), Tønsberg. *15.9.1914:* Wrecked at Lagskaer while on passage from Grangemouth to Gefle.

27. LINDSAY (1889-1895) Ship

Tonnages: 580 gross, 559 net, 838 deadweight.
Dimensions: 144.0 x 33.1 x 18.5 feet.
1863: Built by A.B. Bull, Fagerheim, Tønsberg, as LINDSAY for his own trading account, and after his death in *1879* owned by his widow until purchased *6.4.1889* by Wilh. Wilhelmsen. Price paid 35,000.00 kr. *18.2.1895:* Abandoned, waterlogged, in the North Atlantic while on passage from Apalachiola, U.S.A., to Sutton Bridge, England.

28. FOLDIN (II) (1889-1892) Ship
Tonnages: 872 gross, 808 net, 1,212 deadweight.
Dimensions: 173.3 x 34.5 x 19.7 feet.
10.1873: Launched by Trakey, Maitland, N.S., Canada as LILLIAN M. VIGUS
for G. Vigus, Halifax, N.S. *1885:* Sold to Geo. J. Troop, Halifax, N.S. *30.4.1889:*
Purchased by Wilh. Wilhelmsen and renamed FOLDIN. Price paid 60,000.00
kr. *11.1892:* Wrecked near Bragança, Brazil, while on passage from Newport,
Mon., to Para.

TRANSIT   *W.S.P.L.*

29. TRANSIT (I) (1889-1905)
Tonnages: 1,334 gross, 1,027 net, 2,000 deadweight.
Dimensions: 250.0 x 35.0 x 15.6 feet.
Machinery: 3-cylinder triple expansion steam engines of 750 i.h.p. by North
Eastern Marine Engineering Co. Ltd., Newcastle. Service speed 9 knots.
The first steamship to be built for Wilh. Wilhelmsen. Steel hull.
19.3.1889: Launched by Wood, Skinner & Co., Newcastle (Yard No. 13).
30.4.1889: Completed. Price paid 326,977.24 kr. *1905:* Sold to T. Tasaka,
Japan and renamed TAKESHIMA MARU. *1909:* Sold to S. Uyeda, Japan, and
subsequently managed by H. Koyanagi & Co. *1915:* Sold to S. Koyanagi,
Japan. *1920:* Sold to Busai Kisen K.K., Japan. *17.1.1922:* Left Dairen for Moji
and disappeared with all hands.

30. TANCRED (I) (1889-1897)
Tonnages: 1,238 gross, 786 net, 1,700 deadweight.
Dimensions: 221.3 x 33.2 x 15.8 feet.
Machinery: 2-cylinder compound steam engines of 540 i.h.p. by J. Jones
& Sons, Liverpool. Service speed 8.5 knots.
13.3.1880: Launched by W.H. Potter & Son, Liverpool (Yard No. 91), as
BENALLA for Joseph Hoult & Co., Liverpool. *2.10.1880:* Sank at Ponta
Delgada, Azores, after being in collision with the British s.s. ROBINIA,
1,816/76, when her anchor chain parted during a storm. At the time she was
on passage from New Orleans to Bayonne. She was later sold by auction
''as lay'' for about £150 and was refloated by J.C. Furtado. *5.1.1881:*
Registered at Ponta Delgada in the ownership of J.C. Furtado, F.S. d'Avellar

and E.S. d'Avellar under the name AÇORIANO. *7.1883:* J.C. Furtado sold his interest to his partners who on *19.2.1885* sold her to A. Ben Saude who on *28.2.1885* resold her to Empresa Nacional de Nav. a Vapôr, Portugal. *1888:* Sold to John Wood & Co., West Hartlepool and renamed BENALLA. *1889:* Purchased by Wilh. Wilhelmsen and renamed TANCRED. Price paid 240,000.00 kr. *30.11.1897:* Wrecked on Cockburn Island, Formosa (Taiwan), while on passage from Manila to Japan.

31. COSMO (1889-1898) Ship
Tonnages: 1,249 gross, 1,220 net, 1,742 deadweight.
Dimensions: 200.0 x 37.3 x 23.3 feet.
6.1877: Launched by H. Dinning, Quebec, Canada, as COSMO for H. Fry, Quebec. *1883:* Sold to James G. Ross, Quebec. *1889:* Owners became James G. Ross & Co., who went into liquidation. *16.7.1889:* Purchased by Wilh. Wilhelmsen. Price paid 123,000.00 kr. *1898:* Sold to Christopher Andresen, Christiania (Oslo). *28.1.1899:* Left Savannah for Hamburg and disappeared.

32. TØNSBERG (I) (1889-1894)
Tonnages: 1,395 gross, 1,096 net, 2,134 deadweight.
Dimensions: 262.1 x 35.0 x 15.3 feet.
Machinery: 3-cylinder triple expansion steam engines of 775 i.h.p. by North Eastern Marine Engineering Co. Ltd., Newcastle. Service speed 9 knots.
9.9.1889: Launched by Wood, Skinner & Co., Newcastle (Yard No. 16). *10.1889:* Completed. Price paid 365,338.65 kr. *27.11.1894:* Stranded at Tarifa after being in collision in the Straits of Gibraltar while on passage from le Havre to Leghorn.

TORDENSKJOLD

33. TORDENSKJOLD (I) (1889-1903)
Tonnages: 1,186 gross, 904 net, 1,700 deadweight.
Dimensions: 225.5 x 32.6 x 15.7 feet.
Machinery: 3-cylinder triple expansion steam engines of 550 i.h.p. by North Eastern Marine Engineering Co. Ltd., Newcastle. Service speed 9 knots.
7.11.1889: Launched by T. & W. Smith, North Shields (Yard No. 99). *17.12.1889:* Completed. Price paid 340,000.00 kr. *1903:* Sold to M. Nishikawa, Japan and renamed CHIYODA MARU No. 2. *1909:* Sold to C. Tsukamoto, Japan. *11.1917:* Went ashore but was later refloated, repaired and returned to service in the ownership of K. Kawachi, Japan. *11.4.1920:* Foundered off Iwate.

CHIPMAN

34. CHIPMAN (1890-1899) Barque
Tonnages: 1,124 gross, 1,083 net, 1,625 deadweight.
Dimensions: 191.2 x 36.6 x 22.5 feet.
1877: Built by J. & C. Short, St. Stephen, N.B., Canada, as CHIPMAN for Zachariah Chipman, St. Stephen, N.B., Canada. *1883:* Joint owners became his widow Mary E. Chipman and John D. Chipman. *1889:* Sole owner became John D. Chipman. *1890:* Sold to J.R. de Wolfe, St. Andrews, N.B., Canada. *6.4.1890:* Purchased by Wilh. Wilhelmsen. Price paid 106,000.00 kr. *17.6.1899:* Struck by lightning and set on fire at Pensacola, Fla., U.S.A. Scuttled and later condemned.

TELLUS

35. TELLUS (I) (1890-1907)
Tonnages: 2,522 gross, 1,612 net, 4,050 deadweight.
Dimensions: 302.0 x 40.1 x 20.6 feet.
Machinery: 3-cylinder triple expansion steam engines of 1,300 i.h.p. by George Clark Ltd., Sunderland. Service speed 9.5 knots.
19.4.1890: Launched by Osbourne, Graham & Co., Sunderland (Yard No. 84). *4.6.1890:* Completed. Price paid 684.658.65 kr. *21.9.1907:* Wrecked on North Spit, at the entrance to Grays Harbour, while on passage from Nanaimo, B.C. to Portland, Oregon with a cargo of coal.

36. TAURUS (I) (1891-1904)
Tonnages: 2,123 gross, 1,367 net, 3,025 deadweight.
Dimensions: 278.8 x 37.3 x 18.7 feet.
Machinery: 3-cylinder triple expansion steam engines of 1,100 i.h.p. by Central Marine Engine Works, West Hartlepool. Service speed 9 knots.
26.12.1890: Launched by William Gray & Co. Ltd., West Hartlepool (Yard No. 406). *14.2.1891:* Completed. Price paid 487,807.94 kr. *1904:* Sold to Toba Tekko Goshi Kaisha (later Toba Zosensho Goshi Kaisha), Japan and renamed TOBA MARU. *1913:* Sold to K. Iwagami, Japan, and in *1914* renamed SAPPORO MARU No. 3. *1915:* Sold to Inugami Goshi Kaisha (later Inugami Keigoro), Japan. *17.2.1923:* Wrecked off Noto Peninsula while carrying a cargo of coke.

37. CORINGA (1891-1905)
Tonnages: 2,120 gross, 1,366 net, 3,000 deadweight.
Dimensions: 318.4 x 38.4 x 26.4 feet.
Machinery: *1867-1875:* 2-cylinder inverted direct acting steam engines of 2,255 i.h.p. by Denny & Co., Dumbarton. *1875-1891:* 2-cylinder compound steam engines by Denny & Co., Dumbarton. *1891-1895:* 4-cylinder quadruple expansion steam engines of 950 i.h.p. by Fleming & Ferguson, Paisley. *1895-on:* 3-cylinder triple expansion steam engines of 1,100 i.h.p. by North Eastern Marine Engineering Co. Ltd., Sunderland. Service speed 10 knots.
Laid down by William Denny & Brothers, Dumbarton, as Yard No. 122 for

their own account. *5.11.1866:* Purchased on the stocks by Peninsular & Oriental Steam Navigation Company, London and *21.3.1867* launched as BANGALORE. *21.2.1868:* Completed. *1875:* Re-engined. *1886:* Sold to Hadji Cassum Joosub, Bombay. *1889:* Sold to Baladina & Co., Bombay. *1890:* Sold to Macbeth & Gray, Glasgow. *1891:* Purchased by Wilh. Wilhelmsen, re-engined and renamed CORINGA. *1895:* Again re-engined. *18.3.1905:* Abandoned by her crew and foundered near the Azores while on passage from Cadiz to Halifax, N.S.

38. GUERNSEY (I) (1891-1897)
Tonnages: 2,848 gross, 1,838 net, 4,500 deadweight.
Dimensions: 314.2 x 40.6 x 22.2 feet.
Machinery: 3-cylinder triple expansion steam engines of 1,200 i.h.p. by Central Marine Engine Works, West Hartlepool. Service speed 10 knots.
14.11.1890: Launched by William Gray & Co. Ltd., West Hartlepool (Yard No. 404) as GUERNSEY for J.C. Nielsen & Sir William Gray. *1.1891:* Completed. *5.5.1891:* Purchased by A.N. Hansen, Copenhagen, Denmark and registered at Tønsberg in the ownership of a company in which Wilh. Wilhelmsen were a shareholder and of which they were managers. *10.7.1897:* Sold to D/S Østersøen A/S (P.L. Fisker, later A/S Rhederisyndikatet, managers), Denmark and renamed CIMBRIA. *7.11.1910:* Sold to A/S D/S Atlantic (C. K. Hansen, manager), Denmark and renamed GURRE. *29.5.1912:* Sold to D/S Dannebrog (same manager), Denmark. *26.10.1916:* Sold to D/S Patria A/S (O. Kongsted, manager), Denmark. *20.3.1917:* Torpedoed and sunk in the North Sea in a position 58.20 N, 01.15 E by the German submarine U 59 while on passage from Galveston (and Kirkwall) to Aalborg with a cargo of oil cake. 24 members of her crew were lost.

39. ST. ANDREWS (I) (1891-1905)
Tonnages: 3,065 gross, 1,980 net, 4,580 deadweight.
Dimensions: 325.2 x 41.5 x 22.8 feet.
Machinery: 3-cylinder triple expansion steam engines of 1,400 i.h.p. by Central Marine Engine Works, West Hartlepool. Service speed 10 knots.
7.9.1891: Launched by William Gray & Co. Ltd., West Hartlepool (Yard No. 423), for A.N. Hansen & Co., Copenhagen, Denmark. *10.1891:* Completed and registered at Tønsberg in the ownership of a company in which Wilh. Wilhelmsen were a shareholder and of which they were managers. *28.10.1905:* Sold to W. Kunstmann, Germany and renamed NIPPONIA. *9.10.1908:* Sank near the Haaks Lightship, off Texel, after being in collision with the German s.s. PRETORIA, 13,234/97, while on passage from Luleå to Rotterdam with a cargo of ore.

40. MICHIGAN (1893-1900)
Tonnages: 2,833 gross, 1,799 net, 4,500 deadweight.
Dimensions: 300.0 x 40.2 x 24.5 feet.
Machinery: 2-cylinder compound steam engines of 1,430 i.h.p. by Blair & Co. Ltd., Stockton. Service speed 10 knots.
16.4.1881: Launched by William Gray & Co., West Hartlepool (Yard No. 235) as SURREY for Atlantic Transport Company (Hooper & Williams, later Hooper, Murrell & Williams, managers), London. *1.1888:* Renamed MICHIGAN. *22.2.1888:* Sold to Bernard S.S. Co. Ltd. (Williams, Torrey & Feild, Ltd., managers), London. *12.3.1889:* Sold to Christopher Furness, West Hartlepool. *29.4.1889:* Sold to R.L. Gillchrest & Co., Liverpool. *1889:* Sold to Clarence

MICHIGAN

R. Gillchrest, London. *26.3.1890:* Sold to Charles Lilburn, London. *14.4.1890:* Sold to C.A. Beyts, later Beyts, Craig & Co., London. *1893:* Purchased by Wilh. Wilhelmsen. *1900:* Sold to L. Luckenbach, later Luckenbach S.S. Co., United States, renamed HARRY LUCKENBACH and fitted to carry oil in bulk. In *1903* the owners became Luckenbach Transportation & Wrecking Co., in *1908* the Estate of L. Luckenbach and in *1909* E.F. Luckenbach, all U.S.A. *6.1.1918:* Torpedoed and sunk in the Bay of Biscay, 2 miles N.N.W. of Penmarc'h by the German submarine U 93. Eight members of her crew were lost.

41. COROMANDEL (1893-1895)

Tonnages: *1870-1878:* 1,698 gross, 1,155 net. *1879-on:* 2,184 gross, 1,370 net, 3,500 deadweight.
Dimensions: *1870-1878:* 270.0 x 34.0 x 17.7 feet. *1879-on:* 346.5 x 34.2 x 17.5 feet.
Machinery: *1870-1889:* Two 2-cylinder compound steam engines by the shipbuilders, driving twin screws. *1889-on:* Two 3-cylinder triple expansion steam engines totalling 1,250 i.h.p. by Blaikie Brothers, Aberdeen, driving the twin screws. Service speed 10 knots.
4.1870: Launched by J. & W. Dudgeon, London as LA PAMPA for A. Oneta, Italy. *1874:* Transferred to Italo-Platense Cia., Argentina, in which Oneta was interested. *1876:* Sold to Verminck et Cie., France and subsequently renamed COROMANDEL. *1878-1879:* Lengthened by 76.5 feet. *3.1881:* Registered at Calcutta in the ownership of Banchu Ramaser Garu and renamed EMPRESS OF INDIA. *1886:* Sold to George J. Scott, Calcutta. *1889:* Sold to McFarlane, Strang & Co. Ltd., Glasgow and re-engined. *1893:* Sold to Macbeth & Gray, Glasgow. *1893:* Purchased by Wilh. Wilhelmsen and renamed COROMANDEL. *15.2.1895:* Wrecked at Las Palmas while on passage from the Clyde to Rio de Janeiro.

42. TERRIER (I) (1894-1909)
Tonnages: 1,605 gross, 1,008 net, 2,236 deadweight.
Dimensions: 255.0 x 35.5 x 15.6 feet.
Machinery: 3-cylinder triple expansion steam engines of 715 i.h.p. by George
Clark Ltd., Sunderland. Service speed 10 knots.
6.12.1893: Launched by J. Blumer & Co., Sunderland (Yard No. 128). *1.1894:*
Completed. Price paid 301,495.79 kr. Captain W. Wilhelmsen was master
of the ship for some time. *1909:* Sold to K. Kishimoto, Japan and renamed
SHIN-YU MARU. *1912:* Sold to K. Fukagawa, Japan. *1914:* Sold to S.
Nakamura, Japan. *1919:* Sold to Kuribayashi Shosen K.K., Japan. *1932:* Sold
to G.L. Shaw, Shanghai (British flag) and renamed SHINYU. *2.3.1942:* Scuttled
at Sourabaya.

43. ENRIQUE (1894-1898)
Tonnages: 2,298 gross, 1,495 net, 3,600 deadweight.
Dimensions: 325.3 x 34.7 x 25.3 feet.
Machinery: 2-cylinder compound steam engines of 1,210 i.h.p. by the
shipbuilders. Service speed 9 knots.
6.1878: Launched by Earle's Shipbuilding & Engineering Co. Ltd., Hull (Yard
No. 218) as ENRIQUE for G.H. Fletcher & Co., Liverpool and registered at
Bilbao, Spain. *1884:* Owners became Compania de Navegacion La Flecha,
Spain. *1894:* Purchased by Wilh. Wilhelmsen. *1898:* Sold to Merli & Lugaro,
Italy and renamed RIGHI. *1900:* Sold to Beraldo, Devoto & Pittaluga, Italy
and renamed ONESTA. *8.1901:* Broken up at Genoa.

44. TIGER (1895-1917)
Tonnages: 3,273 gross, 2,116 net, 5,100 deadweight.
Dimensions: 323.9 x 46.5 x 16.8 feet.
Machinery: 3-cylinder triple expansion steam engines of 1,480 i.h.p. by Blair
& Co. Ltd., Stockton. Service speed 10 knots.
9.4.1895: Launched by Ropner & Son, Stockton (Yard No. 304). *5.1895:*
Completed. Price paid 534,645.45 kr. *7.5.1917:* Torpedoed and sunk off Bilbao
by the German submarine UC 69 while on passage from Agua Amarga to
Cardiff with iron ore.

TIGER off Dartmouth   *Norsk Sjøfartsmuseum*

71

45. TYR (I) (1895-1921)
Tonnages: 2,225 gross, 1,417 net, 3,310 deadweight.
Dimensions: 284.8 x 40.0 x 17.6 feet.
Machinery: 3-cylinder triple expansion steam engines of 1,100 i.h.p. by George Clark Ltd., Sunderland. Service speed 10 knots.
23.7.1895: Launched by J. Blumer & Co., Sunderland (Yard No. 133). *31.8.1895:* Completed. Price paid 397,711.11 kr. *9.1921:* Sold to Emil R. Retzlaff, Germany and renamed WOTAN. *6.1931:* Sold to ''Sedina'' Schiffahrts-G.m.b.H., Germany. *1934:* Sold to M. Stern A.G., Essen, for scrapping.

WATERLOO   *Norsk Sjøfartsmuseum*

46. WATERLOO (1895-1914)
Tonnages: 1,283 gross, 795 net, 2,000 deadweight.
Dimensions: 254.4 x 33.1 x 18.7 feet.
Machinery: 2-cylinder compound steam engines of 750 i.h.p. by the shipbuilders. Service speed 9 knots.
6.5.1879: Launched by The London & Glasgow Engineering & Iron Shipbuilding Co. Ltd., Govan (Yard No. 211) as WATERLOO for Allan C. Gow & Co., Glasgow. *1894:* Sold to Macbeth & Gray, Glasgow. *1895:* Purchased by Wilh. Wilhelmsen. *5.12.1914:* Foundered off Lands End, while on passage from Newport, Mon. to Rouen with a cargo of coal.

47. TALISMAN (I) (1896-1921)
Tonnages: 1,878 gross, 1,178 net, 2,750 deadweight.
Dimensions: 270.0 x 39.5 x 14.4 feet.
Machinery: 3-cylinder triple expansion steam engines of 880 i.h.p. by Blair & Co. Ltd., Stockton. Service speed 9 knots.
28.2.1896: Launched by Ropner & Son, Stockton (Yard No. 318). *3.1896:* Completed. Price paid 369,295.19 kr. *29.6.1921:* Sold to A/S D. Finne's Rederi (D. Finne, manager), Oslo and renamed FIOL. *1924:* Sold to D/S A/S Oslo's Rederi (J. W. Klüver, manager), Tønsberg and renamed OSLO. *1927:* Sold to Chi-Tung S.S. Co., China and renamed CHI-TUNG. *1931:* Sold to Central S.N. Co. (L. F. Jovino, manager), Italy and renamed CHIN NING. *1934:* Sold to Hwa Ning S.S. Co., China and renamed CHING NING. *1938:* Sunk in the Yang-tse River as a blockship during the Sino-Japanese war.

TALISMAN   *Norsk Sjøfartsmuseum*

48. NORMAN ISLES (1896-1909)
Tonnages: 3,455 gross, 2,190 net, 5,610 deadweight.
Dimensions: 341.2 x 45.6 x 24.7 feet.
Machinery: 3-cylinder triple expansion steam engines of 1,700 i.h.p. by the
shipbuilders. Service speed 10 knots.
28.5.1896: Launched by William Doxford & Sons Ltd., Sunderland (Yard No.
244) for A.N. Hansen & Co., Copenhagen, Denmark. *1896:* Completed and
registered at Tønsberg in the ownership of a company in which Wilh.
Wilhelmsen were a shareholder and of which they were managers. *1909:*
Sold to Wilton's Engineering & Slipway Company, Netherlands. *1910:* Sold
to Stoomvaart Maatschappij Walcheren (W. Ruys & Zonen, managers),
Netherlands and renamed WALCHEREN. *1916:* Sold to D/S Nordanger (H.
Westfal-Larsen, manager), Bergen and renamed NORDANGER. *27.9.1919:*
Left Newport News for Antwerp with a cargo of coal and disappeared.
12.5.1920: Posted missing.

49. THEMIS (I) (1897-1906)
Tonnages: 1,921 gross, 1,208 net, 2,574 deadweight.
Dimensions: 270.0 x 39.5 x 15.3 feet.
Machinery: 3-cylinder triple expansion steam engines of 1,000 i.h.p. by George
Clark Ltd., Sunderland. Service speed 10 knots.
4.12.1896: Launched by Osbourne, Graham & Co., Sunderland (Yard No. 103).
1.1897: Completed. Price paid 373,954.39 kr. *14.12.1906:* Wrecked near
Scarlet Point, Vancouver, B.C. while on passage, in fog, from Prince of Wales
Island to Vancouver.

TITANIA

50. TITANIA (I) (1897-1916)
Tonnages: 3,613 gross, 2,315 net, 6,000 deadweight.
Dimensions: 350.1 x 46.0 x 24.7 feet.
Machinery: 3-cylinder triple expansion steam engines of 1,350 i.h.p. by the shipbuilders. Service speed 10 knots.
31.8.1897: Launched by William Doxford & Sons Ltd., Sunderland (Yard No. 256). *1897:* Completed. Price paid 635,390.56 kr. *1916:* Sold to Madrigal & Co., Philippine Islands and renamed SUSANA. *1918:* Sold to F.I.A.T. Corporation, U.S.A. *1920:* Sold to Societa di Navigazione Industria e Commercio, Italy. *1923:* Sold to Soc. Marittima e Commerciale Italiana, Italy. *1926:* Broken up in Italy.

51. GUERNSEY (II) (1898-1922)
Tonnages: 4,375 gross, 2,808 net, 7,100 deadweight.
Dimensions: 365.6 x 50.3 x 26.5 feet.
Machinery: 3-cylinder triple expansion steam engines of 1,900 i.h.p. by the shipbuilders. Service speed 10 knots.
21.6.1898: Launched by William Doxford & Sons Ltd., Sunderland (Yard No. 262) for A.N. Hansen & Co., Copenhagen, Denmark. *3.8.1898:* Completed

GUERNSEY discharging a cargo of wood at Sydney, N.S.W.   *W.S.P.L., Dufty*

74

and registered at Tønsberg in the ownership of a company in which Wilh. Wilhelmsen were a shareholder and of which they were managers. *2.12.1922:* Sold to Emil R. Retzlaff, Germany and renamed WALSUNG. *1923:* Registered in the ownership of Dampfer Reederei "Merkur" (1922) G.m.b.H. (Emil R. Retzlaff, manager), Germany. *21.1.1925:* Wrecked at Stangholmen Light near Trannoy while on passage from Stettin to Narvik in ballast.

52. DUNNET (1898-1899)
Tonnages: 3,594 gross, 2,332 net, 5,000 deadweight.
Dimensions: 389.0 x 42.1 x 28.8 feet.
Machinery: 2-cylinder compound steam engines of 1,320 i.h.p. by R. & W. Hawthorn, Newcastle. Service speed 10 knots.
7.10.1873: Launched by C. Mitchell & Co., Newcastle (Yard No. 290) as HANKOW for E.H. Watts, London. *21.2.1874:* Completed. Owners subsequently became Watts, Milburn & Co., London. *1880:* Sold to W. Milburn & Co., London. *1897:* Sold to Aberdeen Atlantic Shipping Co. Ltd. (John Rust & Son, managers), Aberdeen. *1898:* Purchased by Wilh. Wilhelmsen and renamed DUNNET. *6.4.1899:* Sailed from Barry bound for Genoa, and disappeared. Believed to have foundered in the Bay of Biscay.

TROLD

53. TROLD (1898-1915)
Tonnages: 3,247 gross, 2,036 net, 5,450 deadweight.
Dimensions: 325.0 x 47.0 x 25.6 feet.
Machinery: 3-cylinder triple expansion steam engines of 1,500 i.h.p. by W. Allan & Co. Ltd., Sunderland. Service speed 10 knots.
6.8.1898: Launched by J. Priestman & Co., Sunderland (Yard No. 75). *12.1898:* Completed. Price paid 679,345.93 kr. *1915:* Sold to Axel Robt. Bildt Aktiebolaget, Sweden, and renamed AVANTI. *1915:* Sold to Olaf Orvig, Bergen and renamed THOMAS KRAG. *1917:* Sold to A/S Thomas Krag (J. O. Østervold, manager), Bergen. *1923:* Sold to A/S D/S Thomas Krag (Laur Christiansen, manager), Bergen. *1927:* Sold to George Constantine Lemos, Greece and renamed DESPINA LEMOS. *1930:* Sold to J.D. Chandris, Greece and renamed DIMITRIOS CHANDRIS. *1933:* Broken up at Venice by Ernesto Breda.

THYRA

54. THYRA (1899-1914)
Tonnages: 3,742 gross, 2,419 net, 6,200 deadweight.
Dimensions: 339.0 x 48.0 x 17.9 feet.
Machinery: 3-cylinder triple expansion steam engines of 1,650 i.h.p. by Blair & Co. Ltd., Stockton. Service speed 10 knots.
First ship on the Africa-Australia-New Zealand service.
30.11.1898: Launched by Osbourne, Graham & Co., Sunderland (Yard No. 106).
1.1899: Completed. Price paid 656,012.26 kr. *11.6.1914:* Wrecked at Duncansby Head while on passage from the Tyne and Dundee to New York with general cargo.

55. THORDIS (I) (1899-1906)
Tonnages: 3,735 gross, 2,414 net, 6,200 deadweight.
Dimensions: 339.0 x 48.0 x 19.4 feet.
Machinery: 3-cylinder triple expansion steam engines of 1,600 i.h.p. by Blair & Co. Ltd., Stockton. Service speed 10 knots.
29.3.1899: Launched by Osbourne, Graham & Co., Sunderland (Yard No. 108).
5.1899: Completed. Price paid 697,790.98 kr. Captain W. Wilhelmsen was, for some time, her master. *4.3.1906:* Wrecked at Port Stephens, N.S.W. when inward bound from Newcastle, N.S.W. with a cargo of coal.

THORDIS

56. DUNMORE (1899-1900)
Tonnages: 3,730 gross, 2,459 net, 6,100 deadweight.
Dimensions: 350.5 x 43.1 x 28.7 feet.
Machinery: 2-cylinder compound steam engines of 1,650 i.h.p. by Blair &
Co. Ltd., Stockton. Service speed 9 knots.
24.6.1884: Launched by McIntyre & Co. Ltd., Newcastle (Yard No. 3) as
BALTIMORE for S.S. ''Baltimore'' Ltd. (W. Johnston & Co., managers),
Liverpool. *1899:* Purchased by Wilh. Wilhelmsen and renamed DUNMORE.
1900: Sold to Macbeth & Gray, Glasgow and renamed BALTIMORE. *1900:*
Renamed DUNMORE. *1901:* Owners became Macbeth & Co. Ltd., Glasgow.
19.1.1906: Abandoned in the North Atlantic, off the Newfoundland Banks,
and foundered while on passage from Cardiff to Newport News with a cargo
of coal.

57. DUNRAE (1899-1899)
Tonnages: 2,740 gross, 1,583 net.
Dimensions: 328.0 x 40.4 x 27.1 feet.
Machinery: 2-cylinder compound steam engines of 426 n.h.p. by G.Forrester
& Co., Liverpool.
6.1882: Launched by T. Royden & Sons, Liverpool (Yard No. 213) as ALESIA
for Cie. Française de Navigation à Vapeur (Cyprien Fabre et Cie., managers),
France. *1899:* Purchased by Wilh. Wilhelmsen and renamed DUNRAE.
9.9.1899: Foundered off Elba Island while on a voyage from Elba to Glasgow
with iron ore.

ALDERNEY *Norsk Sjøfartsmuseum*

58. ALDERNEY (1899-1920)
Tonnages: 3,090 gross, 1,987 net, 5,100 deadweight.
Dimensions: 325.0 x 48.5 x 21.7 feet.
Machinery: 3-cylinder triple expansion steam engines of 1,200 i.h.p. by Central
Marine Engine Works, West Hartlepool. Service speed 10 knots.
11.7.1899: Launched by William Gray & Co. Ltd., West Hartlepool (Yard No.
587) as DRUMBAIN for W. Christie & Co., London, but sold while fitting out

to A.N. Hansen & Co., Copenhagen, Denmark. *31.8.1899:* Completed as ALDERNEY and registered at Tønsberg in the ownership of a company in which Wilh. Wilhelmsen were a shareholder and of which they were managers. *1920:* Sold to D/S Atlanterhavet (initially managed by O.J. Eskildsen), Denmark and renamed HVIDEHAVET. *1923:* Sold to Essex Line Ltd. (Meldrum & Swinson, managers), London and renamed ESSEX CHASE. *1929:* Sold to Fricis Grauds, Latvia and renamed EVERGUNAR. *18.1.1932:* Wrecked near Sømnes, north of Rørvik, while on passage from Amsterdam to Trondheim in ballast. The wreck was subsequently broken up by Stavanger shipbreakers.

59. SALERNO (1901-1905)
Tonnages: 2,672 gross, 1,683 net, 4,000 deadweight.
Dimensions: 301.0 x 40.0 x 22.6 feet.
Machinery: 2-cylinder compound steam engines of 1,320 i.h.p. by T. Richardson & Sons, Hartlepool. Service speed 9 knots.
29.3.1884: Launched by William Gray & Co., West Hartlepool (Yard No. 289) as LINCOLN CITY for C. Furness (Direct Scandinavia & America S.S. Company), West Hartlepool. *29.5.1884:* Completed. *1885:* Sold to T. Wilson, Sons & Co., Hull and renamed CHICAGO. *1898:* Renamed SALERNO. *1901:* Sold to Macbeth & Gray, Glasgow. *1901:* Purchased by Wilh. Wilhelmsen. *30.6.1905:* Wrecked on Lichfield Shoal, off Halifax, N.S. while on passage from Cadiz to St. John, N.B.

TANCRED   *Ambrose Greenway collection*

60. TANCRED (II) (1902-1922)
Tonnages: 3,474 gross, 2,231 net, 6,000 deadweight.
Dimensions: 334.0 x 48.0 x 24.8 feet.
Machinery: 3-cylinder triple expansion steam engines of 1,426 i.h.p. by North Eastern Marine Engineering Co. Ltd., Newcastle. Service speed 10 knots.
4.9.1902: Launched by Tyne Iron Shipbuilding Co. Ltd., Newcastle (Yard No. 140). *2.10.1902:* Completed. Price paid 695,330.56 kr. *2.12.1922:* Sold to Emil R. Retzlaff, Germany and renamed HAGEN. *1924:* Sold to A.G. für Handel und Verkehr (Lexzau, Scharbau & Co., managers), Germany and renamed HERTA ENGELINE FRITZEN. *1934:* Broken up by Bremer Vulkan Schiffbau und Maschinenfabrik, Vegesack.

61. TERJE VIKEN (1902-1916)
Tonnages: 3,579 gross, 2,304 net, 6,050 deadweight.
Dimensions: 335.0 x 48.0 x 25.4 feet.
Machinery: 3-cylinder triple expansion steam engines of 1,426 i.h.p. by North Eastern Marine Engineering Co. Ltd., Newcastle. Service speed 10 knots.
18.10.1902: Launched by Tyne Iron Shipbuilding Co. Ltd., Newcastle (Yard No. 141). *1902:* Completed. Price paid 697,658.43 kr. *16.4.1916:* Sank off Cascaes Bay, River Tagus, after striking a mine which had been laid by the German submarine U 73. She had been on passage from Galveston to Lisbon with a cargo of wheat.

62. TUNGUS (I) (1903-1922)
Tonnages: 1,753 gross, 1,039 net, 2,370 deadweight.
Dimensions: 260.0 x 36.6 x 12.4 feet.
Machinery: 3-cylinder triple expansion steam engines of 1,000 i.h.p. by North Eastern Marine Engineering Co. Ltd., Sunderland. Service speed 10 knots.
3.3.1903: Launched by Sunderland Shipbuilding Co. Ltd., Sunderland (Yard No. 217). *3.1903:* Completed. Price paid 415,695.75 kr. *7.1922:* Sold to Douglas S.S. Co. Ltd., Hong Kong and renamed HAI FOONG. *1926:* Sold to San Peh S.N. Co. Ltd., China and renamed WAN HSIANG. *4.3.1934:* Collided with and sank the Chinese s.s. SHAWHSING, 1,237/95, off Shanghai. *20.8.1937:* Sunk in the Whangpoo River, Shanghai as a blockship during the Sino-Japanese war.

SARK   *W.S.P.L.*

63. SARK (1903-1923)
Tonnages: 3,560 gross, 2,304 net, 6,100 deadweight.
Dimensions: 340.0 x 48.0 x 25.4 feet.
Machinery: 3-cylinder triple expansion steam engines of 1,500 i.h.p. by North Eastern Marine Engineering Co. Ltd., Sunderland. Service speed 10 knots.
25.7.1903: Launched by Sunderland Shipbuilding Co., Ltd. Sunderland (Yard No. 218) for A.N. Hansen & Co., Copenhagen, Denmark. *9.1903:* Completed and registered at Tønsberg in the ownership of a company in which Wilh. Wilhelmsen were a shareholder and of which they were managers. *11.1.1923:* Sold to Emder Dampfer Kompagnie Nübel & Fritzen A.G., Germany and renamed RADBOD. *1925:* Sold to A.G. für Handel und Verkehr (Lexzau, Scharbau & Co., managers), Germany and renamed KATHARINA DOROTHEA FRITZEN. *29.1.1933:* Arrived at Kiel to be broken up by Deutsche Werke A.G.

TORDENSKJOLD   W.S.P.L.

64. TORDENSKJOLD (II) (1903-1922)
Tonnages: 3,572 gross, 2,296 net, 6,100 deadweight.
Dimensions: 335.0 x 48.0 x 25.5 feet.
Machinery: 3-cylinder triple expansion steam engines of 1,426 i.h.p. by North
Eastern Marine Engineering Co. Ltd., Newcastle. Service speed 10 knots.
21.10.1903: Launched by Tyne Iron Shipbuilding Co. Ltd., Newcastle (Yard
No. 146). *14.11.1903:* Completed. Price paid 668,483.65 kr. *2.12.1922:* Sold
to Emil R. Retzlaff, Germany and renamed HUNDING. *1924:* Sold to A.G.
für Handel und Verkehr (Lexzau, Scharbau & Co., managers), Germany and
renamed KATHARINA DOROTHEA FRITZEN. *2.1.1925:* Wrecked at Skudesnes
while on passage from Rotterdam to Narvik in ballast.

65. TRICOLOR (I) (1904-1905)
Tonnages: 3,843 gross, 2,498 net, 6,500 deadweight.
Dimensions: 350.0 x 48.1 x 17.9 feet.
Machinery: 3-cylinder triple expansion steam engines of 1,650 i.h.p. by Blair
& Co. Ltd., Stockton. Service speed 10 knots.
28.7.1904: Launched by Tyne Iron Shipbuilding Co. Ltd., Newcastle (Yard No.
150). *9.1904:* Completed. Price paid 696,670.52 kr. *25.7.1905:* Wrecked near
Cape Mendocino Light, Eureka, California, while on passage, in fog, from
Nanaimo, B.C. to San Francisco, U.S.A. with a cargo of coal.

THODE FAGELUND on charter to Dupont   W.S.P.L.

66. THODE FAGELUND (I) (1904-1917)
Tonnages: 4,352 gross, 2,826 net, 7,150 deadweight.
Dimensions: 355.0 x 50.0 x 20.0 feet.
Machinery: 3-cylinder triple expansion steam engines of 1,810 i.h.p. by Blair
& Co. Ltd., Stockton. Service speed 10 knots.
12.10.1904: Launched by J. Priestman & Co., Sunderland (Yard No. 107).
11.1904: Completed. Price paid 719,503.89 kr. *12.3.1917:* Torpedoed and sunk
off Ostend in a position 51.40 N, 02.58 E by the German submarine UB 27
while on passage from Shanghai to Rotterdam with a cargo of sesame seed.

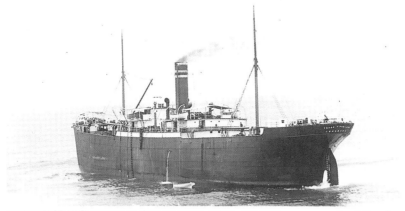

THODE FAGELUND aground on Cronulla Beach, N.S.W., 22.1.1908   *Ian J. Farquhar*

67. JETHOU (1905-1934)
Tonnages: 4,284 gross, 2,781 net, 7,060 deadweight.
Dimensions: 370.4 x 50.0 x 25.8 feet.
Machinery: 3-cylinder triple expansion steam engines of 1,465 i.h.p. by Central
Marine Engine Works, West Hartlepool. Service speed 10 knots.
22.12.1904: Launched by William Gray & Co. Ltd., West Hartlepool (Yard No.
697) for A.N. Hansen, Copenhagen, Denmark. *8.2.1905:* Completed and
registered at Tønsberg in the ownership of a company in which Wilh.
Wilhelmsen were a shareholder and of which they were managers. *25.4.1934:*
Sold to Italian General Shipping Ltd., Italy for scrapping and arrived at Genoa
4.7.1934 to be broken up.

JETHOU

HERM

68. HERM (1905-1920)
Tonnages: 3,902 gross, 2,516 net, 6,600 deadweight.
Dimensions: 344.8 x 49.9 x 18.0 feet.
Machinery: 3-cylinder triple expansion steam engines of 1,650 i.h.p. by D. Rowan & Co., Glasgow. Service speed 10 knots.
28.12.1904: Launched by Russell & Co., Port Glasgow (Yard No. 539) for A.N. Hansen & Co., Copenhagen, Denmark. *2.1905:* Completed and registered at Tønsberg in the ownership of a company in which Wilh. Wilhelmsen were a shareholder and of which they were managers. *1920:* Sold to A/S D/S Atlanterhavet (O.J. Eskildsen, manager), Denmark and renamed SYDHAVET. *1923:* Sold to M. & L.G. Embiricos (later M.G. Embiricos), Greece and renamed ELENI G. EMBIRICOS. *1934:* Sold to Italian shipbreakers. *29.9.1934:* Arrived at Savona to be broken up.

TABOR   *W.S.P.L.*

69. TABOR (I) (1905-1924)
Tonnages: 3,708 gross, 2,392 net, 6,160 deadweight.
Dimensions: 346.5 x 50.9 x 24.7 feet.
Machinery: 3-cylinder triple expansion steam engines of 1,760 i.h.p. by North Eastern Marine Engineering Co. Ltd., Sunderland. Service speed 10 knots.
10.3.1905: Launched by J. Priestman & Co., Sunderland (Yard No. 110). *20.4.1905:* Completed. Price paid 650,627.87 kr. *3.3.1924:* Sold to D/S A/S Tabor (A. Bruusgaard, manager), Drammen. *1928:* Sold to A.G. Constantinidis and P.J. Iatrou, Greece and renamed TO KYMA. *1929:* A.G. Constantinidis became the sole owner. *1933:* Sold to Italian shipbreakers. *22.12.1933:* Arrived at Savona to be broken up.

TAURUS during World War I

70. TAURUS (II) (1905-1935)
Tonnages: 4,262 gross, 2,765 net, 7,387 deadweight.
Dimensions: 355.0 x 50.1 x 20.0 feet.
Machinery: 3-cylinder triple expansion steam engines of 1,870 i.h.p. by Blair & Co. Ltd., Stockton. Service speed 10 knots.
22.3.1905: Launched by Tyne Iron Shipbuilding Co. Ltd., Newcastle (Yard No. 153). *4.1905:* Completed. Price paid 719,425.66 kr. *2.7.1935:* Sold for £8,000 to Achille Lauro, Italy and renamed SANTAGATA. The sale price was agreed on the understanding that the ship would be scrapped, but as she was in fact used for further trading, an additional amount of £300 was paid to Wilh. Wilhelmsen in 1.1940. *4.8.1943:* Bombed and sunk at Naples by Allied aircraft. After the war the wreck was scrapped as it lay.

TRANSIT on her way to Nome, Alaska, with 600 gold prospectors on board

71. TRANSIT (II) (1906-1911)
Tonnages: 1,691 gross, 1,057 net, 2,500 deadweight.
Dimensions: 260.0 x 36.7 x 20.9 feet.
Machinery: 3-cylinder triple expansion steam engines of 1,225 i.h.p. by the shipbuilders. Service speed 9 knots.
15.11.1905: Launched by Fredriksstad Mekaniske Verksted A/S, Fredrikstad (Yard No. 102). *18.1.1906:* Completed. Price paid 394,461.66 kr. *30.8.1911:* Wrecked on the east coast of Kamchatka while outward bound from Petropavlovsk for Ust and Kamchatsk with general cargo.

83

ST. ANDREWS

72. ST. ANDREWS (II) (1906-1920)
Tonnages: 2,984 gross, 1,899 net, 4,900 deadweight.
Dimensions: 325.0 x 46.7 x 21.4 feet.
Machinery: 3-cylinder triple expansion steam engines of 1,300 i.h.p. by George
Clark Ltd., Sunderland. Service speed 10 knots.
11.12.1905: Launched by J. Blumer & Co., Sunderland (Yard No. 184) for A.N.
Hansen & Co., Copenhagen, Denmark. *1.1906:* Completed and registered at
Tønsberg in the ownership of a company in which Wilh. Wilhelmsen were
a shareholder and of which they were managers. *1920:* Sold to D/S
Atlanterhavet (O.J. Eskildsen, manager), Denmark and renamed
SORTEHAVET. *1923:* Sold to Wilh. Kunstmann, Germany and renamed
ARTHUR KUNSTMANN. *1938:* Sold to Johs. Fritzen & Sohn vorm W.
Kunstmann, Germany and renamed GERTRUD FRITZEN.
2.5.1945: Attacked by Typhoon aircraft of No. 184 Squadron off Travemunde
when outward bound from Lübeck for Flensburg with 3,000 tons of sulphur
and between 80 and 100 refugees from Rostock. Sank in five minutes in
shallow water with the loss of at least five refugees and a number of flak
gunners. *2.1946:* Salved by Weichsel & Co., Lübeck, and delivered by
Flenderwerke to Kiel. *18.6.1946:* Left Kiel for Emden to load munitions.
13.7.1946: Scuttled with her cargo in the Skagerrak.

73. TRAFALGAR (I) (1906-1922)
Tonnages: 2,187 gross, 1,384 net, 3,710 deadweight.
Dimensions: 290.0 x 42.2 x 20.5 feet.
Machinery: 3-cylinder triple expansion steam engines of 1,100 i.h.p. by Blair
& Co. Ltd., Stockton. Service speed 10 knots.
First ship on the New York-South America service.
10.2.1906: Launched by J. Crown & Sons Ltd., Sunderland (Yard No. 118).
3.1906: Completed. Price paid 464,741.55 kr. *21.10.1922:* Sold to D/S A/S
Ørsnæs (Jens Lund & Co. A/S, managers), Tønsberg. *1925:* Sold to San Peh
Steam Navigation Co. Ltd., China, and renamed TAISHAN. *26.11.1934:* Left
Tsingtao for Shanghai with a cargo of coal and disappeared after reporting
by radio the following day. *2.12.1934:* Bodies of some of her crew members
were found about 100 miles south of Tsingtao.

84

74. TIMES (1906-1922)
Tonnages: 2,096 gross, 1,328 net, 3,550 deadweight.
Dimensions: 290.0 x 42.2 x 20.4 feet.
Machinery: 3-cylinder triple expansion steam engines of 1,100 i.h.p. by J. Dickinson & Sons, Ltd., Sunderland. Service speed 10 knots.
11.5.1906: Launched by J. Priestman & Co., Sunderland (Yard No. 116). *29.5.1906:* Completed. Price paid 474,223.12 kr. *21.10.1922:* Sold to D/S A/S Ørsnæs (Jens Lund & Co. A/S, managers), Tønsberg. *1925:* Sold to Fukuzawa Masukichi, Japan and renamed TIMES MARU. *1931:* Renamed TAIKYU MARU. *1937:* Sold to Taikyu Kisen K.K., Japan. *16.6.1945:* Mined and sunk in the Tsushima Strait off Karatsu in a position 33.58 N, 130.34 E.

TRICOLOR

75. TRICOLOR (II) (1906-1925)
Tonnages: 4,019 gross, 2,597 net, 6,700 deadweight.
Dimensions: 351.2 x 50.1 x 25.5 feet.
Machinery: 3-cylinder triple expansion steam engines of 1,815 i.h.p. by Blair & Co. Ltd., Stockton. Service speed 10 knots.
24.3.1906: Launched by Tyne Iron Shipbuilding Co. Ltd., Newcastle (Yard No. 158). *16.5.1906:* Completed. Price paid 698,856.40 kr. *14.3.1925:* Sold to Emder Dampfer Kompagnie Nübel & Fritzen A.G., later Emder Dampfer Kompagnie (W. Nübel, manager), Germany and renamed WITTEKIND. *14.1.1944:* Bombed and sunk off Lister by British aircraft while on passage from Narvik to Germany. 29 of her crew were lost.

76. THORDIS (II) (1906-1911)
Tonnages: 1,749 gross, 1,091 net, 2,500 deadweight.
Dimensions: 264.7 x 39.0 x 11.1 feet.
Machinery: 3-cylinder triple expansion steam engines of 950 i.h.p. by Richardsons, Westgarth & Co. Ltd., Middlesbrough. Service speed 10 knots.
10.1906: Completed by Fevigs Jernskibsbyggeri, Fevig, Arendal (Yard No. 59). Price paid 446,474.54 kr. *5.7.1911:* Wrecked in the Sea of Okhotsk near Gizhiga while on passage from Petropavlovsk to Vladivostock.

77. THELMA (1906-1921)
Tonnages: 1,350 gross, 847 net, 2,100 deadweight.
Dimensions: 260.0 x 38.1 x 16.7 feet.
Machinery: 3-cylinder triple expansion steam engines of 1,000 i.h.p. by the shipbuilders. Service speed 10 knots.
31.10.1906: Launched by Laxevaags Maskin-og Jernskibsbyggeri, Bergen (Yard No. 82). *11.1906:* Completed. Price paid 354,289.60 kr. *10.12.1921:* Sold to Rederi A/B Gefion (Joh. Gorthon, manager), Sweden, and renamed STIG. *1924:* Renamed STIG GORTHON. *7.1927:* Sold to Rederi A/B Brubor (Ragnar Brunkman, manager), Sweden, and renamed MERGUS. *5.1951:* Sold to Førnyade Rederi-A/B Commercial (Helge Johnsson, manager), Sweden and renamed VÄRING. *10.1955:* Sold to Rederi-A/B Signe (John Andersson, manager), Sweden and renamed SIGNE. *11.12.1959:* Sprang a leak and sank at Helsingborg where she was being used as a grain store. Subsequently raised and sold *26.1.1960* to Vereenigde Utrechtsche Ijzerhandel N.V., Utrecht to be broken up. *5.2.1960:* Arrived at Rotterdam in tow of the tug MAAS. *6.1960:* Demolition commenced.

ELSA at Bristol during World War I   *Norsk Sjøfartsmuseum*

78. ELSA (1906-1918)
Tonnages: 3,581 gross, 2,304 net, 6,100 deadweight.
Dimensions: 335.0 x 48.1 x 25.5 feet.
Machinery: 3-cylinder triple expansion steam engines of 1,426 i.h.p. by North Eastern Marine Engineering Co. Ltd., Newcastle. Service speed 10 knots.
25.10.1904: Launched by Tyne Iron Shipbuilding Co. Ltd., Newcastle (Yard No. 151) as ELSA for A.C. Mohr & Son, Bergen. *17.11.1904:* Completed. *1906:* Purchased by Wilh. Wilhelmsen. Price paid 648,000.00 kr. *24.1.1918:* Torpedoed and sunk five miles E.S.E of Dartmouth by the German submarine UB 31 while on passage from Sourabaya and Cardiff to Christiania (Oslo) with general cargo and coal.

79. HEIMDAL (1907-1910)

Tonnages: 2,998 gross, 1,856 net, 5,000 deadweight.
Dimensions: 314.0 x 41.3 x 21.5 feet.
Machinery: 3-cylinder triple expansion steam engines of 1,375 i.h.p. by the shipbuilders. Service speed 9 knots.
21.11.1889: Launched by Palmers' Shipbuilding & Iron Co. Ltd., Jarrow (Yard No. 631) as EGREMONT CASTLE for Lancaster Shipowners' Co. Ltd. (later Lancashire Shipping Co. Ltd.) (W.J. Chambers, later James Chambers & Co., managers), Liverpool. *1.1890:* Completed. *1902:* Sold to Macbeth & Co. Ltd., Glasgow and registered at Sydney, New South Wales. *1907:* Purchased by Wilh. Wilhelmsen and renamed HEIMDAL. *20.6.1910:* Wrecked on Sable Island, N.S. while on passage from Santos to the U.K. in ballast.

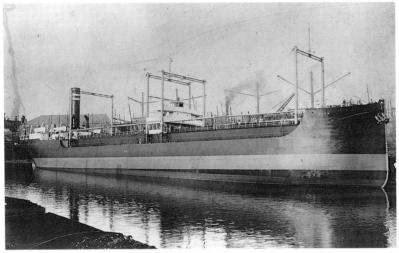

THOR   *Norsk Sjøfartsmuseum*

80. THOR (1907-1917)

Tonnages: 4,739 gross, 2,889 net, 7,600 deadweight.
Dimensions: 359.9 x 52.6 x 24.7 feet.
Machinery: 3-cylinder triple expansion steam engines of 2,030 i.h.p. by Blair & Co. Ltd., Stockton. Service speed 10 knots.
9.9.1907: Launched by Ropner & Sons Ltd., Stockton (Yard No. 439). *1907:* Completed. Price paid 875,883.25 kr. She was the first Wilhelmsen bulk carrier and was at the time of completion the largest steamship under the Norwegian flag. *18.11.1917:* Abandoned in a sinking condition N.W. of Hawaii in a position 34 N, 161 W after being overwhelmed by a hurricane while on a voyage from San Francisco to Hong Kong with general cargo.

81. TORSDAL (1908-1916)

Tonnages: 3,620 gross, 2,299 net, 6,000 deadweight.
Dimensions: 350.0 x 43.1 x 19.3 feet.
Machinery: 3-cylinder triple expansion steam engines of 1,760 i.h.p. by North Eastern Marine Engineering Co. Ltd., Newcastle. Service speed 10 knots.
19.7.1894: Launched by Tyne Iron Shipbuilding Co. Ltd., Newcastle (Yard No. 104) as STRATHNEVIS for Burrell & Son, Glasgow. *8.1894:* Completed. *14.4.1899:* Sold to Tate Steamers Ltd. (A. Tate & Co., managers), Glasgow.

1.12.1903: Sold to J. Mackay (Macbeth & Co. Ltd., managers), Glasgow. *1908:* Macbeth & Co. Ltd. became owners. *1908:* Purchased by Wilh. Wilhelmsen and renamed TORSDAL. *28.10.1916:* Torpedoed and sunk 25 miles S.E. of Cape St. Vincent by the German submarine U 63 while on passage from Civitavecchia to Barry in ballast.

TUDDAL   *Norsk Sjøfartsmuseum*

82. TUDDAL (1909-1917)
Tonnages: 3,510 gross, 2,218 net, 5,700 deadweight.
Dimensions: 330.0 x 45.0 x 18.6 feet.
Machinery: 3-cylinder triple expansion steam engines of 1,700 i.h.p. by Blair & Co. Ltd., Stockton. Service speed 10 knots.
5.9.1895: Launched by Ropner & Son, Stockton (Yard No. 310) as DUNOTTAR for Macbeth & Gray, Glasgow. *9.1895:* Completed. *1901:* Owners became Macbeth & Co. Ltd. *1909:* Purchased by Wilh. Wilhelmsen and renamed TUDDAL. *14.8.1917:* Torpedoed and sunk off Ushant in a position 46.45 N, 07.00 W by the German submarine UB 40 while on passage from Havana to le Havre with a cargo of sugar.

83. CUZCO (1910-1917)
Tonnages: 4,302 gross, 2,773 net, 7,100 deadweight.
Dimensions: 375.0 x 50.0 x 25.9 feet.
Machinery: 3-cylinder triple expansion steam engines of 1,870 i.h.p. by D. & W. Henderson & Co., Glasgow. Service speed 9 knots.
10.6.1899: Launched by Napier & Miller Ltd., Glasgow (Yard No. 85) as CUZCO for New York & Pacific Steam Ship Co. Ltd., London. *11.1899:* Completed. *17.8.1910:* Purchased by Wilh. Wilhelmsen. *28.2.1917:* Stranded on the coast of Chile and declared a constructive total loss. Subsequently salved and towed to Callao. *1920:* Sold to Nafra Italiana, Italy. In *1921* this firm went into liquidation and she was taken over by Banca Italiana di Sconto (Roma Societa di Nav., managers), Italy. Banca Italiana di Sconto themselves subsequently went into liquidation. *1932:* Sold to shipbreakers at Genoa.

TERRIER

84. TERRIER (II) (1911-1934)
Tonnages: 5,122 gross, 3,163 net, 8,400 deadweight.
Dimensions: 400.0 x 52.0 x 27.4 feet.
Machinery: 3-cylinder triple expansion steam engines of 2,310 i.h.p. by Blair & Co. Ltd., Stockton. Service speed 10 knots.
30.12.1910: Launched by Joseph L. Thompson & Sons Ltd., Sunderland (Yard No. 478). *2.1911:* Completed. Price paid 811,559.80 kr. *12.6.1934:* Sold to Far Eastern S.S. Co. Ltd. A/S (J. Gran, manager), Bergen and renamed MABUHAY I. *1938:* Sold to Koun Kisen K.K. (Yamashita Kisen K.K., managers), Japan and renamed RYUNAN MARU. *1939:* Sold to Matumoto Masaiti, Japan. *20.10.1942:* Torpedoed and sunk east of Kii Channel, Japan, in a position 34.09 N, 136.46 E by the United States submarine DRUM.

85. TELLUS (II) (1911-1915)
Tonnages: 7,395 gross, 4,131 net, 13,000 deadweight.
Dimensions: 445.0 x 60.0 x 29.2 feet.
Machinery: 3-cylinder triple expansion steam engines of 2,400 i.h.p. by the shipbuilders. Service speed 10 knots.
31.1.1911: Launched by William Doxford & Sons Ltd., Sunderland (Yard No. 417). *8.3.1911:* Completed. Price paid 1,125,165.39 kr. At the time of completion she was the largest cargo steamship in the world. *11.1915:* Went

aground at Nemuro, near Yokohama, while on passage from New York to Vladivostock. *1.1916:* Refloated and by *22.1.1916* had arrived at Hanasaki. *2.4.1916:* Arrived at Shanghai for repairs and subsequently sold to A/S Elizabeth IV (O. Wikberg, manager), Drammen and renamed ELIZABETH IV. *8.9.1916:* Captured by the German submarine U 34 N.E. of Menorca in a position 41.14 N, 06.24 E while on passage from Java to Marseilles with a cargo of sugar and scuttled with explosive charges.

THEMIS during World War I

86. THEMIS (II) (1911-1917)
Tonnages: 7,402 gross, 4,134 net, 13,000 deadweight.
Dimensions: 445.0 x 60.0 x 29.2 feet.
Machinery: 3-cylinder triple expansion steam engines of 2,400 i.h.p. by the shipbuilders. Service speed 10 knots.
30.3.1911: Launched by William Doxford & Sons Ltd., Sunderland (Yard No. 419). *25.4.1911:* Completed. Price paid 1,125,925.20 kr. *12.10.1917:* Torpedoed and sunk about 20 miles North of Cape Bon, Tunisia, in a position 37.23 N, 11.05 E. by the German submarine UB 51 while on passage, in convoy, from Karachi to Marseilles with a cargo of grain..

87. ATNA (1911-1925)
Tonnages: 4,682 gross, 2,873 net, 8,520 deadweight.
Dimensions: 390.0 x 53.5 x 26.1 feet.
Machinery: 3-cylinder triple expansion steam engines of 2,900 i.h.p. by the shipbuilders. Service speed 11 knots.
Accommodation for 7 first class passengers. She, TYSLA and RENA were the first ships designed to carry passengers.
First ship on the Scandinavian Line.
6.7.1911: Launched by William Doxford & Sons Ltd., Sunderland (Yard No. 424). *16.8.1911:* Completed - the first liner in the fleet. Price paid 939,810.87 kr. *4.4.1925:* Sold to Schulte & Bruns, Germany. *27.6.1925:* Delivered and renamed GODFRIED BUEREN. *10.1929:* Owners became "Atlas" Reederei A.G., Germany. *18.1.1941:* Sank 20 miles east of Limfjorden, Denmark, after striking a mine.

TYSLA

88. TYSLA (I) (1911-1914)
Tonnages: 4,676 gross, 2,879 net, 8,300 deadweight.
Dimensions: 390.0 x 53.5 x 26.1 feet.
Machinery: 3-cylinder triple expansion steam engines of 2,900 i.h.p. by the shipbuilders. Service speed 11 knots.
Passengers: 7.
17.8.1911: Launched by William Doxford & Sons Ltd., Sunderland (Yard No. 430). *2.10.1911:* Completed. Price paid 939,964.03 kr. *7.8.1914:* Became the first Norwegian ''war loss'' of World War I when she sank near Flushing after striking a Dutch mine while on passage from Port Pirie to Antwerp. Three of her crew were killed.

RENA

89. RENA (1911-1934)
Tonnages: 4,686 gross, 2,885 net, 8,520 deadweight.
Dimensions: 390.0 x 53.5 x 26.2 feet.
Machinery: 3-cylinder triple expansion steam engines of 2,900 i.h.p. by the shipbuilders. Service speed 11 knots.
Passengers: 8.
First ship on the Scandinavian Joint Service.
26.8.1911: Launched by William Doxford & Sons Ltd., Sunderland (Yard No. 435). *23.11.1911:* Completed. Price paid 990,922.59 kr. *19.6.1934:* Sold to the Grimstad Shipbreaking Company and subsequently scrapped at Grimstad.

91

90. LOSNA (1912-1921)
Tonnages: 4,187 gross, 2,665 net, 6,700 deadweight.
Dimensions: 360.0 x 50.2 x 17.9 feet.
Machinery: 3-cylinder triple expansion steam engines of 2,000 i.h.p. by North Eastern Marine Engineering Co. Ltd., Newcastle. Service speed 11 knots.
16.4.1904: Launched by Sir Raylton Dixon & Co. Ltd., Middlesbrough (Yard No. 507) as ADMIRAL BØRRESEN for V. Torkildsen, Bergen. *14.6.1904:* Completed. *26.9.1912:* Purchased by Wilh. Wilhelmsen and renamed LOSNA. Price paid 620,000.00 kr. *27.11.1921:* Wrecked 20 miles east of Great Fish Point, South Africa, while on passage from Viborg to Cape Town and Delagoa Bay with a cargo of timber.

VINSTRA *Ian J. Farquhar*

91. VINSTRA (1913-1935)
Tonnages: 4,668 gross, 2,932 net, 8,213 deadweight.
Dimensions: 410.0 x 52.2 x 25.7 feet.
Machinery: 3-cylinder triple expansion steam engines of 2,100 i.h.p. by D. Rowan & Co., Glasgow. Service speed 11 knots.
1.10.1910: Launched by Russell & Co., Port Glasgow (Yard No. 618) as DRUMCRAIG for Astral Shipping Co. Ltd. (J. Chadwick & Sons, managers), Liverpool. *10.1910:* Completed. *1913:* Purchased by Wilh. Wilhelmsen and renamed VINSTRA. Price paid 1,187,433.68 kr. *28.12.1935:* Sold to A/B Oceanfart (Birger Krogius, manager), Finland and renamed HERAKLES. *1942:* Seized by the Germans. *8.1943:* Damaged by air attack while lying at Åbo. *5.1945:* Recovered, repaired and returned to service. *1950:* Sold to Rederi A/B Curt Mattson, Finland. *1951:* Transferred to Rederi A/B Trident (Curt Mattson, manager), Finland. *1958:* Sold to Hong Kong Salvage & Towing Co. Ltd. for scrapping. *15.11.1958:* Arrived at Hong Kong. *11.12.1958:* Demolition commenced.

92. SAN JOAQUIN (1913-1929) Tanker
Tonnages: 6,987 gross, 4,421 net, 10,360 deadweight.
Dimensions: 425.5 x 57.1 x 33.1 feet.
Machinery: 3-cylinder triple expansion steam engines of 2,250 i.h.p. by George Clark Ltd., Sunderland. Service speed 10 knots.
The first Wilhelmsen tanker.

14.11.1913: Launched by Sir James Laing & Sons Ltd., Sunderland (Yard No. 644). *21.12.1913:* Completed. Price paid 1,862,527.25 kr. *6.6.1929:* Sold to A/S Hektor (N. Bugge, manager), Tønsberg and renamed MELVILLE. *1935:* Sold to Hellenic Tramp S.S. Co. Ltd. (S. Iossifoglu, manager), Greece and renamed IOLCOS. *1937:* Sold to Finchley S.S. Co. Ltd (J. N. Vassiliou, manager), London and renamed WOODFORD. *1.9.1937:* Torpedoed and sunk 24 miles off Benicarlo, Spain, by the Italian submarine DIASPRO while on a voyage from Constantza to Valencia during the Spanish Civil War with a cargo of fuel oil.

MEXICANO

93. MEXICANO (1914-1934)
Tonnages: 3,694 gross, 2,312 net, 5,824 deadweight.
Dimensions: 346.0 x 46.8 x 24.8 feet.
Machinery: 3-cylinder triple expansion steam engines of 2,030 i.h.p. by J. Dickinson & Sons Ltd., Sunderland. Service speed 11 knots.
First ship on the U.S.A., Cuba and Mexico service.
6.12.1911: Launched by Sir James Laing &. Sons Ltd., Sunderland (Yard No. 634) as MEXICANO for Norge Mexico Gulf Linien (G. M. Bryde, manager) and registered at Christiania (Oslo). *17.2.1912:* Completed. *1.1914:* Taken over by Wilh. Wilhelmsen when Norge Mexico Gulf Linien was acquired, and re-registered at Tønsberg. Price paid 892,971.52 kr. *11.4.1934:* Sold to Lindholmen-Motala, Gothenburg, for scrapping, but re-sold for further trading to Glückmans Metallaffär, later Rederi A/S Ruth, both of which were managed by Leopold Glückman, Sweden, and renamed RUTH. *7.5.1942:* Badly damaged by allied air attack off Vlieland while on passage from Rotterdam to Gothenburg with a cargo of coal, and beached to avoid sinking. Condemned as beyond repair.

NORUEGA

94. NORUEGA (1914-1924)
Tonnages: 3,459 gross, 2,192 net, 5,800 deadweight.
Dimensions: 330.9 x 46.1 x 15.2 feet.
Machinery: 3-cylinder triple expansion steam engines of 1,850 i.h.p. by Richardsons, Westgarth & Co. Ltd., Middlesbrough. Service speed 10 knots.
17.10.1908: Launched by Fevigs Jernskibsbyggeri, Fevig, Arendal (Yard No. 67) as NORUEGA for Norge Mexico Gulf Linien (G. M. Bryde, manager) and registered at Christiania (Oslo). *1.1909:* Completed. *1.1914:* Taken over by Wilh. Wilhelmsen when Norge Mexico Gulf Linien was acquired, and re-registered at Tønsberg. Price paid 797,009.17 kr. *30.4.1924:* Sold to Soc. Algérienne de Navigation pour l'Afrique du Nord (Charles Schiaffino et Cie., managers), France and renamed SCHIAFFINO. *1925:* Renamed MARIE LOUISE SCHIAFFINO. *1937:* Sold to André Puech, France and renamed BRISBANE. *8.6.1938:* Badly damaged by air attack while lying at Denia during the Spanish Civil War. Beached, but a constructive total loss and later cut up for scrap during port clearance.

LA HABRA   *Norsk Sjøfartsmuseum*

95. LA HABRA (1914-1936) Tanker
Tonnages: 7,021 gross, 4,437 net, 10,360 deadweight.
Dimensions: 424.8 x 57.0 x 33.2 feet.
Machinery: 3-cylinder triple expansion steam engines of 2,250 i.h.p. by
George Clark Ltd., Sunderland. Service speed 10 knots.
26.1.1914: Launched by Sir James Laing & Sons Ltd., Sunderland (Yard No.
645). *4.3.1914:* Completed. Price paid 1,895,127.33 kr. *26.10.1936:* Sold to
Magnus Konow & Co., Oslo and renamed APACHE. *1937:* Sold to Esturia
S.S. Co. Ltd. (S. Catsell, manager), London and renamed ESTURIA. *1939:*
Sold to Harris & Dixon Ltd., London. *1947:* Sold to ''Corrado'' Soc. di Nav.,
Italy and renamed RINA CORRADO. *4.4.1955:* Arrived at Troon to be scrapped
by the West of Scotland Shipbreaking Co. Ltd.

MARICOPA   *Norsk Sjøfartsmuseum*

96. MARICOPA (1914-1929) Tanker
Tonnages: 6,960 gross, 4,417 net, 10,300 deadweight.
Dimensions: 425.2 x 57.0 x 33.1 feet.
Machinery: 3-cylinder triple expansion steam engines of 2,250 i.h.p. by the
shipbuilders. Service speed 10 knots.
27.4.1914: Launched by Palmers' Shipbuilding & Iron Co. Ltd., Jarrow (Yard
No. 836). *16.5.1914:* Completed. Price paid 2,030,883.20 kr. *25.1.1929:* Sold
to Falkland Shipowners Ltd., London, renamed ANGLO NORSE and converted
into a Whale Oil Refinery. *20.6.1941:* Purchased by the Ministry of War
Transport (Chr. Salvesen & Co., managers). *19.8.1941:* In collision with the
Canadian s.s. LANARK, 1,904/23 while on passage from Curaçao to the Tyne
with a cargo of oil and put in to the Tyne with hull damage. *31.8.1941:* Caught
fire while under repair and beached. Her ammunition magazine exploded and
she was scuttled. *3.9.1941:* Refloated and subsequently repaired and renamed
EMPIRE NORSE. *14.6.1946:* Returned to Falkland Shipowners Ltd., and
reverted to the name ANGLO NORSE. *5.1950:* Sold to Armement Baleinier
S.A., France. *1956:* Renamed JANINA. *15.1.1957:* Abandoned, ablaze, N.W.
of Oporto, Portugal, in a position 41.43 N, 09.30 W after fire had broken out
during a voyage from Odessa to Åbo with a cargo of oil. *18.1.1957:* Sank.

BELRIDGE   *Norsk Sjøfartsmuseum*

97. BELRIDGE (1914-1935) Tanker

Tonnages: 7,020 gross, 4,420 net, 10,300 deadweight.
Dimensions: 425.1 x 57.0 x 33.1 feet.
Machinery: 3-cylinder triple expansion steam engines of 2.250 i.h.p. by
George Clark Ltd., Sunderland. Service speed 10 knots.
29.4.1914: Launched by Sir James Laing & Sons Ltd.. Sunderland (Yard No.
647). *6.6.1914:* Completed. Price paid 2,048,320.73 kr. *10.1.1935:* Sold to
Skibs A/S Apache (Magnus Konow & Co., managers), Oslo and renamed
APACHE. *1936:* Sold to Petros M. Nomikos Ltd., Greece and renamed
PETRAKIS NOMIKOS. *17.4.1941:* Beached near Piraeus after being badly
damaged by air attack while lying at Ambelaki. *3.4.1941:* Bombed again and
suffered further damage. Later salved by the Germans, repaired at Venice
and renamed WILHELMSBURG, managed by Atlantic Rhederei F. & W. Joch.
7.7.1943: Torpedoed and sunk off Lemnos by H.M. Submarine RORQUAL.

AMERICA   *Norsk Sjøfartsmuseum*

98. AMERICA (II) (1914-1915)
Tonnages: 3,707 gross, 2,415 net, 5,800 deadweight.
Dimensions: 357.5 x 48.0 x 27.2 feet.
Machinery: 3-cylinder triple expansion steam engines of 2,220 i.h.p. by North Eastern Marine Engineering Co. Ltd., Newcastle. Service speed 11 knots.
10.1914: Completed by Sørlandets Skibsbyggeri, Fevig, Arendal, from whom she had been ordered by Norge Mexico Gulf Linien before the Line was acquired by Wilh. Wilhelmsen. Price paid 1,297,000.57 kr. *2.5.1915:* Torpedoed and sunk in the North Sea east of Aberdeen in a position 57.23 N, 01.10 E by the German submarine U 41 while on passage from Boston and Sunderland to Bergen with general cargo.

TYSLA   *Ian J. Farquhar*

99. TYSLA (II) (1914-1935)
Tonnages: 4,297 gross, 2,691 net, 8,386 deadweight.
Dimensions: 405.0 x 53.4 x 25.5 feet.
Machinery: 3-cylinder triple expansion steam engines of 2,150 i.h.p. by Blair & Co. Ltd., Stockton. Service speed 11 knots.
19.11.1914: Completed by Northumberland Shipbuilding Co. Ltd., Newcastle (Yard No. 219) having been purchased while under construction. Price paid 1,273,108.50 kr. *8.6.1935:* Sold to John D. Chandris, Greece and renamed AGIOS VLASIOS. *1939:* Sold to Yamashita Kisen K.K., Japan and renamed SUGIYAMA MARU. *15.11.1944:* Torpedoed and sunk S.E. of Hainan Island in a position 15.14 N, 112.13 E by the American submarine BARBEL.

100. CUBANO (I) (1915-1915)
Tonnages: 4,337 gross, 2,805 net, 7,350 deadweight.
Dimensions: 375.7 x 52.2 x 25.5 feet.
Machinery: 3-cylinder triple expansion steam engines of 1,925 i.h.p. by J.G. Kincaid & Co. Ltd., Greenock. Service speed 10 knots.
8.2.1912: Launched by Greenock & Grangemouth Dockyard Co. Ltd., Greenock (Yard No. 336) as STRATHMORE for Strathmore S S. Co. Ltd. (Burrell & Son, managers), Glasgow. *4.1915:* Purchased by Wilh. Wilhelmsen and renamed CUBANO. Price paid 1,201,395.00 kr. *3.6.1915:* Sunk by gunfire by the German submarine U 35 fifteen miles N.E. of the Flannan Islands, Outer Hebrides, while on a voyage from Christiania (Oslo) to the East Indies with general cargo.

BONNA

101. BONNA (1915-1922)
Tonnages: 4,255 gross, 2,711 net, 7,100 deadweight.
Dimensions: 365.0 x 50.8 x 26.0 feet.
Machinery: 3-cylinder triple expansion steam engines of 2,000 i.h.p. by Central Marine Engine Works, West Hartlepool. Service speed 10 knots.
2.3.1911: Launched by William Gray & Co. Ltd., West Hartlepool (Yard No.785) as HANS B. for Akties. Borgen (G. E. Stoesen, manager), Bergen. *13.4.1911:* Completed. *6.1915:* Purchased by Wilh. Wilhelmsen and renamed BONNA. Price paid 1,542,648.00 kr. *8.8.1922:* Sold to G. Nicolaou (later N. Nicolaou and subsequently N.G. Nicolaou), Greece and renamed AGIOS GEORGIOS. *1935:* Sold to G. Pantaleon & Sons (later D. Pantaleon Sons, subsequently Pantaleon Navigation, and then P. & B. Pantaleon), Greece. *1960:* Sold to Arcadia Shipping Corporation, Greece. *23.1.1964:* Arrived at Split to be scrapped by Brodospas who commenced work the following month.

YARRA

102. ARTEMIS / YARRA (1915-1927)
Tonnages: 5,076 gross, 3,068 net, 9,600 deadweight.
Dimensions: 410.0 x 54.0 x 26.4 feet.
Machinery: 3-cylinder triple expansion steam engines of 2,200 i.h.p. by Blair
& Co. Ltd., Stockton. Service speed 10 knots.
First ship on the Far East service.
22.8.1910: Launched by Ropner & Sons Ltd., Stockton (Yard No. 453) as
ARTEMIS for Akties. Chr. Michelsen & Co., Bergen. *9.9.1910:* Completed.
7.1915: Purchased by Wilh. Wilhelmsen and subsequently renamed YARRA.
Price paid 2,189,000.00 kr. *3.12.1927:* Severely damaged by fire at Gizo,
Solomon Islands, whilst loading copra during a voyage from Newcastle, N.S.W.
to Antwerp with ivory and zinc ore. Beached and *9.12.1927* abandoned as
a constructive total loss. *26.4.1928:* Refloated and subsequently sold and
towed to Kobe for demolition.

MIRITA

103. ZURITA / MIRITA (1916-1934) Tanker
Tonnages: 5,845 gross, 3,655 net, 8,700 deadweight.
Dimensions: 407.0 x 52.4 x 31.5 feet.
Machinery: 3-cylinder triple expansion steam engines of 2,200 i.h.p. by
George Clark Ltd., Sunderland. Service speed 10 knots.
19.1.1916: Launched by Sir James Laing & Sons Ltd., Sunderland (Yard No.
652) as ZURITA. *28.7.1916:* Completed, having been renamed MIRITA, port
of registry London, and by arrangement consequent upon war requisition
placed under the management of H.E. Moss & Co., Liverpool, being registered
in the ownership of Wm. Molyneux Cohan, senior partner in that firm. Price
paid 1,437,172.01 kr. *9.1919:* Returned to Wilh. Wilhelmsen. *14.11.1934:* Sold
to Glenfield Syndicate Ltd., London and renamed GLENFIELD. *1935:* Sold
to Hellenic Tramp S.S. Co. Ltd. (S. Iossifoglu, manager), Greece and renamed
IONIA. *1937:* Sold to Finchley S.S. Co. Ltd. (J. N. Vassiliou, manager), London
and renamed ROMFORD. *1937:* Sold to Cia. Primera de Nav. Ltda., Panama
and renamed CLAIRY. *21.5.1940:* Attacked by German aircraft when in
Boulogne Roads during a voyage from Giuria and New York to Dunkirk with
crude oil, set on fire and abandoned the following day.

104. RINDA (I) (1916-1917)
Tonnages: 5,509 gross, 2,620 net, 7,700 deadweight.
Dimensions: 385.0 x 53.7 x 31.6 feet.
Machinery: 3-cylinder triple expansion steam engines of 2,400 i.h.p. by J.
Dickinson & Sons Ltd., Sunderland. Service speed 11 knots.
18.4.1916: Launched by Joseph L. Thompson & Sons Ltd., Sunderland (Yard
No. 512). *5.12.1916:* Completed. Price paid 1,385,004.24 kr. Requisitioned

by the British Government, although not placed under the British flag, and, by arrangement, managed by Furness, Withy & Co. Ltd. *9.1.1917:* Wrecked in Edinburgh Channel, Thames Estuary, while bound from Newcastle to Naples.

MANTILLA

105. MEXPETRO / MANTILLA (1917-1939) Tanker
Tonnages: 5,671 gross, 3,495 net, 9,100 deadweight.
Dimensions: 407.0 x 52.2 x 31.4 feet.
Machinery: 3-cylinder triple expansion steam engines of 2,200 i.h.p. by North Eastern Marine Engineering Co. Ltd., Newcastle. Service speed 10.5 knots.
16.6.1916: Launched by Sir W.G. Armstrong, Whitworth & Co. Ltd., Newcastle (Yard No. 886) as MEXPETRO. *12.1916:* Renamed MANTILLA. *12.1.1917:* Completed and by arrangement consequent upon war requisition placed under the management of H.E. Moss & Co. (registered owner W.M. Cohan). Price paid 1,480,134.52 kr. *6.1920:* Returned to Wilh. Wilhelmsen. *3.1939:* Sold to John T. Essberger, Germany and renamed NORDMEER. *3.9.1939:* Lying at Willemstad, but *9.12.1939* broke out and returned to Germany. *1940:* Taken over by the German Navy. *26.8.1944:* Scuttled in the River Gironde. *2.12.1946:* Refloated and subsequently repaired. It was initially proposed that she would be sold to Soc. Française des Petroliers who intended to rename her THIERACHE. However in *1948* she was purchased by S.A. Les Petroles d'Outremer, France and renamed ARTVINE. *9.8.1954:* Arrived in the Tyne to be scrapped at Dunston by Clayton & Davie Ltd.

106. OHIO (1917-1917)
Tonnages: 5,524 gross, 3,530 net, 7,700 deadweight.
Dimensions: 385.0 x 53.7 x 31.6 feet.
Machinery: 3-cylinder triple expansion steam engines of 2,200 i.h.p. by J. Dickinson & Sons Ltd., Sunderland. Service speed 11 knots.
15.6.1916: Launched by Joseph L. Thompson & Sons Ltd., Sunderland (Yard No. 513) as OHIO. *9.3.1917:* Completed, having been renamed ORTONA, port of registry London, and by arrangement consequent upon war requisition placed under the management of Furness, Withy & Co. Ltd. (registered owners The Gulf Line Ltd.), London. Price paid 1,356,150.28 kr. *21.6.1917:* Torpedoed and sunk 140 miles S.S.W. of the Fastnet in a position 49.01 N, 09.55 W by the German submarine U 150 while on a voyage from Philadelphia to London with general cargo.

BESSA at Hull

107. BESSA (1917-1936)
Tonnages: 7,815 gross, 5,847 net, 11,650 deadweight.
Dimensions: 410.9 x 56.2 x 38.4 feet.
Machinery: 3-cylinder triple expansion steam engines of 2,500 i.h.p. by Union Iron Works Company, San Francisco, Cal. Service speed 11 knots.
20.1.1917: Launched by Union Iron Works Company, Alameda, Cal. (Yard No. 139). *3.1917:* Completed. Price paid 7,133,942.85 kr. *4.12.1936:* Sold to Rederi A/S Henneseid (Thoralf Holta, manager), Porsgrunn. *1937:* Renamed BINNA. *1939:* Sold to Yosiaki Tamaya, Japan and renamed TAMAKI MARU. *1941:* Sold to Nissan Kisen K.K., Japan and renamed NISSYU MARU. *18.7.1944:* Torpedoed and sunk N.W. of the Bonin Islands in a position 28.43 N, 139.24 E by the American submarine COBIA.

108. HERCULES (1917-1921)
Tonnages: 3,789 gross, 2,439 net, 6,700 deadweight.
Dimensions: 339.0 x 48.0 x 17.9 feet.
Machinery: 3-cylinder triple expansion steam engines of 1,760 i.h.p. by George Clark Ltd., Sunderland. Service speed 10 knots.
15.12.1902: Launched by Osbourne, Graham & Co., Sunderland (Yard No. 120) as HERCULES for Venus Steam Shipping Co. Ltd., Newcastle. *26.2.1903:* Completed. Shortly afterwards Venus Steam Shipping Co. Ltd. went into liquidation. *1904:* Sold to A/S D/S Hercules (J. Christensen, manager), Bergen. *1915:* Sold to L. Kloster, Stavanger. *1.1917:* Purchased by Wilh. Wilhelmsen. Price paid 4,559,592.06 kr. *1921:* Sold to Bruusgaard & Kjøsterud, Drammen. *1922:* Sold to A/S Neptun (B. Hanssen, manager), Oslo. *1926:* Sold to Skibs A/S Steam (J. G. Larssen, manager), Oslo. *8.1933:* Sold to Italian shipbreakers. *27.9.1933:* Passed Gibraltar bound for Spezia for scrapping.

109. MADRONO (1917-1929) Tanker

Tonnages: 5,894 gross, 3,697 net, 8,600 deadweight.
Dimensions: 407.5 x 52.4 x 31.6 feet.
Machinery: 3-cylinder triple expansion steam engines of 2,200 i.h.p. by George Clark Ltd., Sunderland. Service speed 10 knots.
11.11.1916: Launched by Palmers' Shipbuilding & Iron Co. Ltd., Jarrow (Yard No. 846). *4.1917:* Completed and by arrangement consequent upon war requisition placed under the management of H.E. Moss & Co., Liverpool (registered owner W.M. Cohan). Price paid 1,413,117.03 kr. *10.1919:* Returned to Wilh. Wilhelmsen. *19.12.1929:* Sold to Skibs A/S ''Madrono'' (Hans Borge, manager), Tønsberg. *1938:* Sold to A/S Norsk Rutefart (A.I. Langfeldt & Co., managers), Kristiansand. *4.7.1942:* Captured in the Indian Ocean in a position 29.50 S, 70.00 E by the German raider THOR while on passage from Melbourne to Abadan in ballast. Prize crew placed on board, renamed ROSSBACH and sailed to Yokohama. Allocated to Waried Tankschiff Rhederei G.m.b.H. *7.5.1944:* Torpedoed and sunk in the Kii Channel, Japan, in a position 33.14 N, 134.40 E by the American submarine BURRFISH.

SIMLA

Ian J. Farquhar

110. SIMLA (1917-1940)

Tonnages: 6,031 gross, 3,810 net, 9,430 deadweight.
Dimensions: 405.3 x 53.5 x 33.5 feet.
Machinery: 3-cylinder triple expansion steam engines of 2,500 i.h.p. by J. Dickinson & Sons Ltd., Sunderland. Service speed 11.5 knots.
Passengers: 4.
19.4.1916: Launched by Sir James Laing & Sons Ltd., Sunderland (Yard No. 656) as SIMLA. *1.6.1917:* Completed, having been renamed GLASTONBURY, port of registry London, and by arrangement consequent upon war requisition placed under the management of Furness, Withy & Co. Ltd., London (registered owners Norfolk & North American Steam Shipping Co. Ltd.). Price paid 1.403,998.39 kr. *1.6.1920:* Returned to Wilh. Wilhelmsen and renamed SIMLA. *22.9.1940:* Torpedoed and sunk west of Bloody Foreland, Ireland in a position 55.08 N, 17.40 W by the German submarine U 100 while on passage from Philadelphia to the River Tees with steel and scrap metal. Five of her crew were lost.

MESNA

Ian J. Farquhar

111. MESNA (1917-1924)
Tonnages: 5,424 gross, 3,431 net, 9,000 deadweight.
Dimensions: 385.0 x 53.7 x 31.6 feet.
Machinery: 3-cylinder triple expansion steam engines of 2,200 i.h.p. by North Eastern Marine Engineering Co. Ltd., Sunderland. Service speed 11 knots.
8.12.1916: Launched by Joseph L. Thompson & Sons Ltd., Sunderland (Yard No. 514) as MESNA. *11.6.1917:* Completed, having been renamed ABERCORN, port of registry London, and by arrangement consequent upon war requisition placed under the management of Furness, Withy & Co. Ltd., London (registered owners Norfolk & North American Steam Shipping Co. Ltd.). Price paid 1,508,533.40 kr. *20.3.1920:* Returned to Wilh. Wilhelmsen and renamed MESNA. *4.9.1924:* Wrecked on Hakaufisi Reef, near Nukualofa, Tonga Islands, in a position 20.09S, 174.55E while on passage from Haiphong to the U.K. with a cargo of zinc ore and copra.

112. MIRLO (I) (1917-1918) Tanker
Tonnages: 6,978 gross, 4,417 net, 10,360 deadweight.
Dimensions: 425.0 x 57.0 x 33.1 feet.
Machinery: 3-cylinder triple expansion steam engines of 2,250 i.h.p. by George Clark Ltd., Sunderland. Service speed 11 knots.
8.11.1916: Launched by Sir James Laing & Sons Ltd., Sunderland (Yard No. 660) *23.8.1917:* Completed and by arrangement consequent upon war requisition placed under the management of H.E. Moss & Co., Liverpool (registered owner W.M. Cohan). Price paid 2,038,273.56 kr. *16.8.1918:* Torpedoed, set on fire and sunk half a mile S. by E. of Cape Hatteras by the German submarine U 117 while on passage from New Orleans to London with gasolene and refined oil. Nine members of her crew were lost.

MENDOCINO

113. MENDOCINO (1917-1935) Tanker
Tonnages: 7,032 gross, 4,412 net, 10,360 deadweight.
Dimensions: 425.0 x 57.0 x 33.1 feet.
Machinery: 3-cylinder triple expansion steam engines of 2,250 i.h.p. by George Clark Ltd., Sunderland. Service speed 10 knots.
22.1.1917: Launched by Sir James Laing & Sons Ltd., Sunderland (Yard No. 661). *2.11.1917:* Completed and by arrangement consequent upon war requisition placed under the management of H.E. Moss & Co., Liverpool (registered owner W.M. Cohan). Price paid 2,026,478.55 kr. *6.1919:* Returned to Wilh. Wilhelmsen. *12.8.1935:* Sold to A/S Viking (Lundegaard & Sønner, managers) Farsund. *3.1939:* Sold to John T. Essberger, Germany and renamed KARIBISCHES MEER. *10.1939:* Taken over by the German Navy. *21.8.1944:* Scuttled in the River Seine near Rouen. *20.4.1946:* Refloated. *15.8.1946:* Beached at Henouville for scrapping.

RINDA

Ian J. Farquhar

104

114. SJOA / RINDA (II) (1917-1941)
Tonnages: 6,029 gross, 3,820 net, 9,430 deadweight.
Dimensions: 405.3 x 53.5 x 33.5 feet.
Machinery: 3-cylinder triple expansion steam engines of 2,500 i.h.p. by J Dickinson & Sons Ltd., Sunderland. Service speed 11.5 knots.
Passengers: 4.
4.4.1917: Launched by Sir James Laing & Sons Ltd., Sunderland (Yard No. 659) as SJOA. *14.12.1917:* Completed, having been renamed APPLEBY, port of registry London, and by arrangement consequent upon war requisition placed under the management of Furness, Withy & Co. Ltd., London (registered owners Norfolk & North American Steam Shipping Co. Ltd.). Price paid 1,518,766.06 kr. *16.6.1920:* Returned to Wilh. Wilhelmsen and renamed RINDA. *9.1939:* Mined off Terschelling, but brought into port and repaired. *30.5.1941:* Torpedoed and sunk off Liberia in a position 06.52 N, 16.25 W by the German submarine U 38 while on passage from Haifa and Table Bay to Freetown and the U.K. with general cargo. Thirteen of her crew were lost.

MONTANA   *Norsk Sjøfartsmuseum*

115. MONTANA (1918-1937) Tanker
Tonnages: 7,031 gross, 4,411 net, 10,624 deadweight.
Dimensions: 425.0 x 57.0 x 33.1 feet.
Machinery: 3-cylinder triple expansion steam engines of 2,500 i.h.p. by George Clark Ltd., Sunderland. Service speed 10 knots.
4.7.1917: Launched by Sir James Laing & Sons Ltd., Sunderland (Yard No. 662). *14.1.1918:* Completed and by arrangement consequent upon war requisition placed under the management of H.E. Moss & Co., Liverpool (registered owner W.M. Cohan). Price paid 2,382,963.89 kr. *11.1920:* Returned to Wilh. Wilhelmsen. *25.10.1937:* Sold to Th. Brøvig, Farsund and renamed KETTY BRØVIG. *2.2.1941:* Captured near the Seychelles by the German raider ATLANTIS while on passage from Bahrain to Lourenço Marques with diesel and fuel oil. Prize crew placed on board and used as a supply ship until scuttled *4.3.1941* after being intercepted off Italian Somaliland by the cruisers H.M.S. LEANDER and H.M.A.S. CANBERRA.

116. THODE FAGELUND (II) (1920-1941)
Tonnages: 5,757 gross, 3,604 net, 8,325 deadweight.
Dimensions: 395.0 x 53.3 x 32.7 feet.
Machinery: 3-cylinder triple expansion steam engines of 2,900 i.h.p. by Palmers' Shipbuilding & Iron Co. Ltd., Jarrow. Subsequently fitted with a low pressure exhaust steam turbine. Service speed 12 knots.
Passengers: 8.

THODE FAGELUND

7.8.1920: Launched by Sir James Laing & Sons Ltd.,Sunderland (Yard No. 678). *29.10.1920:* Completed. Price paid 4,134,503.75 kr. *17.11.1941:* Torpedoed and sunk 60 miles east of East London by the Vichy French submarine LE HEROS while on passage from Chittagong and Madras to Table Bay and the U.K. with iron, jute and tea.

117. TROUBADOUR (I) (1920-1953)
Tonnages: 5,808 gross, 3,668 net, 8,385 deadweight.
Dimensions: 395.1 x 53.3 x 24.7 feet.
Machinery: 3-cylinder triple expansion steam engines of 2,900 i.h.p. by Palmers' Shipbuilding & Iron Co. Ltd., Jarrow. Subsequently fitted with a low pressure exhaust steam turbine. Service speed 12 knots.
Passengers: 4.

TROUBADOUR

15.7.1920: Launched by Joseph L. Thompson & Sons Ltd., Sunderland (Yard No. 532). *4.11.1920:* Completed. Price paid 4,289,522.85 kr. *19.1.1953:* Sold to A/S Lab and D/S A/S Danto (H. Tangvald-Pedersen, manager), Porsgrunn and renamed TANGHOLM. *1956:* Sold to Kam Kee Navigation Co. Ltd., Hong Kong. *1958:* Renamed SHUN FAT. *24.10.1960:* Arrived at Hong Kong to be scrapped by Shiu Wing Co. Ltd. *25.1.1961:* Demolition commenced.

DELAWARE

118. DELAWARE (1920-1928)
Tonnages: *1920-1928:* 4,501 gross, 2,787 net, 7,000 deadweight. *1929-on:* 5,453 gross, 3,287 net.
Dimensions: *1920-1928:* 363.4 x 52.2 x 31.1 feet. *1929-on:* 401.5 x 52.2 x 31.0 feet.
Machinery: 3-cylinder triple expansion steam engines of 2,200 i.h.p. by Richardsons, Westgarth & Co. Ltd., Sunderland. Service speed 10 knots.
23.12.1920: Completed by Furness Shipbuilding Co. Ltd., Haverton Hill-on-Tees (Yard No. 21) having been purchased from the Furness, Withy Group while under construction. Price paid 5,634,532.82 kr. *9.6.1928:* Went aground at Argosgrund, near Orskar, while on passage from Sanda to New Orleans with a cargo of woodpulp and manganese ore. Abandoned as a constructive total loss. *3.9.1928:* The afterpart was refloated and towed to Kiel where a new forepart was fitted by Howaldtswerke A.G. which increased her length to 401.5 feet and her gross tonnage to 5,453. *1929:* Sold to Norddeutscher Lloyd, Germany and renamed TUBINGEN. *1934:* Sold to Hamburg-Bremer Afrika-Linie G.m.b.H. (Woermann-Linie A.G. Deutsche Ost Afrika-Linie, managers), Germany. *18-19.4.1945:* Attacked and damaged by Halifax aircraft off Skagen in position 57.41 N, 10.36 E. She subsequently sailed, with speed much reduced, for Flensburg for repairs. *24.4.1945:* Attacked, together with her two escort vessels, by another Halifax aircraft of Coastal Command in position 57.12 N, 10.42 E. Fire broke out in her wooden cargo frames, developed out of control and she subsequently sank.

CUBANO   *W.S.P.L.*

119. CUBANO (II) (1921-1940)
Tonnages: 5,810 gross, 3,639 net, 8,420 deadweight.
Dimensions: 395.1 x 53.3 x 24.7 feet.
Machinery: 3-cylinder triple expansion steam engines of 2,900 i.h.p. by
Palmers' Shipbuilding & Iron Co. Ltd., Jarrow. Subsequently fitted with a low
pressure exhaust steam turbine. Service speed 12 knots.
28.9.1920: Launched by Joseph L. Thompson & Sons Ltd., Sunderland (Yard
No. 533). *9.3.1921:* Completed. Price paid 5,114,396.93 kr. *19.10.1940:*
Torpedoed S.W. of Iceland in a position 57.55 N, 24.57 W by the German
submarine U 124 while on a voyage from Manchester to Montreal in ballast.
20.10.1940: Abandoned. Two members of her crew were lost.

LOUISIANA   *Ambrose Greenway collection*

120. LOUISIANA (1921-1928)
Tonnages: 4,498 gross, 2,767 net, 7,000 deadweight.
Dimensions: 362.6 x 52.2 x 31.1 feet.
Machinery: 3-cylinder triple expansion steam engines of 2,200 i.h.p. by Richardsons, Westgarth & Co. Ltd., Sunderland. Service speed 10 knots.
11.11.1920: Launched by Furness Shipbuilding Co. Ltd., Haverton Hill-on-Tees (Yard No. 22) having been purchased while under construction for the Furness, Withy Group. *18.3.1921:* Completed. Price paid 5,398,400.61 kr. *7.3.1928:* Sold to Ozean Dampfer A.G., Germany and renamed NORD-FRIESLAND. *1.1931:* Sold to Norddeutscher Lloyd, Germany and renamed MÜNSTER. *1935:* Chartered to Hamburg-Südamerikanische Dampfschifffahrts-Gesellschaft, Germany. *1.3.1938:* Purchased by Hamburg-Südamerikanische Dampfschifffahrts-Gesellschaft and renamed CORRIENTES. *9.1939:* Laid up and interned at Las Palmas, Canary Islands. *9.1942:* Sold to the Spanish Government. *1944:* Sold to Naviera Aznar S.A., Spain and renamed MONTE MONCAYO. *1.1955:* Sold to Maritima Madrilena S.A., Spain and renamed TAJUNA. *11.12.1957:* Went aground at Mazarron after her anchor chain had parted during a storm while on passage from Valencia to Mazarron in ballast. *8.1958:* Reported that the remaining parts of the hull were to be towed to Carthagena for demolition.

TOLUMA arriving at St. Lucia for bunkers, 9.8.1922

121. TOLUMA (I) (1921-1932)
Tonnages: 7,041 gross, 5,234 net, 10,800 deadweight.
Dimensions: 417.8 x 54.4 x 36.0 feet.
Machinery: 4-cylinder quadruple expansion steam engines of 2,600 i.h.p. by North Eastern Marine Engineering Co. Ltd., Newcastle. Service speed 12 knots.
17.12.1906: Launched by Short Bros. Ltd., Sunderland (Yard No. 736) as CHIPANA for New York & Pacific Steam Ship Co. Ltd., London. *13.3.1907:* Completed. *6.1921:* Purchased by Wilh. Wilhelmsen and renamed TOLUMA. *1932:* Sold to the Union Shipbreaking Company, U.S.A. *1933:* Scrapped at Baltimore.

TUGELA

Alex Duncan

122. TUGELA (I) (1921-1945)
Tonnages: 5,559 gross, 3,462 net, 7,918 deadweight.
Dimensions: 380.4 x 52.2 x 33.6 feet.
Machinery: 3-cylinder triple expansion steam engines of 2,900 i.h.p. by the shipbuilders. Subsequently fitted with a low pressure exhaust steam turbine. Service speed 12 knots.
Passengers: 8.
First ship on the Barber Line.
11.2.1921: Launched by Palmers' Shipbuilding & Iron Co. Ltd., Jarrow (Yard No. 916). *5.8.1921:* Completed. Price paid 6,193,899.85 kr. *4.1940:* Scuttled at Oslo, but later raised by the Germans and managed for them by Rob. M. Sloman jr., Hamburg. *28.4.1943:* Again scuttled at Oslo by Norwegian ''underground'' forces. Later raised by the German Navy. *24.3.1945:* Sank after striking a mine near Florö.

123. STEIN (1921-1923)
Tonnages: 123 gross, 65 net, 150 deadweight.
Dimensions: 106.0 x 17.5 x 6.2 feet.
Machinery: Oil engine of 150 i.h.p. Service speed 9 knots.
1904: Completed by Gebr. Sachsenberg, Rosslau as the non-propelled river barge NINDORF for German owners. *1911:* Purchased by Niels F. Bye, Skien, fitted with an Atlas diesel engine and renamed STEIN. *1918:* Sold to A/S Lokaltransport (Fearnley & Wilhelmsen, managers), Oslo. *1921:* Purchased by Wilh. Wilhelmsen. *9.11.1923:* Sold to K. Jacobsen, Denmark and renamed EBBA. *19.3.1924:* Went aground on Sjællands Reef. Later refloated and broken up.

124. AMERICA (III) (1921-1936)
Tonnages: 4,917 gross, 3,062 net, 7,560 deadweight.
Dimensions: 362.0 x 51.6 x 31.2 feet.
Machinery: Two 6-cylinder four stroke cycle single acting oil engines totalling 2,200 i.h.p. by the shipbuilders, driving twin screws. Service speed 9 knots. Wilhelmsen's first sea-going motorship.

AMERICA

16.3.1921: Launched by Akers Mekaniske Verksted A/S, Oslo (Yard No. 389). *22.9.1921:* Completed. Price paid 4,054,762.78 kr. *17.6.1936:* Sold to E.B.Aaby, later E.B. Aaby's Rederi A/S, Oslo and renamed TENTO. *6.5.1944:* Sank in Kiel Bay after striking a mine while on passage to Norway with a cargo of coal. The wreck was later blown up.

125. TANA (I) (1921-1941)
Tonnages: 5,535 gross, 3,448 net, 8,153 deadweight.
Dimensions: 380.4 x 52.2 x 33.6 feet.
Machinery: Two steam turbines totalling 2,500 i.h.p. by the shipbuilders, replaced in *9.1928* by two new steam turbines totalling 2,500 i.h.p by Parsons Marine Steam Turbine Co. Ltd., Newcastle. Both sets of turbines were double

TANA

reduction geared to a single screw shaft. Service speed 11 knots.
Passengers: 6.
Wilhelmsen's first steam turbine ship.
24.3.1921: Launched by Palmers' Shipbuilding & Iron Co. Ltd., Jarrow (Yard No. 917). *10.10.1921:* Completed. Price paid 5,810,866.75 kr. *4.7.1941:* Taken over at Safi by the Vichy French whilst on passage from Liverpool to Panama and renamed STE. SIMONE. *11.1942:* Taken over by the Germans and renamed TANA. *24.5.1943:* Sunk by Allied air attack off Olbia, Sardinia. Later raised, but *10.12.1946* foundered in a position 41.20 N, 10.57 E while bound in tow for Genoa.

MIRLO

126. MIRLO (II) (1922-1942) Tanker
Tonnages: 7,455 gross, 4,415 net, 11,334 deadweight.
Dimensions: 441.0 x 57.5 x 34.1 feet.
Machinery: 3-cylinder triple expansion steam engines of 2,800 i.h.p. by the shipbuilders. Service speed 10.5 knots.
29.11.1920: Launched by Sir W.G. Armstrong, Whitworth & Co. Ltd., Newcastle (Yard No. 976). *31.1.1922:* Completed. Price paid 8,793,090.00 kr. *11.8.1942:* While serving as a Royal Fleet Auxiliary torpedoed and sunk 870 miles W.S.W. of Freetown, in a position 06.04 N, 25.53 W by the German submarine U 130. She was at the time on passage from Curaçao and Trinidad to Freetown with fuel oil and diesel. Her crew was saved.

127. TENERIFFA (I) (1922-1941)
Tonnages: 5,655 gross, 3,496 net, 9,555 deadweight.
Dimensions: 425.5 x 55.2 x 35.8 feet.
Machinery: Two 6-cylinder 4 S.C.S.A. oil engines totalling 3,100 i.h.p. by the shipbuilders, driving twin screws. Service speed 11.5 knots.
Passengers: 10.
15.12.1921: Launched by Burmeister & Wain's Maskin-og Skibsbyggeri A/S, Copenhagen (Yard No. 320). *3.5.1922:* Completed. Price paid 5,238,789.88 kr. *26.2.1941:* Sank in the Bristol Channel in a position 51.06 N, 04.49 W after being bombed by a German aircraft while on passage from Newport, Mon. to Milford Haven and St. John, N.B. with a cargo of china clay and general.

TENERIFFA   *Ian J. Farquhar*

128. THALATTA (I) (1922-1948)

Tonnages: 5,671 gross, 3,492 net, 9,563 deadweight.
Dimensions: 425.5 x 55.2 x 27.9 feet.
Machinery: Two 6-cylinder 4 S.C.S.A. oil engines totalling 3,100 i.h.p. by the shipbuilders, driving twin screws. Service speed 11.5 knots.
7.5.1922: Launched by Burmeister & Wain's Maskin-og Skibsbyggeri A/S, Copenhagen (Yard No. 321). *29.7.1922:* Completed. Price paid 5,758,334.66 kr. *5.7.1948:* Went aground off Suvadiva Atoll, in the Maldive Islands while on a voyage from Shanghai to Oslo with passengers and general cargo. Reported later in the month to have been (unofficially) renamed AQUA QUEEN. *26.10.1948:* Refloated and *9.11.1948* arrived at Colombo where examination showed her to be beyond economical repair. *20.4.1949:* Declared a constructive total loss. *31.7.1949:* Sold by insurance underwriters to A. Ebrahim & Co., Bombay for scrapping. *11.1949:* Demolition began at Darukhana, Bombay.

THALATTA   *Alex Duncan*

TIRADENTES   *Norsk Sjøfartsmuseum*

129. TIRADENTES (1922-1950)
Tonnages: 4.960 gross, 2,913 net, 8,557 deadweight.
Dimensions: 401.2 x 54.2 x 26.9 feet.
Machinery: Two 6-cylinder 4 S.C.S.A. oil engines totalling 3,100 i.h.p. by Algemeine Electricitäts Gesellschaft, Berlin, driving twin screws. Service speed 11 knots.
43,474 cu. ft. of refrigerated cargo space.
Passengers: 10.
24.6.1922: Launched by Deutsche Werft A.G., Hamburg (Yard No. 10). *24.9.1922:* Completed. Price paid 3,260,991.83 kr. *23.8.1950:* Sold to H. Vogemann, Germany and renamed VOGTLAND. *1956:* Sold to the Ministry of Transport, London and loaded at Cairnryan with a cargo of bombs. *30.5.1956:* Scuttled in the North Atlantic.

130. TENNESSEE (I) (1922-1940)
Tonnages: 5,667 gross, 3,492 net, 9,555 deadweight.
Dimensions: 425.5 x 55.2 x 35.8 feet.
Machinery: Two 6-cylinder 4 S.C.S.A. oil engines totalling 3,100 i.h.p. by the shipbuilders, driving twin screws. Service speed 11.5 knots.
Passengers: 10.
1.8.1922: Launched by Burmeister & Wain's Maskin-og Skibsbyggeri A/S, Copenhagen (Yard No. 324). *28.9.1922:* Completed. Price paid 4,981.655.40 kr. *25.5.1940:* Wrecked in Roana Bay, Mainland, Orkney Islands, while returning to Kirkwall after being in collision in a position 58.59 N, 02.27 W with the British s.s. BARON FAIRLIE, 6,706/25, while on passage in convoy from Calcutta and Kirkwall to Leith with general cargo.

TENNESSEE

131. TITANIA (II) (1923-1937)

Tonnages: 4,765 gross, 2,834 net, 7,618 deadweight.
Dimensions: 400.6 x 54.2 x 26.3 feet.
Machinery: Two 6-cylinder 4 S.C.S.A. oil engines totalling 3,100 i.h.p. by
Algemeine Electricitäts Gesellschaft, Berlin, driving twin screws. Service
speed 10 knots.
14.11.1922: Launched by Deutsche Werft A.G., Hamburg (Yard No. 60).
11.2.1923: Completed. Price paid 3,571,012.02 kr. *27.1.1937:* Sold to Bruun
& von der Lippe's Rederi (Bruun & von der Lippe, managers), Tønsberg and
renamed VIGRID. *1937:* Sold to Skibs A/S Gdynia (Olav Ringdal, manager),
Oslo. *24.6.1941:* Torpedoed and sunk S.S.E. of Cape Farewell in about 54.30
N, 41.30 W by the German submarine U 371 while on passage from New
Orleans to Belfast and Manchester with 6,000 tons of general cargo. 21 of
her crew were lost together with a gunner and four passengers.

TITANIA at Rotterdam, 15.7.1925

TALISMAN in the 1930's   *W.S.P.L.*

132. TALISMAN (II) (1923-1936)
Tonnages: 4,765 gross, 2,833 net, 7,618 deadweight.
Dimensions: 400.6 x 54.2 x 26.3 feet.
Machinery: Two 6-cylinder 4 S.C.S.A. oil engines totalling 3,100 i.h.p. by
Algemeine Electricitäts Gesellschaft, Berlin, driving twin screws. Service
speed 10 knots.
27.1.1923: Launched by Deutsche Werft A.G., Hamburg (Yard No. 61).
10.4.1923: Completed. Price paid 3,513,868.80 kr. *3.11.1936:* Sold to Bruun
& von der Lippe's Rederi A/S (Bruun & von der Lippe, managers), Tønsberg
and renamed VIGILANT. *1937:* Sold to Skibs A/S Gdynia (Olav Ringdal,
manager), Oslo. *1940:* Renamed RINGSTAD. *24.1.1942:* Torpedoed and sunk
off Cape Race in a position 45.50 N, 51.04 W by the German submarine
U 333 while on passage from Cardiff to St. John, N.B., with china clay. 27
of her crew and three passengers were lost.

TALISMAN outward bound from Havana

TAMPA

133. TAMPA (I) (1923-1958)
Tonnages: 4,701 gross, 2,794 net, 7,019 deadweight.
Dimensions: 357.6 x 51.2 x 30.7 feet.
Machinery: 6-cylinder 4 S.C.S.A. oil engine of 2,500 i.h.p. by Algemeine
Electricitäts Gesellschaft, Berlin. Service speed 11 knots.
Passengers: 8.

14.7.1923: Launched by Deutsche Werft A.G., Hamburg (Yard No. 46). *15.9.1923:* Completed. Price paid 1,748,287.14 kr. *1940:* Seized by the Germans, but in *5.1945* recovered at Horten. *15.3.1958:* Sold to Cia. Mar. ''Med-Cont'' Ltda., Costa Rica (Loucas Matsas & Sons, Greece, managers) and renamed GEORGIOS M. *22.6.1959:* Grounded in the Andaman Islands during bad weather while on a voyage from Rangoon to Colombo with a cargo of rice and although she refloated she foundered *23.6.1959* whilst trying to return to Rangoon.

TORTUGAS

134. TORTUGAS (I) (1923-1942)
Tonnages: 4,697 gross, 2,852 net, 7,019 deadweight.
Dimensions: 357.6 x 51.2 x 30.7 feet.
Machinery: 6-cylinder 4 S.C.S.A. oil engine of 2,500 i.h.p. by Algemeine Electricitäts Gesellschaft, Berlin. Service speed 11 knots.
Passengers: 12.
30.8.1923: Launched by Deutsche Werft A.G., Hamburg (Yard No. 47). *2.11.1923:* Completed. Price paid 1,679,060.05 kr. *18.11.1942:* Torpedoed and sunk east of Barbados in a position 12.39 N, 54.59 W by the German submarine U 67 while on passage from Calcutta and Table Bay to Trinidad and the Clyde with general cargo.

135. TAIWAN (I) (1924-1950)
Tonnages: 5,502 gross, 3,359 net, 9,159 deadweight.
Dimensions: 426.8 x 55.2 x 27.6 feet.
Machinery: Two 6-cylinder 4 S.C.S.A. oil engines totalling 3,100 i.h.p. by Algemeine Electricitäts Gesellschaft, Berlin, driving twin screws. Service speed 11.5 knots.
9.2.1924: Launched by Deutsche Werft A.G., Hamburg (Yard No. 64). *5.7.1924:* Completed. Price paid 2,613,118.32 kr. *21.4.1946:* In collision in the Gulf of Suez with the steam tanker BRITISH HUSSAR, 6,954/23 when leaving Suez Roads during a voyage from Quilon to New York and beached with her decks awash. *15.5.1946:* Refloated, and subsequently repaired and returned to service. *14.3.1950:* Stranded near St. John's Island, Red Sea, in a position 23.43 N, 36.15 E while on passage from Basra to Gothenburg with a cargo of grain and general. She was refloated *15.3.1950* but had to be abandoned in a position 23.44 N, 35.50 E and then sank.

TAIWAN   *Alex Duncan*

136. TUNGSHA (I) (1924-1948)

Tonnages: 5,505 gross, 3,359 net, 9,170 deadweight.
Dimensions: 426.8 x 55.2 x 27.6 feet.
Machinery: Two 6-cylinder 4 S.C.S.A. oil engines totalling 3,100 i.h.p. by
Algemeine Electricitäts Gesellschaft, Berlin, driving twin screws. Service
speed 11.5 knots.
Passengers: 12.
First ship on the Scandinavian-Middle East Line.
14.6.1924: Launched by Deutsche Werft A.G., Hamburg (Yard No. 65).
9.8.1924: Completed. Price paid 3,725,249.69 kr. *8.12.1948:* Sold to Olaf
Pedersen's Rederi (Olaf Pedersen, manager), Oslo and continued running on
charter to Wilh. Wilhelmsen. *1951:* Renamed SUNNY QUEEN. *1957:* Sold
to Marconquista Cia. Nav. S.A., Liberia and renamed ROULA. *21.2.1960:*
Arrived at Osaka to be scrapped by Banno Tsusho K.K. who commenced
work *20.4.1960* at Kinoe, Hiroshima Prefecture.

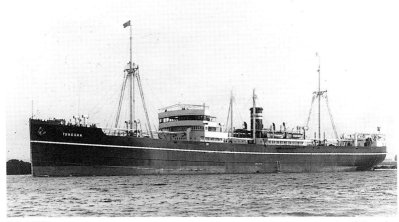

TUNGSHA   *Ian J. Farquhar*

TOURCOING at Cape Town   *W.S.P.L.*

137. TOURCOING (I) (1924-1942)
Tonnages: 5,798 gross, 3,578 net, 9,590 deadweight.
Dimensions: 435.9 x 56.2 x 27.8 feet.
Machinery: Two 8-cylinder 4 S.C.S.A. oil engines totalling 5,100 i.h.p. by
Burmeister & Wain's Maskin-og Skibsbyggeri A/S, Copenhagen, driving twin
screws. Service speed 13 knots.
Passengers: 12.
22.7.1924: Launched by Odense Staalskibsvaerft, Odense (Yard No. 17).
22.10.1924: Completed. Price paid 4,369,983.04 kr. *24.8.1942:* Sank off
Swinemünde after striking a mine while on passage from Gdynia to Oslo.

TOPEKA

138. TOPEKA (I) (1925-1943)
Tonnages: 4,991 gross, 3,030 net, 6,385 deadweight.
Dimensions: 366.3 x 51.2 x 31.4 feet.
Machinery: Two 6-cylinder 4 S.C.S.A. oil engines totalling 2,500 i.h.p. by the shipbuilders driving twin screws. Service speed 10.5 knots.
12.1.1925: Launched by Deutsche Werke A.G., Kiel (Yard No. 198). *24.3.1925:* Completed. Price paid 1,721,116,72 kr. *4.10.1943:* Bombed and set on fire north of Sandnessjøen by Allied aircraft. Grounded but refloated and towed to Stavanger. On examination she was found to be beyond economical repair and was sold for scrapping. *27.11.1945:* Left Stavanger bound in tow for Gothenburg, but *1.12.1945* broke adrift in heavy weather and went aground on Jaeren becoming a total loss.

TANCRED   *Ian J. Farquhar*

139. TANCRED (III) (1925-1940)
Tonnages: 6,094 gross, 3,722 net, 9,840 deadweight.
Dimensions: 442.6 x 58.2 x 27.6 feet.
Machinery: Two 6-cylinder 4 S.C.S.A. oil engines totalling 5,000 i.h.p. by Algemeine Electricitäts Gesellschaft, Berlin, driving twin screws. Service speed 13 knots.
Passengers: 8.
6.6.1925: Launched by Deutsche Werft A.G., Hamburg (Yard No. 66). *25.7.1925:* Completed. Price paid 4,192,086.55 kr. *26.9.1940:* Torpedoed and then shelled and sunk 600 miles W.N.W. of Valencia, Ireland in a position 53.32 N, 24.35 W by the German submarine U 32 while on passage from Liverpool to New York in ballast.

140. TOURAINE (1925-1940)
Tonnages: 5,811 gross, 3,579 net, 9,590 deadweight.
Dimensions: 435.9 x 56.2 x 27.8 feet.
Machinery: Two 8-cylinder 4 S.C.S.A. oil engines totalling 5,100 i.h.p. by Burmeister & Wain's Maskin-og Skibsbyggeri A/S, Copenhagen, driving twin screws. Service speed 13 knots.
Passengers: 12.

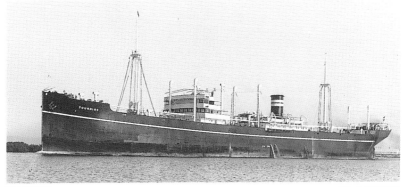

TOURAINE   *Ian J. Farquhar*

17.1.1925: Launched by Odense Staalskibsvaerft, Odense (Yard No. 18).
8.8.1925: Completed. Price paid 3,744,531.13 kr. *7.10.1940:* Torpedoed and
sunk west of Bloody Foreland, Ireland in a position 55.12 N, 10.18 W by the
German submarine U 59 while on passage from Glasgow to Sydney, N.S.
in ballast.

TRICOLOR

141. TRICOLOR (III) (1925-1931)
Tonnages: 6,119 gross, 3,737 net, 10,000 deadweight.
Dimensions: 442.6 x 58.2 x 27.6 feet.
Machinery: Two 6-cylinder 4 S.C.S.A. oil engines totalling 5,000 i.h.p. by
Algemeine Electricitäts Gesellschaft, Berlin, driving twin screws. Service
speed 13.5 knots.
5.8.1925: Launched by Deutsche Werft A.G., Hamburg (Yard No. 81).
17.10.1925: Completed. Price paid 2,441,144.70 kr. *5.1.1931:* Sank four miles
off Colombo after an explosion had occurred in her cargo while she was on
a voyage from Oslo to Yokohama. Six members of her crew were lost.

142. TRANSIT (III) (1925-1929)
Tonnages: 210 gross, 104 net, 250 deadweight.
Dimensions: 99.8 x 20.5 x 9.1 feet.
Machinery: 4-cylinder 2 S.C.S.A. oil engine of 150 i.h.p. by Motorenwerke
Mannheim A.G., Mannheim. Service speed 10 knots.

11.1923: Completed by J. Frerichs & Co. A.G., Einswarden (Yard No. 376) as MONTAN for Ernst Komrowski, Germany. *15.7.1925:* Purchased by Wilh. Wilhelmsen and renamed TRANSIT. *26.9.1929:* Capsized and sank off Strømtangen Lighthouse while on passage from Fredrikstad to Oslo.

TRIANON   *J. Y. Freeman*

143. TRIANON (I) (1926-1959)
Tonnages: 5,805 gross, 3,579 net, 9,590 deadweight.
Dimensions: 435.9 x 56.2 x 27.8 feet.
Machinery: Two 8-cylinder 4 S.C.S.A. oil engines totalling 5,100 i.h.p. by Burmeister & Wain's Maskin-og Skibsbyggeri A/S, Copenhagen, driving twin screws. Service speed 13 knots.
31.10.1925: Launched by Odense Staalskibsvaerft, Odense (Yard No. 19). Price paid 3,669,625.24 kr. *28.2.1926:* Completed. *8.9.1959:* Arrived at Hong Kong and *11.9.1959* sold to Oriental Steel & Rolling Mills Co., Hong Kong for scrapping. *10.10.1959:* Delivered to the shipbreakers.

TEMERAIRE

144. TEMERAIRE (I) (1926-1926)
Tonnages: 6,120 gross, 3,695 net, 9,488 deadweight.
Dimensions: 442.2 x 58.2 x 27.5 feet.
Machinery: Two 6-cylinder 4 S.C.S.A. oil engines totalling 5,100 i.h.p. by Maschinenfabrik Augsburg-Nürnberg A.G., Augsburg, driving twin screws. Service speed 11 knots.

25.8.1925: Launched by Flender A.G., Lübeck (Yard No. 126) *1.3.1926:* Completed. Price paid 2,972,035.41 kr. *20.9.1926:* Wrecked on Brämö Island in the Gulf of Bothnia near Sundsvall, while on passage from Gefle to Sundsvall during a voyage from Westervik to Sydney.

TIJUCA   *W.S.P.L.*

145. TIJUCA (I) (1926-1952)
Tonnages: 5,498 gross, 3,082 net, 8,662 deadweight.
Dimensions: 418.0 x 54.5 x 27.5 feet.
Machinery: Two 6-cylinder 4 S.C.S.A. oil engines totalling 4,000 i.h.p. by Burmeister & Wain's Maskin-og Skibsbyggeri A/S, Copenhagen, driving twin screws. Service speed 12 knots.
1926-1936: 57,952 cu. ft. of refrigerated cargo space.
Passengers: 7.
2.9.1925: Launched by Chantier et Ateliers de St. Nazaire (Penhoët) S.A., Grand Quevilly, Rouen (Yard No. E 5). *2.3.1926:* Completed. Price paid 3,597,586.29 kr. *12.1.1941:* Struck a mine in the Bristol Channel when outward bound from Avonmouth for Trinidad, but was able to proceed to Barry. *8.4.1952:* Sold to Olaf Pedersen's Rederi A/S (Olaf Pedersen, manager), Oslo and subsequently renamed SUNNY PRINCE. *1958:* Sold to The People's Republic of China and renamed HOPING SSU SHI PA. Deleted from ''Lloyd's Register'' 1976-77 in the absence of up-to-date information about her continued existence.

TIGRE   *Fotoflite incorporating Skyfotos*

146. TIGRE (I) (1926-1959)
Tonnages: 5,498 gross, 3,070 net, 8,662 deadweight.
Dimensions: 418.0 x 54.5 x 27.5 feet.
Machinery: Two 6-cylinder 4 S.C.S.A. oil engines totalling 4,000 i.h.p. by the shipbuilders driving twin screws. Service speed 12 knots.
57,952 cu. ft. of refrigerated cargo space.
17.12.1925: Launched by Chantier et Ateliers de St. Nazaire (Penhoët) S.A., Grand Quevilly, Rouen (Yard No. F 5). *31.5.1926:* Completed. Price paid 3,502,164.40 kr. *21.8.1959:* Sold for demolition to United Mineral Trading Company, Monrovia, Liberia. *22.8.1959:* Handed over at Osaka to Japanese shipbreakers. *27.8.1959:* Demolition commenced.

TOLEDO

147. TOLEDO (I) (1926-1958)
Tonnages: 4,598 gross, 2,727 net, 7,109 deadweight.
Dimensions: 376.2 x 52.5 x 27.1 feet.
Machinery: 6-cylinder 4 S.C.S.A. oil engines of 3,000 i.h.p. by Burmeister & Wain's Maskin-og Skibsbyggeri A/S, Copenhagen. Service speed 11.5 knots.
23.4.1926: Launched by Odense Staalskibsvaerft, Odense (Yard No. 23). *31.7.1926:* Completed. Price paid 2,723,125.39 kr. *21.11.1958:* Sold to Einar M. Gaard A/S, Sigurd Haavik A/S and Trygve Klovning (Einar M. Gaard A/S, managers), Haugesund and renamed GARDVIK. *7.3.1964:* Arrived at Hong Kong to be broken up by Leung Yau Shipbreaking Co. Ltd.

TOLEDO at Cape Town. Note shortened funnel   *W.S.P.L.*

TARONGA   *Ian J. Farquhar*

148. TARONGA (I) (1927-1933)
Tonnages: 6,732 gross, 4,038 net, 9,730 deadweight.
Dimensions: 461.4 x 60.6 x 29.0 feet.
Machinery: Two 8-cylinder 4 S.C.S.A. oil engines totalling 7,000 i.h.p. by the
shipbuilders driving twin screws. Service speed 14.5 knots.
Passengers: 12.
20.6.1927: Launched by Deutsche Werke A.G., Kiel (Yard No. 210). *7.9.1927:*
Completed. Price paid 3,363,056.25 kr. *15.1.1933:* Beached on fire at Perim
Island after fire had broken out in No.5 hold during a voyage from Rabaul
to Oslo with a cargo of copra, wheat, hides and wool. *12.2.1933:* Refloated,
leaking badly and efforts were made to discharge her wheat cargo. *25.2.1933:*
Surveyed but considered to be a total loss and broken up.

TALLEYRAND   *W.S.P.L.*

149. TALLEYRAND (I) (1927-1940)
Tonnages: 6,732 gross, 4,038 net, 10,010 deadweight.
Dimensions: 461.4 x 60.6 x 29.0 feet.
Machinery: Two 8-cylinder 4 S.C.S.A. oil engines totalling 7,000 i.h.p. by the
shipbuilders driving twin screws. Service speed 14.5 knots.
Passengers: 12.
28.7.1927: Launched by Deutsche Werke A.G., Kiel (Yard No. 211). *20.10.1927:*
Completed. Price paid 3,069,377.22 kr. *2.8.1940:* Captured S.E. of Mauritius
in about 31.00 S, 67.00 E by the German raider ATLANTIS while on passage
from Sydney, N.S.W. and Fremantle to Cape Town and the U.K. *3.8.1940:*
Sunk. Her crew was transferred to TIRRANNA (No. 173) and three of them
were lost when the latter ship was sunk by H.M. Submarine TUNA.

TEMERAIRE   W.S.P.L.

150. TEMERAIRE (II) (1927-1955)
Tonnages: 6,465 gross, 3,926 net, 9,488 deadweight.
Dimensions: 452.8 x 60.2 x 28.0 feet.
Machinery: Two 8-cylinder 4 S.C.S.A. oil engines totalling 7,740 i.h.p. by the shipbuilders driving twin screws. Service speed 14.5 knots.
Passengers: 12.
28.5.1927: Launched by Chantier et Ateliers de St. Nazaire (Penhoët) S.A., St. Nazaire (Yard No. U 5). *17.12.1927:* Completed. Price paid 3,250,718.18 kr. *28.1.1955:* Sold to H. Vogemann, Germany, and renamed VOGESEN. *13.11.1958:* Arrived at Hamburg to be scrapped by Eisen & Metall K.G., Lehr & Co.

151. TORONTO (I) (1928-1951)
Tonnages: 5,018 gross, 2,883 net, 6,608 deadweight.
Dimensions: 381.8 x 52.2 x 27.7 feet.
Machinery: Two 6-cylinder 4 S.C.S.A. oil engines totalling 4,000 i.h.p. by the shipbuilders driving twin screws. Service speed 12.5 knots.
Passengers: 10.

TORONTO   *Norsk Sjøfartsmuseum*

17.8.1927: Launched by Chantier et Ateliers de St. Nazaire (Penhoët) S.A., Grand Quevilly, Rouen (Yard No. V 5). *30.1.1928:* Completed. Price paid 2,127,252.29 kr. *3.10.1951:* Sold to A/S D/S "Fjeld" (Anton Meidell, manager), Bergen. *1952:* Renamed HORDNES. *22.5.1956:* Sank off Swinoujscie after striking a wreck while on a voyage from Murmansk to Stettin with a cargo of apatite. *21.9.1956:* Refloated and later towed to Kiel, arriving there *6.2.1957,* but condemned and *19.3.1957* sold to Eckhardt & Co.for scrapping. *23.3.1957:* Arrived at Hamburg. *30.9.1957:* Eckhardt & Co. commenced demolition.

TAI YANG   *Norsk Sjøfartsmuseum*

152. TAI YANG (1929-1962)
Tonnages: 7,084 gross, 3,903 net, 12,400 deadweight.
Dimensions: 461.4 x 60.6 x 29.0 feet.
Machinery: *1929-1952:* Two 8-cylinder 4 S.C.S.A. oil engines totalling 7,000 i.h.p. by the shipbuilders driving twin screws. Service speed 14.5 knots. *1952-on:* Two 5-cylinder 2 S.C.S.A. oil engines totalling 8,000 i.h.p. by Howaldtswerke A.G., Hamburg, driving the twin screws. Service speed 15 knots.
Passengers: 8.
14.7.1928: Launched by Deutsche Werke A.G., Kiel (Yard No. 220). *18.3.1929:* Completed. Price paid 3,668,298.14 kr. *1952:* Re-engined by Howaldtswerke A.G. with M.A.N. oil engines. *22.2.1962:* Sold to Cia. Nav. Mousse S.A. (Achilles Frangistas, manager), Lebanon and renamed MOUSSE. *1969:* Sold to Mousse Shipping Co. Ltd., Cyprus. *1970:* Sold to Chinese shipbreakers. *16.3.1970 :* Delivered at Shanghai for demolition.

153. TEMPLAR (II) (1929-1961)
Tonnages: 6,749 gross, 4,047 net, 12,475 deadweight.
Dimensions: 461.4 x 60.6 x 29.0 feet.
Machinery: *1929-1953:* Two 8-cylinder 4 S.C.S.A. oil engines totalling 7,000 i.h.p. by the shipbuilders driving twin screws. Service speed 14.5 knots. *1953-on:* Two 5-cylinder 2 S.C.S.A. oil engines totalling 8,000 i.h.p. by Howaldtswerke A.G., Hamburg, driving the twin screws. Service speed 15 knots.
Passengers: 12.

TEMPLAR

19.1.1929: Launched by Deutsche Werke A.G., Kiel (Yard No. 221). *25.3.1929:* Completed. Price paid 3,074,709.39 kr. *10.8.1940:* Seized by the Germans at Oslo and from *23.11.1940* served as SPERRBRECHER 17. *17 5.1945:* Re-taken, damaged, at Kiel and towed to Malmö for repairs prior to returning to service on *5.7.1947. 10.1.1948:* Suffered an underwater explosion, and believed mined, when in a position 52.48 N, 04.31 E during a voyage from Macassar and Rotterdam to Oslo and arrived at Stavanger *13.1.1948* with deck and engine damage. *1953:* Re-engined by Howaldtswerke A.G. with M.A.N. oil engines. *15.12.1961:* Sold to Achilles Frangistas, Lebanon and renamed KATERINA. *1967:* Sold to Rea Shipping Co. Ltd., Cyprus. *20.1.1972:* Delivered to China National Machinery Import & Export Corporation at Shanghai for demolition.

TEMPLAR in the 1950's with shortened funnel   *Fotoflite incorporating Skyfotos*

TAI YIN on trials, 4.6.1929

154. TAI YIN (1929-1961)
Tonnages: 7,077 gross, 3,891 net, 12,340 deadweight.
Dimensions: 461.4 x 60.6 x 29.0 feet.
Machinery: *1929-1951:* Two 8-cylinder 4 S.C.S.A. oil engines totalling 7,000 i.h.p. by the shipbuilders driving twin screws. Service speed 14.5 knots. *1951-on:* Two 7-cylinder 2 S.C.S.A. oil engines totalling 8,000 i.h.p. by Howaldtswerke A.G., Kiel, driving the twin screws. Service speed 15 knots.
Passengers: 8.
First ship on the Barber Wilhelmsen Line.
27.2.1929: Launched by Deutsche Werke A.G., Kiel (Yard No. 222). *5.6.1929:* Completed. Price paid 3,520,134.45 kr. *1951:* Re-engined by Howaldtswerke A.G., Kiel with M.A.N. oil engines. *1961:* Sold to the Hanwa Co., Osaka, Japan, for scrapping. *11.8.1961:* Delivered at Osaka and demolition commenced *25.8.1961* at Sakurajima.

155. TAI PING (I) (1929-1940)
Tonnages: 7,019 gross, 3,868 net, 9,860 deadweight.
Dimensions: 461.9 x 60.6 x 28.9 feet.
Machinery: Two 8-cylinder 4 S.C.S.A. oil engines totalling 7,300 i.h.p. by the shipbuilders driving twin screws. Service speed 14.5 knots.
21,965 cu. ft. of refrigerated cargo space.
Passengers: 12.
16.3.1929: Launched by Kockums Mekaniska Verkstads A/B, Malmö (Yard No. 159). *15.6.1929:* Completed. Price paid 3,362,842.72 kr. *28.5.1940:* Seized by the Germans at Oslo and served as SPERRBRECHER 14, a supply ship for raiders. Later bought by Unterweser Reederei A.G., Germany and renamed BOCKENHEIM. *12.9.1942:* Mined and sunk at Honningsvaag, but later raised and repaired. *26.8.1944:* Scuttled in the River Gironde near Bordeaux. By *10.7.1946* she was lying at Bassens, having meantime been refloated. She lay there until *29.2.1948* when she left in tow for Pasajes where demolition was completed by *2.1949.*

TAI PING

156. TAI PING YANG (1929-1962)
Tonnages: 7,025 gross, 3,806 net, 12,400 deadweight.
Dimensions: 461.4 x 60.6 x 29.0 feet.
Machinery: *1929-1952:* Two 8-cylinder 4 S.C.S.A. oil engines totalling 7,000 i.h.p. by the shipbuilders driving twin screws. Service speed 14.5 knots. *1952-on:* Two 5-cylinder 2 S.C.S.A. oil engines totalling 8,000 i.h.p. by Howaldtswerke A.G., Hamburg, driving the twin screws. Service speed 15 knots.
Passengers: 10.
4.5.1929: Launched by Deutsche Werke A.G., Kiel (Yard No. 223). *27.8.1929:* Completed and registered in the ownership of Transpacific Corporation, Panama. Price paid 3,686,139.12 kr. *1937:* Re-registered under the Norwegian flag at Tønsberg. *1952:* Re-engined by Howaldtswerke Hamburg A.G. with M.A.N. oil engines. *22.5.1962:* Sold to Olistim Navigation Co. (Achilles Frangistas, manager), Greece and renamed SOPHIA. *1964:* Sold to Lestam Greek Shipping Co. Ltd., Greece. *1969:* Sold to Sophia Shipping Co. Ltd., Cyprus. *1972:* Sold to Istanbul Metalurji Sanayii A.S., Turkey for scrapping. *16.3.1972:* Demolition commenced at Fener.

TAI PING YANG

TAI SHAN under the Panamanian flag

157. TAI SHAN (1929-1960)
Tonnages: 6,962 gross, 3,779 net, 12,060 deadweight.
Dimensions: 461.9 x 60.6 x 28.9 feet.
Machinery: Two 8-cylinder 4 S.C.S.A. oil engines totalling 7,300 i.h.p. by the shipbuilders driving twin screws. Service speed 14.5 knots.
Passengers: 8.
10.8.1929: Launched by Kockums Mekaniska Verkstads A/B, Malmö (Yard No. 160). *16.10.1929:* Completed and registered in the ownership of Transpacific Corporation, Panama. Price paid 3,391,847.10 kr. *1937:* Re-registered at Tønsberg under the Norwegian flag. *17.3.1960:* Sold to Nichimen Co., Osaka, Japan, for scrapping. *23.7.1960:* Arrived at Mihara and demolition commenced *25.7.1960* at Kihara, Mihara-shi.

TUDOR   W.S.P.L.

158. TUDOR (I) (1930-1940)
Tonnages: 6,607 gross, 4,045 net, 10,260 deadweight.
Dimensions: 461.9 x 60.6 x 28.9 feet.
Machinery: Two 8-cylinder 4 S.C.S.A. oil engines totalling 7,300 i.h.p. by the shipbuilders driving twin screws. Service speed 14.5 knots.
Passengers: 12.
18.1.1930: Launched by Kockums Mekaniska Verkstads A/B, Malmö (Yard No. 163). *9.4.1930:* Completed. Price paid 3,185,385.95 kr. *19.6.1940:* Torpedoed and sunk N.W. of Cape Finisterre in a position 45.10 N, 11.50 W by the German submarine U 48 while on passage from Sydney and Gibraltar to the U.K. with a cargo of steel. One member of her crew was lost.

132

THERMOPYLÆ W.S.P.L.

159. THERMOPYLÆ (I) (1930-1942)
Tonnages: 6,655 gross, 4,088 net, 10,564 deadweight.
Dimensions: 461.4 x 60.6 x 29.0 feet.
Machinery: Two 6-cylinder 4 S.C.S.A. oil engines totalling 7,700 i.h.p. by the shipbuilders driving twin screws. Service speed 15 knots.
Passengers: 12.
5.4.1930: Launched by Burmeister & Wain's Maskin-og Skibsbyggeri A/S, Copenhagen (Yard No. 569). *10.6.1930:* Completed. Price paid 3,256,153.73 kr. *19.1.1942:* Sunk by a convoy escort in position 34.03 N, 24.16 E to avoid an explosion of her ammunition cargo after she had been set on fire by German bombing south of Crete. She had been on passage between Alexandria and Malta in Convoy MW 8A with military stores and troops. Three members of her crew were lost.

160. TRITON (I) (1930-1942)
Tonnages: 6,607 gross, 4,045 net, 10,130 deadweight.
Dimensions: 461.9 x 60.6 x 28.9 feet.
Machinery: Two 8-cylinder 4 S.C.S.A. oil engines totalling 7,300 i.h.p. by the shipbuilders driving twin screws. Service speed 14.5 knots.

TRITON

Passengers: 12
26.3.1930: Launched by Kockums Mekaniska Verkstads A/B, Malmö (Yard No. 164). *19.6.1930:* Completed. Price paid 3,191,513.85 kr. *17.8.1942:* Torpedoed and sunk N.E. of the Azores in a position 39.31 N, 22.43 W by the German submarine U 566 while on passage from Sydney, N.S.W. and Freetown to Belfast Lough and Avonmouth with general cargo.

TROJA   *J. Y. Freeman*

161. TROJA (I) (1930-1962)
Tonnages: 6,650 gross, 4,084 net, 10,706 deadweight.
Dimensions: 461.4 x 60.6 x 29.0 feet.
Machinery: Two 8-cylinder 4 S.C.S.A. oil engines totalling 6,550 i.h.p. by the shipbuilders driving twin screws. Service speed 14.5 knots.
Passengers: 11.
2.10.1930: Launched by Burmeister & Wain's Maskin-og Skibsbyggeri, Copenhagen (Yard No. 572). *27.11.1930:* Completed. Price paid 3,132,635.50 kr. *2.4.1962:* Sold to Mardita Cia. Naviera S.A. (Michail A. Karageorgis, manager), Greece and renamed IOANNA. *1964:* Transferred to Panamanian registry. *20.3.1966:* Suffered an engine room explosion when in the Red Sea about 200 miles from Jeddah in a position 24.06 N, 36.12 E during a voyage from Tarragona to Rangoon with a cargo of soya bean oil. Fire ensued but was extinguished *22.3.1966. 25.3.1966:* Arrived in tow at Suez. Examination showed her to be beyond economical repair and she was declared a constructive total loss and sold to S.p.A. Cantieri Navali del Golfo for scrapping. *18.11.1966:* Arrived in tow at Spezia and demolition commenced the following month.

162. TRICOLOR (IV) (1933-1956)
Tonnages: 6,850 gross, 4,208 net, 10,225 deadweight.
Dimensions: 479.1 x 61.1 x 29.0 feet.
Machinery: Two 6-cylinder 2 S.C.D.A. oil engines totalling 10,000 i.h.p. by Gebr. Stork & Co. N.V., Hengelo driving twin screws. Service speed 16.25 knots.
Passengers: 12.
18.2.1933: Launched by N.V. Nederlandsche Scheepsbouw Maatschappij, Amsterdam (Yard No. 224). *27.5.1933:* Completed. Price paid 2,881,066.00 kr. *28.2.1956:* Fire broke out in the jute in No. 3 'tweendeck when she was near Rangoon during a voyage from Chittagong to Oslo with general cargo. She was beached the following day on Liffey Sands but broke in two and became a total loss. *22.9.1956:* Wreck sold to L. Bauer of London who engaged a local salvor to salvage her cargo.

TRICOLOR *Fotoflite incorporating Skyfotos*

163. TARN (I) (1933-1960)

Tonnages: 6,850 gross, 4,209 net, 10,225 deadweight.
Dimensions: 479.1 x 61.1 x 29.0 feet.
Machinery: Two 6-cylinder 2 S.C.D.A. oil engines totalling 10,000 i.h.p. by Gebr. Stork & Co. N.V., Hengelo driving twin screws. Service speed 16.25 knots.
Passengers: 12.
20.5.1933: Launched by N.V. Nederlandsche Scheepsbouw Maatschappij, Amsterdam (Yard No. 225). *13.9.1933:* Completed. Price paid 2,906,991.69 kr. *26.9.1960:* Sold to Michail A. Karageorgis, Greece and renamed ROULA. *1960:* Sold to Marnuestro Cia. Nav. S.A. (Michail A. Karageorgis, manager), Panama. *1966:* Sold to Taiwan shipbreakers and *20.5.1966* arrived at Kaohsiung. She was, however, reconditioned by Chou's Iron & Steel Company and sold to Ta Lai S.S. Co. Ltd., Panama who renamed her RUTA. *4.1967:* Demolition commenced at Keelung, where she had been lying since the end of 1966.

TARN *W.S.P.L.*

TOULOUSE at anchor in Sydney harbour, 1.1.1952   *David Finch*

164. TOULOUSE (I) (1934-1959)
Tonnages: 7,027 gross, 4,309 net, 10,720 deadweight.
Dimensions: 469.0 x 60.7 x 28.9 feet.
Machinery: Two 8-cylinder 4 S.C.S.A. oil engines totalling 8,000 i.h.p. by the shipbuilders driving twin screws. Service speed 15.5 knots.
Passengers: 10.
7.10.1933: Launched by Deutsche Werke A.G., Kiel (Yard No. 228). *4.1.1934:* Completed. Price paid 2,474,721.18 kr. *28.10.1959:* Sold to Oleada Cia. Naviera (Michail A. Karageorgis, manager), Greece and renamed MICHALAKIS. *26.3.1962:* Fire broke out in No.1 hold when she was about 8 miles north of San Juan, P.R. during a voyage from Callao to Hull with a cargo of fishmeal in paper bags. *27.3.1962:* Put in at San Juan where the fire was extinguished *31.3.1962.* Examination showed her to be beyond economical repair and on *30.7.1962* she was abandoned to insurance underwriters as a constructive total loss. *24.8.1962:* Sold for demolition to Buques y Materiales S.A. *26.8.1962:* Arrived at Bilbao to be broken up.

165. TARONGA (II) (1934-1961)
Tonnages: 7,064 gross, 4,235 net, 10,550 deadweight.
Dimensions: 484.0 x 61.3 x 29.0 feet.
Machinery: 7-cylinder 2 S.C.D.A. oil engine of 9,650 i.h.p. by Burmeister & Wain's Maskin-og Skibsbyggeri A/S, Copenhagen. Service speed 16.25 knots.
Passengers: 12.
20.1.1934: Launched by Odense Staalskibsvaerft, Odense (Yard No. 50). *5.5.1934:* Completed. Price paid 2,716,489.32 kr. *15.8.1940:* Seized by the Germans and employed as SPERRBRECHER 15. *1945:* Recovered at Hamburg entirely burned out following air attack. The hull was reconditioned by Beliard Crighton et Cie., Antwerp and the machinery by Burmeister & Wain, Copenhagen, and in *8.1948* she was ready for service again. *28.10.1961:* Sold to the Sangyo Shinko K.K. for scrapping. *4.11.1961:* Demolition began at Izumi-Ohtsu, near Osaka.

TARONGA

Norsk Sjøfartsmuseum

166. TAURUS (III) (1935-1941)
Tonnages: 4,767 gross, 2,879 net, 7,610 deadweight.
Dimensions: 408.6 x 55.3 x 25.2 feet.
Machinery: 7-cylinder 2 S.C.D.A. oil engine of 4,800 i.h.p. by the shipbuilders.
Service speed 13.5 knots.
Passengers: 12.
23.10.1935: Launched by Akers Mekaniske Verksted A/S, Oslo (Yard No. 466).
14.12.1935: Completed. Price paid 2,153,342.32 kr. *6.6.1941:* Bombed by a German aircraft and sunk off Montrose, Scotland in a position 56.47 N, 02.15 W while on passage from Port Harcourt and Freetown to Hull with a cargo of groundnuts, palm kernels and cocoa.

TAURUS

Norsk Sjøfartsmuseum

TALABOT at Cape Town

167. TALABOT (II) (1936-1942)
Tonnages: 6,798 gross, 4,178 net, 10,740 deadweight.
Dimensions: 479.1 x 62.3 x 28.9 feet.
Machinery: 7-cylinder 2 S.C.D.A. oil engine of 9,650 i.h.p. by the shipbuilders.
Service speed 16.25 knots.
Passengers: 12.
5.11.1935: Launched by A/B Götaverken, Gothenburg (Yard No. 492).
20.3.1936: Completed. Price paid 2,986,510.31 kr. *26.3.1942:* Bombed and set on fire by enemy aircraft while lying at Valletta, Malta, and scuttled to prevent her ammunition cargo exploding. *3.1949:* Refloated, towed out to deep water and scuttled.

TAMERLANE

138

168. TAMERLANE (I) (1936-1962)
Tonnages: 6,778 gross, 4,140 net, 10,750 deadweight.
Dimensions: 479.1 x 62.3 x 29.0 feet.
Machinery: 8-cylinder 2 S.C.D.A. oil engine of 9,600 i.h.p. by the shipbuilders.
Service speed 16.25 knots.
840 cu. ft. of refrigerated cargo space.
Passengers: 12.
First ship on the Barber West African Line.
10.1.1936: Launched by Kockùms Mekaniska Verkstads A/B, Malmö (Yard No. 188). *28.5.1936:* Completed. Price paid 2,982,945.50 kr. *1.6.1962:* Sold to Conpac Schiffahrts G.m.b.H. (Helmut Bastian, manager), West Germany and renamed ALISIOS. *12.1963:* Sold to Ulises Maritime Co. S.A., Panama. *1967:* Sold to Naviera Maritima Fluvial S.A., Peru. *20.12.1971:* Handed over at Shanghai to Chinese shipbreakers.

TABOR *Norsk Sjøfartsmuseum*

169. TABOR (II) (1936-1943)
Tonnages: 4,768 gross, 2,875 net, 7,610 deadweight.
Dimensions: 408.6 x 55.3 x 25.2 feet.
Machinery: 7-cylinder 2 S.C.D.A. oil engine of 4,800 i.h.p. by the shipbuilders.
Service speed 13.5 knots.
Passengers: 12.
27.5.1936: Launched by Akers Mekaniske Verksted A/S, Oslo (Yard No. 468). *31.7.1936:* Completed. Price paid 2,291,293.52 kr. *9.3.1943:* Torpedoed and sunk S.E. of Cape Agulhas in a position 38.30 S, 23.10 E by the German submarine U 506 while on passage from Aden to Cape Town. Twelve of those on board were lost.

TARIFA at Cape Town   *W.S.P.L.*

170. TARIFA (I) (1936-1944)
Tonnages: 7,229 gross, 4,426 net, 10,850 deadweight.
Dimensions: 493.6 x 63.3 x 29.0 feet.
Machinery: Two 8-cylinder 2 S.C.S.A. oil engines totalling 10,600 i.h.p. by
F. Schichau G.m.b.H., Elbing driving twin screws. Service speed 16.25 knots.
Passengers: 12.
20.8.1936: Launched by F. Schichau G.m.b.H., Danzig (Yard No. 1357).
7.11.1936: Completed. Price paid 2,896,475.45 kr. *7.3.1944:* Torpedoed and
sunk some 250 miles east of Socotra in a position 12.48 N, 58.44 E by the
German submarine U 510 while on passage from Aden to Melbourne.

TATRA

171. TATRA (I) (1937-1962)
Tonnages: 4,766 gross, 2,804 net, 7,580 deadweight.
Dimensions: 412.0 x 55.5 x 25.6 feet.
Machinery: 8-cylinder 2 S.C.S.A. oil engine of 5,150 i.h.p. by F. Schichau
G.m.b.H., Elbing. Service speed 14 knots.
Passengers: 10.
31.10.1936: Launched by F. Schichau G.m.b.H., Danzig (Yard No. 1378).
4.2.1937: Completed. Price paid 2,029,264.93 kr. *13.9.1962:* Sold to
Marfianza Cia. Nav. S.A. (Michail A. Karageorgis S.A., managers), Greece
and renamed KALAMATA. *1965:* Transferred to Panamanian registry.
9.9.1968: Arrived at Kaohsiung to be scrapped by Taiwan shipbreakers.

TITANIA   *J. Y. Freeman*

172. TITANIA (III) (1937-1961)
Tonnages: 6,704 gross, 4,081 net, 10,090 deadweight.
Dimensions: 479.1 x 62.3 x 28.8 feet.
Machinery: Two 7-cylinder 2 S.C.D.A. oil engines totalling 11,600 i.h.p. by
the shipbuilders driving twin screws. Service speed 17 knots.
820 cu. ft. of refrigerated cargo.
Passengers: 12.
11.2.1937: Launched by Kockums Mekaniska Verkstads A/B, Malmö (Yard
No. 198). *4.5.1937:* Completed. Price paid 3.446,160.10 kr. *28.11.1961:* Sold
to Marvuelo Cia. Nav. S.A. (Michail A. Karageorgis S.A., subsequently Michail
A. Karageorgis (Hellas) Ltd., managers), Greece and renamed ARISTOTELIS.
14.5.1969: Delivered at Shanghai to Chinese shipbreakers.

173. TALISMAN (III) (1937-1950)
Tonnages: 6,701 gross, 4,056 net, 10,100 deadweight.
Dimensions: 479.1 x 62.3 x 28.8 feet.
Machinery: Two 7-cylinder 2 S.C.D.A. oil engines totalling 11,600 i.h.p. by
the shipbuilders driving twin screws. Service speed 17 knots.
1,640 cu. ft. of refrigerated cargo space.
25.8.1937: Launched by Kockums Mekaniska Verkstads A/B, Malmö (Yard
No. 199). *29.10.1937:* Completed. Price paid 3,451,763.69 kr. *12.5.1950:*
Abandoned by her crew and passengers after fire had broken out in the engine
room when she was about 80 miles off Shimizu after leaving there for Hong
Kong. *14.5.1950:* Towed to near Shimizu by the American naval tanker
SHAWNEE TRAIL. *18.5.1950:* Took on a severe list but righted and *7.6.1950*
refloated. *15.8.1950:* Arrived in tow at Yokohama for examination. *17.9.1950:*

TALISMAN   *W.S.P.L.*

Condemned and sold to Mitsui Sempaku K.K., Japan, to whom she was
delivered *16.11.1950* and who had her rebuilt at Kobe. *1951:* Renamed
ASAKASAN MARU. *1959:* Sold to Toyo Kaiun K.K., Japan. *1966:* Sold to
Hei An Shipping Co. Ltd., Taiwan and renamed CHUN AN. *1967:* Sold to Cia.
Nav. Fu An Ltda., Panama. *1968:* Sold to Tienho Nav. (Panama) Ltd. S.A.,
Panama and renamed TIEN HO. *1969:* Sold for scrapping to Koshin Sangyo
K.K. *23.6.1969:* Demolition began at Osaka.

TRAFALGAR

174. TRAFALGAR (II) (1938-1942)
Tonnages: 5,542 gross, 3,301 net, 8,690 deadweight.
Dimensions: 438.0 x 57.3 x 25.6 feet.
Machinery: 8-cylinder 2.S.C.D.A. oil engine of 6,600 i.h.p. by Gebr. Stork &
Co. N.V., Hengelo. Service speed 15 knots.
Passengers: 12.
23.10.1937: Launched by N.V. Nederlandsche Scheepsbouw Maatschappij
N.V., Amsterdam (Yard No. 268). *16.2.1938:* Completed. Price paid
3,211,570.21 kr. *15.10.1942:* Torpedoed and sunk about 1,100 miles N.E. of
Guadeloupe in a position 25.30 N, 52.00 W by the German submarine
U 129 while on passage from Buenos Aires to New York with general cargo.

142

TIRRANNA   W.S.P.L.

175. TIRRANNA (I) (1938-1940)
Tonnages: 7,230 gross, 4,410 net, 10,850 deadweight.
Dimensions: 493.6 x 63.3 x 29.0 feet.
Machinery: Two 8-cylinder 2 S.C.S.A. oil engines totalling 10,600 i.h.p. by
F. Schichau G.m.b.H., Elbing driving twin screws. Service speed 16.25 knots.
2,200 cu. ft. of refrigerated cargo space.
Passengers: 12.
11.12.1937: Launched by F. Schichau G.m.b.H., Danzig (Yard No. 1396).
10.3.1938: Completed. Price paid 3,302,542.19 kr. *10.6.1940:* Captured S.E.
of Mauritius in about 23.00 S, 69.00 E by the German raider ATLANTIS, while
on passage from Sydney, N.S.W. and Melbourne to Mombasa and the U.K.
22.9.1940: While endeavouring to run the blockade to Bordeaux, torpedoed
and sunk in the Gironde Estuary by H.M. Submarine TUNA with the loss
of 87 of the 292 persons on board.

TORRENS   J. Y. Freeman

176. TORRENS (I) (1939-1966)
Tonnages: 6,713 gross, 4,090 net, 10,300 deadweight.
Dimensions: 479.1 x 62.3 x 28.8 feet.
Machinery: Two 7-cylinder 2 S.C.D.A. oil engines totalling 11,600 i.h.p. by
the shipbuilders driving twin screws. Service speed 17 knots.
820 cu. ft. of refrigerated cargo space.
Passengers: 12.

5.4.1939: Launched by Kockums Mekaniska Verkstads A/B, Malmö (Yard No. 209). *31.5.1939:* Completed. Price paid 3,655,395.17 kr. During the war, between 1942 and 1946, served as a troopship, operated on behalf of the United States War Shipping Administration by Barber Steamship Lines and the American West African Line. As a troopship she could carry up to 1,702 passengers. She became known as ''The Ship of Good Cheer''. *3.6.1966:* Sold to Dimitra Cia. Nav. S.A. (Michail A. Karageorgis, and latterly E.T. Kolintzas, manager), Greece and renamed GEORGIOS M. *13.4.1970:* Delivered at Hsinkang to Chinese shipbreakers. She had been sold for scrapping to H. Si Chiao El Le Kou, Peking.

TAMESIS

177. TAMESIS (I) (1939-1943)
Tonnages: 7,256 gross, 4,411 net, 10,450 deadweight.
Dimensions: 504.4 x 63.4 x 29.1 feet.
Machinery: Two 9-cylinder 2 S.C.S.A. oil engines totalling 11,950 i.h.p. by F. Schichau G.m.b.H., Elbing driving twin screws. Service speed 17 knots.
Passengers: 12.
13.5.1939: Launched by F. Schichau G.m.b.H., Danzig (Yard No. 1424). *29.9.1939:* Completed. *7.3.1943:* Sank following a collision 200 miles N.E. of Bermuda in a position 35.07 N, 62.45 W with ALCOA GUARD, 4,905/18 while proceeding in convoy from Lobito Bay to New York with general cargo.

Dimensions: From here on are length between perpendiculars (length overall) x breadth extreme x depth to weather deck, together with the draught at summer deadweight. **Machinery:** From here on the brake horse power (b.h.p.) or the shaft horse power (s.h.p.) of the machinery is given.

178. TULANE (I) (1940-1965)
Tonnages: 5,488 gross, 3,240 net, 8,300 deadweight.
Dimensions: 128.01 (138.15 o.a.) x 17.47 x 11.89 m. 7.848 m draught.
Machinery: 5-cylinder 2 S.C.D.A. Burmeister & Wain type oil engine of 5,500 b.h.p. by the shipbuilders. Service speed 15.25 knots.
37.66 cu. m. of refrigerated cargo space.
Passengers: 12.
18.10.1939: Launched by Akers Mekaniske Verksted A/S, Oslo (Yard No. 478). *11.1.1940:* Completed. Price paid 3,551,208.48 kr. *8.1940:* Seized at Oslo

TULANE on trials

by the Germans and from *16.11.1940* employed as SPERRBRECHER 16. *8.4.1943:* Struck a mine at La Pallice and heavily damaged. Bombed whilst undergoing repairs and *11.8.1944* sank after being bombed again the previous day. *1946:* Raised and subsequently repaired. *2.1949:* Returned to service. *11.6.1965:* Sold to Eastcote Cia. Nav. S.A. (Michail A. Karageorgis (Hellas) Ltd., managers), Panama and renamed ARISTANDROS. *1970:* Transferred to Greek registry. *21.9.1971:* Delivered at Shanghai to China National Machinery Import & Export Corporation for scrapping.

179. TORTUGAS (II) (1946-1967)
Tonnages: 5,164 gross, 2,824 net, 7,945 deadweight.
Dimensions: 119.13 (125.69 o.a.) x 18.34 x 11.43 m. 7.570 m draught.
Machinery: Two 6-cylinder 2 S.C.S.A. oil engines totalling 4,150 b.h.p. by Nordberg Manufacturing Co., Milwaukee geared to a single screw shaft. Service speed 14.5 knots.

TORTUGAS   *F. W. Hawks*

17.1.1943: Launched by Pennsylvania Shipyards Inc., Beaumont, Texas (Yard No. 269) as CAPE BARNABAS for the United States War Shipping Administration. *4.1943:* Completed as GENERAL FLEISCHER and bareboat chartered to the Norwegian Government (Norwegian Shipping & Trade Mission, managers). *20.10.1946:* Purchased by Wilh. Wilhelmsen and renamed TORTUGAS. Price paid 4,764,329.85 kr. *16.5.1967:* Sold to Philippine President Lines Inc., Philippine Islands and renamed EMILIO AGUINALDO. Later in *1967* renamed PRESIDENT LAUREL. *1975:* Renamed LUCKY NINE. *28.4.1975:* Sold to Barracuda Shipping Inc. (Gulf Shipping Lines Ltd., managers), Somali Republic. *20.9.1975:* Arrived at Kaohsiung and *26.9.1975* delivered to Nan Feng Steel Enterprise Co. Ltd. for scrapping. *21.9.1975:* Demolition commenced.

TALABOT   *W.S.P.L.*

180. TALABOT (III) (1946-1967)
Tonnages: 6,104 gross, 3,690 net, 9,875 deadweight.
Dimensions: 135.62 (145.90 o.a.) x 18.62 x 12.65 m. 8.236 m draught.
Machinery: 9-cylinder 2 S.C.S.A. Burmeister & Wain oil engine of 8,100 b.h.p. by the shipbuilders. Service speed 16.5 knots.
26.05 cu. m. of refrigerated cargo space.
Passengers: 12.
27.8.1946: Launched by Eriksbergs Mekaniska Verkstads A/B, Gothenburg (Yard No. 326). *25.11.1946:* Completed. Price paid 9,255,190.91 kr. *15.7.1967:* Sold to the Shun Cheong Steam Navigation Co. Ltd., Hong Kong (port of registry London) and renamed BELINDA. *1976:* Transferred to Somali Republic registry. Later in *1976:* Transferred to Panamanian registry. *10.4.1978:* Arrived at Kaohsiung to be scrapped. *9.6.1978:* Yun Shen Steel & Iron Works Co. Ltd commenced demolition.

181. TOURCOING (II) (1947-1967)
Tonnages: 6,780 gross, 4,124 net, 10,515 deadweight.
Dimensions: 143.54 (152.10 o.a.) x 19.00 x 13.09 m. 8.414 m draught.
Machinery: Two 7-cylinder 2 S.C.D.A. M.A.N. oil engines totalling 11,600 b.h.p. by the shipbuilders driving twin screws. Service speed 17 knots.
23.22 cu. m. of refrigerated cargo space.
Passengers: 12.

TOURCOING   *J. Y. Freeman*

6.5.1947: Launched by Kockums Mekaniska Verkstads A/B, Malmö (Yard No. 296). *16.12.1947:* Completed. Price paid 10,385,907.33 kr. *10.10.1967:* Sold to Marnuestro Cia. Nav. S.A. (Michail A. Karageorgis S.A., managers), Greece and renamed ARISTOGENIS. *1973:* Sold to Nissho-Iwai Co. Ltd. for scrapping. *7.3.1973:* Arrived at Kaohsiung and delivered *10.3.1973* to Li Chong Steel & Iron Works Co. Ltd. *10.4.1973:* Demolition began.

TOURNAI   *W.S.P.L.*

182. TOURNAI (1948-1968)
Tonnages: 6,780 gross, 4,124 net, 10,515 deadweight.
Dimensions: 143.54 (152.10 o.a.) x 19.00 x 13.09 m. 8.414 m draught.
Machinery: Two 7-cylinder 2 S.C.D.A. M.A.N. oil engines totalling 11,600 b.h.p. by the shipbuilders driving twin screws. Service speed 17 knots.
23.22 cu. m. of refrigerated cargo space.
Passengers: 12.
15.12.1947: Launched by Kockums Mekaniska Verkstads A/B, Malmö (Yard No. 297). *22.4.1948:* Completed. Price paid 10,635,564.96 kr. *19.8.1968:* Sold to George Manopoulos, Greece and renamed PROTON. *1972:* Sold to Hill Court Shipping Co. S.A., Cyprus and renamed YPERAGIA. *1973:* Sold to Denney Shipping Co. S.A., Cyprus and in *1976* renamed FANEROMENI. *2.11.1978:* Anchored off Karachi prior to beaching at Gadani Beach for demolition by Dewan Sons Ltd. *2.1979:* Work commenced.

TRITON at Cape Town   W.S.P.L.

183. TRITON (II) (1948-1969)

Tonnages: 5,414 gross, 3,117 net, 9,235 deadweight.
Dimensions: 131.30 (141.31 o.a.) x 18.19 x 12.43 m. 8.059 m draught.
Machinery: 7-cylinder 2 S.C.D.A. M.A.N. oil engine of 7,000 b.h.p. by the
shipbuilders. Service speed 16.5 knots.
25.48 cu. m. of refrigerated cargo space.
Passengers: 12.
13.3.1948: Launched by Kockums Mekaniska Verkstads A/B, Malmö (Yard
No. 298). *28.6.1948:* Completed. Price paid 9,597,721.95 kr. *8.3.1969:* Sold
to the Hong Kong Pacific Shipping Co. Ltd. (Hong Kong Islands Shipping Co.
Ltd., managers), Singapore and renamed APLICHAU. *1973:* Transferred to
Panamanian registry. *7.2.1978:* Suffered extensive damage when she was
in collision off Singapore with the Singapore m.v. ILOK, 8,442/57. *24.3.1978:*
Arrived at Kaohsiung for examination and subsequently sold to Chi Shun
Hwa Steel Co. Ltd. for scrapping. *30.9.1978:* Demolition commenced.

TAURUS in Barber Line colours at New York

148

184. TAURUS (IV) (1948-1966)
Tonnages: 5,487 gross, 3,239 net, 8,300 deadweight.
Dimensions: 128.01 (137.84 o.a.) x 17.47 x 11.89 m. 7.848 m draught.
Machinery: 5-cylinder 2 S.C.D.A. Burmeister & Wain oil engine of 5,500 b.h.p.
by the shipbuilders. Service speed 15.25 knots.
37.66 cu. m. of refrigerated cargo space.
Passengers: 12.
6.4.1948: Launched by Akers Mekaniske Verksted A/S, Oslo (Yard No. 482).
17.8.1948: Completed. Price paid 8,984,095.50 kr. *12.5.1966:* Sold to
Beaconsfield Cia. Nav. S.A. (Michail A. Karageorgis, manager), Greece and
renamed ROULA. *20.6.1971:* Arrived at Kaohsiung to be broken up by Yung
Tai Steel and Iron Works Co. Ltd. *10.7.1971:* Demolition began.

TRINIDAD *Norsk Sjøfartsmuseum*

185. TRINIDAD (I) (1948-1966)
Tonnages: 6,838 gross, 3,929 net, 9,064 deadweight.
Dimensions: 120.39 (127.38 o.a.) x 18.34 x 11.43 m. 8.407 m draught.
Machinery: Two steam turbines totalling 4,500 s.h.p. by Westinghouse
Electrical & Manufacturing Company, Pittsburgh, double reduction geared
to a single screw shaft. Service speed 14 knots.
22.7.1943: Launched by Consolidated Steel Corporation Ltd., Wilmington,
Cal. (Yard No. 279) as CAPE MEREDITH for the United States War Shipping
Administration. *1947:* Sold to Trinidad Navigation Co., Panama and renamed
TRINIDAD. *23.9.1948:* Purchased by Wilh. Wilhelmsen. Price paid
6,596,732.65 kr. *23.6.1966:* Sold to Astrovalia Cia. Nav. S.A. (N. & J.
Vlassopulos Ltd., managers), Greece and renamed FROSSINI. *1969:* Sold
to Taiwan shipbreakers. *26.4.1969:* Arrived at Kaohsiung, where demolition
commenced the following month.

186. TARIFA (II) (1948-1969)
Tonnages: 6,386 gross, 3,836 net, 10,140 deadweight.
Dimensions: 138.85 (149.06 o.a) x 19.58 x 12.85 m. 8.254 m draught.
Machinery: 9-cylinder 2 S.C.D.A. Fiat oil engine of 7,500 b.h.p. by Ansaldo
S.A. Stabilimento Meccanico, Genoa-Sampierdarena. Service speed 16.25
knots.
29.02 cu. m. of refrigerated cargo space.
Passengers: 12.

TARIFA

4.4.1948: Launched by Societa Anonima Ansaldo, Genoa-Sestri (Yard No. 877). *30.9.1948:* Completed. Price paid 9,435,006.93 kr. *31.1.1969:* Sold to Shun Cheong Steam Navigation Co. Ltd., Hong Kong, registered under the Somali Republic flag and renamed LORINDA. *5.5.1972:* Delivered at Shanghai to China National Machinery Import & Export Corporation for demolition.

TOMAR   *Fotoflite incorporating Skyfotos*

187. TOMAR (I) (1948-1968)
Tonnages: 6,410 gross, 3,869 net, 10,000 deadweight.
Dimensions: 138.86 (149.67 o.a.) x 19.56 x 12.85 m. 8.229 m draught.
Machinery: 9-cylinder 2 S.C.D.A. Fiat oil engine of 7,500 b.h.p. by Cantieri Riuniti dell' Adriatico, Trieste. Service speed 16.5 knots.
28.66 cu. m. of refrigerated cargo space.
Passengers: 12.

25.3.1948: Launched by Cantieri Riuniti dell' Adriatico, Monfalcone (Yard No. 1737). *5.10.1948:* Completed. Price paid 9,674,520.88 kr. *6.1.1968:* Suffered an explosion and fire in her engine room when she was off Robe, South Australia, during a voyage from Gothenburg to Brisbane with general cargo. The fire was extinguished by her crew and she arrived in the Yarra River in tow *8.1.1968.* After partial discharge she was towed to Sydney where the rest of her cargo was unloaded. *23.2.1968:* Sold to Mitsui & Co., London, for scrapping and *28.2.1968* left in tow, arriving at Kaohsiung prior to *15.4.1968* to be broken up.

TANCRED, 2.7.1970   *M. R. Dippy*

188. TANCRED (IV) (1948-1971)
Tonnages: 6,133 gross, 3,619 net, 9,740 deadweight.
Dimensions: 135.62 (145.90 o.a.) x 18.65 x 12.65 m. 8.236 m draught.
Machinery: 9-cylinder 2 S.C.S.A. Burmeister & Wain oil engine of 8,100 b.h.p. by the shipbuilders. Service speed 16 knots.
695.17 cu. m. of refrigerated cargo space.
Passengers: 12.
6.7.1948: Launched by Eriksbergs Mekaniska Verkstads A/B, Gothenburg (Yard No. 372). *21.10.1948:* Completed. Price paid 12,189,924.32 kr. *1.9.1971:* Sold to Skips A/S Solnes & Co. (Johannes Solstad, manager), Norway and renamed SOL JEAN. *1974:* Transferred to Skips-A/S Solhav & Co., Norway (same manager). *1976:* Sold to Saudi America Line Ltd. (Orri Navigation Lines S.A., managers), Saudi Arabia and renamed AL HADA. *8.12.1976:* Gutted by fire which broke out while she was lying at Jeddah during a voyage to Helsinki and was not extinguished until two days later. *1978:* Sold to Themis Shipping & Trading Corporation S.A., Panama and towed *28.9-19.10.1978* to Piraeus where examination showed her to be beyond economical repair. *8.3.1979:* Arrived in tow at Castellon to be broken up by I.M.Varela Davalillo.

TUDOR

189. TUDOR (II) (1949-1969)

Tonnages: 5,418 gross, 3,118 net, 9,090 deadweight.
Dimensions: 131.30 (141.31 o.a.) x 18.19 x 12.53 m. 8.059 m draught.
Machinery: 7-cylinder 2 S.C.D.A. M.A.N. oil engine of 7,000 b.h.p. by the shipbuilders. Service speed 16.5 knots.
605.30 cu. m. of refrigerated cargo space.
Passengers: 12.
25.10.1948: Launched by Kockums Mekaniska Verkstads A/B, Malmö (Yard No. 299). *7.2.1949:* Completed. Price paid 10,632,835.53 kr. *6.8.1969:* Sold to Solstad Rederi A/S (Johannes Solstad, manager), Skudeneshavn and renamed SOL TULLA. *1975:* Sold to Harper Shipping Co. Ltd., Panama and renamed SEA GLORY. *1978:* Sold to Pakistani shipbreakers. *29.3.1978:* Left Bombay for Gadani Beach where demolition commenced during the following month.

TENNESSEE

190. TENNESSEE (II) (1949-1968)
Tonnages: 4,723 gross, 2,756 net, 7,620 deadweight.
Dimensions: 122.21 (130.77 o.a.) x 16.82 x 11.59 m. 7.792 m draught.
Machinery: 7-cylinder 2 S.C.S.A. oil engine of 5,050 b.h.p. by the shipbuilders.
Service speed 15 knots.
833.64 cu. m. of refrigerated cargo space.
Passengers: 12.
16.11.1948: Launched by A/B Götaverken, Gothenburg (Yard No. 626).
15.2.1949: Completed. Price paid 9,385,197.36 kr. *22.1.1968:* Sold to Kassiopi
Cia. Maritima S.A., Panama, and later in *1968* renamed KASSIOPI. *1970:*
Sold to Natalia Shipping Co. S.A., Greece and renamed EVANGELOS M. *1973:*
Sold to Admiral Shipping Co. Ltd., Greece. *1978:* Sold to Eliki Cia. Nav. S.A.,
Greece. *6.1978:* Laid up at Aegion. *1979:* Sold to International Transactions
& Shipping Co. S.A. (International Transactions & Shipping Services Co. Ltd.,
managers), Panama and renamed MAXIMINUS. *1984:* Sold to Crystal Breeze
Cia. Naviera S.A. (Roussos Brothers, managers), Panama and renamed
TIGER'S TAIL. *6.4.1984:* Anchored off Piraeus following arrival from Aegion
where she had been laid up continuously since *6.1978. 4.7.1984:* Sold for
demolition to Evgenios Baboukos & Sons who commenced work in *9.1984*
at the Frantzeskou Shipyard, Perama.

TEXAS   *Fotoflite incorporating Skyfotos*

191. TEXAS (I) (1949-1968)
Tonnages: 4,719 gross, 2,755 net, 7,620 deadweight.
Dimensions: 122.21 (130.77 o.a.) x 16.82 x 11.59 m. 7.792 m draught.
Machinery: 7-cylinder 2 S.C.S.A. oil engine of 5,050 b.h.p. by the shipbuilders.
Service speed 15 knots.
833.64 cu. m. of refrigerated cargo space.
Passengers: 12.
12.4.1949: Launched by A/B Götaverken, Gothenburg (Yard No. 627).
30.6.1949: Completed. Price paid 9,706,265.95 kr. *23.2.1968:* Sold to Ion
Shipping Co., Liberia and renamed ION. *1971:* Sold to Agility Shipping Co.
S.A., Greece and renamed AGILITY. *6.3.1978:* Laid up at Chalkis. *1979:* Sold
to Crystal Breeze Cia. Naviera S.A. (Roussos Brothers, managers), Greece,
but never traded. *1988:* Sold to Turkish shipbreakers. *19.12.1988:* Arrived
in tow at Aliaga to be broken up.

153

TOPEKA   Norsk Sjøfartsmuseum

192. TOPEKA (II) (1949-1967)
Tonnages: 4,721 gross, 2,761 net, 7,550 deadweight.
Dimensions: 122.05 (130.49 o.a.) x 16.82 x 11.59 m. 7.767 m draught.
Machinery: 7-cylinder 2 S.C.S.A. oil engine of 5,200 b.h.p. by the shipbuilders.
Service speed 15 knots.
808.30 cu. m. of refrigerated cargo space.
Passengers: 12.
21.4.1949: Launched by Burmeister & Wain's Maskin-og Skibsbyggeri A/S,
Copenhagen (Yard No. 694). *13.7.1949:* Completed. Price paid 9,785,792.20
kr. *7.12.1967:* Sold to Marcima Cia. Nav. S.A., Greece and renamed DOROS.
1972: Sold to Perissia Shipping Co. Ltd. (A. Sigalas & Platis Bros., managers),
Cyprus and renamed PANOMERITIS. *6.12.1979:* Arrived at Split to be
scrapped by Brodospas.

TALLEYRAND, 26.4.1969   J. Y. Freeman

154

193. TALLEYRAND (II) (1949-1971)
Tonnages: 6,126 gross, 3,648 net, 9,575 deadweight.
Dimensions: 135.62 (145.90 o.a.) x 18.62 x 12.65 m. 8.217 m draught.
Machinery: 9-cylinder 2 S.C.S.A. Burmeister & Wain oil engine of 8,100 b.h.p.
by the shipbuilders. Service speed 16 knots.
641.37 cu. m. of refrigerated cargo space.
Passengers: 12.
5.5.1949: Launched by Eriksbergs Mekaniska Verkstads A/B, Gothenburg
(Yard No. 382). *11.8.1949:* Completed. Price paid 12,595,550.92 kr. *1971:*
Sold to Colossus Maritime S.A. (Angelos Politis, manager), Greece and
renamed MINERVA. *15.9.1978:* Delivered at Karachi to Dada Steel Industries
for demolition. *10.1978:* Work commenced at Gadani Beach.

TRAFALGAR off the Hook of Holland, 24.6.1970   *Malcolm Cranfield*

194. TRAFALGAR (III) (1949-1971)
Tonnages: 5,503 gross, 3,144 net, 9,270 deadweight.
Dimensions: 131.30 (141.31 o.a.) x 18.78 x 12.43 m. 8.059 m draught.
Machinery: 7-cylinder 2 S.C.D.A. M.A.N. oil engine of 7,000 b.h.p. by the
shipbuilders. Service speed 16.5 knots.
618.04 cu. m. of refrigerated cargo space.
Passengers: 12.
10.6.1949: Launched by Kockums Mekaniska Verkstads A/B, Malmö (Yard
No. 309). *29.9.1949:* Completed. Price paid 11,502,336.56 kr. *13.4.1971:*
Sold to Hong Kong Atlantic Shipping Co. Ltd., Singapore and renamed
NGOMEI CHAU. *1975:* Transferred to the ownership of Hong Kong Islands
Shipping Co. Ltd. (the former managers) and to Panamanian registry.
11.5.1978: Arrived at Kaohsiung to be broken up by Nan Fu Steel Enterprise
Co. Ltd. *15.6.1978:* Demolition commenced.

195. TASCO (1949-1967)
Tonnages: 4,719 gross, 2,760 net, 7,550 deadweight.
Dimensions: 122.05 (130.49 o.a.) x 16.82 x 11.59 m. 7.772 m draught.
Machinery: 7-cylinder 2 S.C.S.A. oil engine of 5,200 b.h.p. by the shipbuilders.
Service speed 15 knots.
880.64 cu. m. of refrigerated cargo space.
Passengers: 12.

TASCO

11.8.1949: Launched by Burmeister & Wain's Maskin-og Skibsbyggeri A/S, Copenhagen (Yard No. 695). *28.10.1949:* Completed. Price paid 9,850,251.19 kr. *5.12.1967:* Sold to Eudora Cia. Naviera, Liberia. *1968:* Renamed PELOPS. *1970:* Sold to Efplia I Shipping Co. S.A., Greece and renamed ELIZABETH. *1976:* Sold to Walton Shipping Co. (Liberia) Ltd., Panama and renamed SEVILLE. *18.7.1977:* Arrived at Karachi for demolition by Pakistani shipbreakers and by *5.10.1977* had moved on to Gadani Beach to be broken up.

196. THERMOPYLÆ (II) (1949-1971)
Tonnages: 7,262 gross, 4,329 net, 10,250 deadweight.
Dimensions: 146.50 (158.59 o.a.) x 19.79 x 13.08 m. 8.407 m draught.
Machinery: Two 10-cylinder 2 S.C.S.A. Burmeister & Wain oil engines totalling 9,600 b.h.p. by the shipbuilders driving twin screws. Service speed 17 knots. 681.98 cu. m. of refrigerated cargo space.
Passengers: 12.
29.6.1949: Launched by Akers Mekaniske Verksted A/S, Oslo (Yard No. 483). *24.11.1949:* Completed. Price paid 14,011,416.66 kr. *24.6.1971:* Sold to Skips-A/S Solvang (Brodrene Olsen A/S, managers) Stavanger and renamed KONGSBORG. *18.8.1972:* Delivered at Kaohsiung to Chi Shun Hwa Steel Co. Ltd. for demolition. *25.10.1972:* Work began.

THERMOPYLÆ   *J. Y. Freeman*

MV "TUNGUS" (1949)

TUNGUS

197. TUNGUS (II) (1949-1969)
Tonnages: 5,499 gross, 3,143 net, 9,270 deadweight.
Dimensions: 131.30 (141.31 o.a.) x 18.80 x 12.43 m. 8.052 m draught.
Machinery: 7-cylinder 2 S.C.D.A. M.A.N. oil engine of 7,000 b.h.p. by the
shipbuilders. Service speed 16.5 knots.
600.70 cu. m. of refrigerated cargo space.
Passengers: 12.
22.9.1949: Launched by Kockums Mekaniska Verkstads A/B, Malmö (Yard
No. 313). *15.12.1949:* Completed. Price paid 11,708,515.28 kr. *29.10.1969:*
Sold to Progress Shipping Co., Liberia and renamed PROGRESS. *1973:* Sold
to Hightide Corp., Liberia and renamed PROGRESO. *1975:* Sold to Seaplace
Inc., Panama and renamed SEAKING I. *20.7.1976:* Fire broke out when she
was off Colombo during a voyage from Kuwait to Colombo. *21.7.1976:* Arrived
at Colombo with damage. *10.9.1976:* Sustained hull damage when she was
struck by a towed barge. Not worth repairing and sold to Walter Ritscher
G.m.b.H., Hamburg, for demolition in Pakistan. *23.2.1977:* Left Colombo in
tow for Karachi under the name KING. *10.3.1977:* Beached at Gadani Beach
for demolition by Metalside Ltd.

198. TAMESIS (II) (1950-1969)
Tonnages: 6,749 gross, 4,041 net, 10,260 deadweight.
Dimensions: 137.42 (147.33 o.a.) x 19.31 x 13.09 m. 8.506 m draught.
Machinery: 6-cylinder 2 S.C.S.A. Doxford oil engine of 6,800 b.h.p. by Fairfield
Shipbuilding & Engineering Co. Ltd., Glasgow. Service speed 16 knots.
554.44 cu. m. of refrigerated cargo space.
Passengers: 12.
5.12.1949: Launched by Charles Connell & Co. Ltd., Glasgow (Yard No. 463).
30.3.1950: Completed. Price paid 13,229,296.03 kr. *7.1969:* Suffered engine
breakdown in the Pacific during a voyage from Hamburg to Dunedin. After
discharge at Dunedin she was sold to Taiwan shipbreakers and arrived at

TAMESIS *J. Y. Freeman*

Kaohsiung *23.10.1969.* She was, however, resold for further trading to Compania Maritima Ta Teh S.A.. Panama and renamed SUCCESSFUL TRADER. *1972:* Sold to Wan Lung Nav. Co. S.A., Panama and renamed WAN FU. *1973:* Sold to Wan Lee S.S. Co. S.A., Panama and renamed WAN LEE. *2.3.1978:* Delivered to Chu Feng Industrial Co. Ltd. for scrapping. *12.5.1978:* Demolition began at Kaohsiung.

199. TARTAR (I) (1951-1963) Tanker
Tonnages: 11,103 gross, 6,421 net, 16,390 deadweight.
Dimensions: 153.93 (163.79 o.a.) x 20.55 x 11.33 m. 8.914 m draught.
Machinery: 5-cylinder 2 S.C.S.A. Burmeister & Wain oil engine of 6,700 i.h.p. by J.G. Kincaid & Co. Ltd., Greenock. Service speed 14 knots.
27.10.1950: Launched by Charles Connell & Co. Ltd., Glasgow (Yard No. 466). *27.1.1951:* Completed. Price paid 13,616,996.56 kr. *11.12.1963:* Sold to Lovisa Ångfartygs A/B (A/B R. Nordström & Co. O/Y, managers), Finland and renamed SUSANNA. *1970:* Sold to Tenacity Seafaring Corporation, Greece and renamed TENACITY. *1971:* Sold to Kydon Cia. Nav. S.A. (Mamitank Shipping Enterprises S.A., managers), Greece and renamed LENA. *23.3.1975:* Steel Scrap Co. commenced demolition at Gadani Beach.

TARTAR

THALATTA

200. THALATTA (II) (1951-1970)
Tonnages: 5,168 gross, 2,921 net, 7,835 deadweight.
Dimensions: 128.02 (138.51 o.a.) x 18.32 x 11.92 m. 7.875 m draught.
Machinery: 7-cylinder 2 S.C.D.A. oil engine of 7,500 b.h.p. by Gebr. Stork
& Co. N.V., Hengelo. Service speed 16.5 knots.
889.71 cu. m. of refrigerated cargo space.
Passengers: 12.
31.1.1951: Launched by Kaldnes Mekaniske Verksted A/S, Tønsberg (Yard No.
133). *21.6.1951:* Completed. Price paid 16,507,561.18 kr. *10.3.1970:* Sold to
Solstad Rederi A/S (Johannes Solstad, manager), Skudeneshavn and
renamed SOL PEMKO. Owners later became S/A Solborg & Co. (same
managers). *1975:* Sold to Solstad R/A (same managers). *1975:* Sold to Hong
Kong Ocean Shipping Co. Ltd. (Hong Kong Islands Shipping Co. Ltd.,
managers), Panama and renamed LUK CHAU. *9.11.1978:* Delivered at
Shanghai to China National Metals & Minerals Import & Export Corporation
who commenced demolition at Nanjing the following month.

TABOR   *W.S.P.L.*

201. TABOR (III) (1952-1968)
Tonnages: 5,483 gross, 3,224 net, 8,340 deadweight.
Dimensions: 128.01 (137.84 o.a.) x 17.47 x 11.89 m. 7.848 m draught.
Machinery: 6-cylinder 2 S.C.D.A. Burmeister & Wain oil engine of 5,600 b.h.p.
by the shipbuilders. Service speed 15.5 knots.
Passengers: 12.
23.10.1951: Launched by Akers Mekaniske Verksted A/S, Oslo (Yard No. 492).
15.1.1952: Completed. Price paid 16,223,527.35 kr. *4.1.1968:* Sold to Ion
Shipping Co., Liberia. *9.1969:* Renamed PELASGOS. *1.5.1972:* Arrived at Vigo
to be broken up by Jose Antonio Sestelo. *6.5.1972:* Demolition commenced.

TAIWAN

202. TAIWAN (II) / TIRRANNA (II) (1952-1966)
Tonnages: 5,463 gross, 3,087 net, 9,150 deadweight.
Dimensions: 131.06 (140.99 o.a.) x 18.77 x 12.42 m. 8.077 m draught.
Machinery: 7-cylinder 2 S.C.D.A. M.A.N. oil engine of 7,000 b.h.p. by the shipbuilders. Service speed 16.5 knots.
596.35 cu. m. of refrigerated cargo space.
Passengers: 12.
12.12.1951: Launched by Kockums Mekaniska Verkstads A/B, Malmö (Yard No. 334). *14.3.1952:* Completed. Price paid 16,017,631.86 kr. *1.1.1959:* Renamed TIRRANNA. *30.1.1966:* Went aground in Finsnesrenna, near Tromsø, during a voyage from Murmansk to Rostock with a cargo of iron ore and broke in two the following day, the afterpart sinking. The remainder of the wreck was later sold to Erik Volckmar, Oslo, for demolition. Most of it was cut into pieces and these were taken to the smelting works at Mo i Rana, but some identifiable parts still remain at the stranding site.

TENERIFFA   *Fotoflite incorporating Skyfotos*

203. TENERIFFA (II) (1952-1970)
Tonnages: 5,150 gross, 2,923 net, 7,835 deadweight.
Dimensions: 128.02 (138.51 o.a.) x 18.32 x 8.87 m. 7.875 m draught.
Machinery: 7-cylinder 2 S.C.D.A. oil engine of 9,000 i.h.p. by Gebr. Stork &
Co. N.V., Hengelo. Service speed 16.5 knots.
882.34 cu. m. of refrigerated cargo space.
Passengers: 12.
19.12.1951: Launched by Kaldnes Mekaniske Verksted A/S, Tønsberg (Yard
No. 134). *23.4.1952:* Completed. Price paid 16,722,343.36 kr. *13.2.1970:*
Sold to Skips A/S Soltun & Co. (Johannes Solstad, manager), Skudeneshavn
and renamed SOL LAILA. *1975:* Transferred to Skips-A/S Solhav & Co. (same
managers). *1975:* Sold to Hong Kong Pacific Shipping Co. Ltd. (Hong Kong
Islands Shipping Co. Ltd., managers), Panama and renamed SUNSHINE
ISLAND. *20.3.1979:* Arrived at Kaohsiung to be broken up. *21.4.1979:* Long
Jong Industry Co. Ltd. commenced demolition.

TALISMAN

204. TALISMAN (IV) (1952-1973)
Tonnages: 6,785 gross, 4,002 net, 10,280 deadweight.
Dimensions: 143.25 (153.46 o.a.) x 19.56 x 13.08 m. 8.432 m draught.
Machinery: 6-cylinder 2 S.C.S.A. Doxford oil engine of 8,500 b.h.p. by Barclay
Curle & Co. Ltd., Glasgow. Service speed 17 knots.
843.55 cu. m. of refrigerated cargo space.
Passengers: 12.
29.2.1952: Launched by Charles Connell & Co. Ltd., Glasgow (Yard No. 471).
20.5.1952: Completed. Price paid 16,719,247.75 kr. *11.1972:* Suffered engine
failure during a voyage from Marseilles to Brisbane and completed her voyage,
from Balboa to Sydney, N.S.W., in tow of TENDER TUNA — q.v. As she was
not worth repairing TENDER TUNA then towed her to Kaohsiung where she
arrived *18.2.1973* to be broken up by Nan Feng Steel & Enterprise Co. Ltd.
12.3.1973: Demolition commenced.

TUNGSHA   *Norsk Sjøfartsmuseum*

205. TUNGSHA (II) (1952-1972)
Tonnages: 5,465 gross, 3,093 net, 9,160 deadweight.
Dimensions: 131.30 (141.31 o.a.) x 18.75 x 12.43 m. 8.065 m draught.
Machinery: 7-cylinder 2 S.C.D.A. M.A.N. oil engine of 7,000 b.h.p. by the
shipbuilders. Service speed 16.5 knots.
596.35 cu. m. of refrigerated cargo space.
Passengers: 12.
8.4.1952: Launched by Kockums Mekaniska Verkstads A/B, Malmö (Yard No.
340). *16.7.1952:* Completed. Price paid 16,253,761.03 kr. *28.9.1972:* Sold
to Solstad Rederi A/S, Skudeneshavn and renamed CONCORDIA FONN.
1973: Sold to Sirines Shipping Co. S.A., Greece and renamed FANEROMENI.
1975: Sold to Simeon Maritime Co. S.A., Greece and renamed LEONIDAS
G. *21.4.1978:* Anchored off Karachi to await demolition at Gadani Beach
where work commenced during the following month.

TAGUS   *W.S.P.L.*

162

206. TAGUS / TOWADA (1953-1977)

Tonnages: 6,397 gross, 3,715 net, 10,400 deadweight.
Dimensions: 143.52 (152.10 o.a.) x 19.61 x 13.09 m. 8.421 m draught.
Machinery: 10-cylinder 2 S.C.S.A. M.A.N. oil engine of 9,000 b.h.p. by the shipbuilders. Service speed 17 knots.
805.33 cu. m. of refrigerated cargo space.
Passengers: 12.
17.11.1952: Launched by Kockums Mekaniska Verkstads A/B, Malmö (Yard No. 346). *27.2.1953:* Completed. Price paid 19,210,226.10 kr. *8.10.1975:* Transferred to Arctic Shipping Singapore (Pte.) Ltd. (Barber Ship Management Ltd., managers), Singapore and renamed TOWADA. *13.8.1977:* Sold to Africont Navigation Shipping Co. S.A., Greece and renamed LAGOS EXPRESS. *6.4.1979:* Arrived at Kaohsiung for demolition by Keun Hwa Iron Steel Works & Enterprise Ltd. *27.4.1979:* Demolition commenced.

TUAREG

207. TUAREG (I) (1953-1965) Tanker

Tonnages: 11,480 gross, 6,569 net, 16,850 deadweight.
Dimensions: 158.49 (167.12 o.a.) x 21.33 x 11.35 m. 9.093 m draught.
Machinery: 6-cylinder 2 S.C.S.A. Burmeister & Wain oil engine of 7,200 b.h.p. by J.G. Kincaid & Co. Ltd., Greenock. Service speed 15 knots.
20.11.1952: Launched by Lithgows Ltd., Port Glasgow (Yard No. 1069). *17.3.1953:* Completed. Price paid 15,554,213.58 kr. *12.3.1965:* Sold to ''Ausonia'' di Nav. dei Fratelli Ravano di Alberto, Italy and renamed SOBRIETAS. *5.2.1970:* Sustained major damage when she encountered a storm about 400 miles off Land's End during a voyage from Amuay Bay to Milford Haven with naphtha. Declared a constructive total loss and sold to Desguaces Maritimos for scrapping. After temporary repairs at Swansea she left there in tow *5.3.1970* bound for Vinaroz where she arrived *18.3.1970* to be broken up.

208. THEMIS (III) / TOYO (1953-1977)

Tonnages: 7,016 gross, 4,126 net, 10,550 deadweight.
Dimensions: 143.41 (155.58 o.a.) x 19.87 x 13.11 m. 8.402 m draught.
Machinery: 10-cylinder 2 S.C.S.A. Burmeister & Wain oil engine of 9,300 b.h.p. by the shipbuilders. Service speed 17.5 knots.
735.10 cu. m. of refrigerated cargo space.
Passengers: 12.

THEMIS in 5.1964

J. Y. Freeman

9.6.1953: Launched by Eriksbergs Mekaniska Verkstads A/B, Gothenburg (Yard No. 439). *27.8.1953:* Completed. Price paid 19,193,901.48 kr. *25.3.1975:* Transferred to Arctic Shipping Singapore (Pte.) Ltd. (Barber Ship Management Ltd., managers), Singapore and renamed TOYO. *20.8.1977:* Sold to Nan Chiao Shipping (Pte.) Ltd. (Sin Chiao Shipping (Pte.) Ltd., managers), Singapore and renamed NEW HORSE. *22.8.1979:* Arrived at Tientsin for demolition by China National Metals & Minerals Import & Export Corporation who commenced work the following month.

THEBEN leaving Hamburg, 5.9.1970

Joachim Pein

209. THEBEN (I) (1953-1977)
Tonnages: 7,010 gross, 4,120 net, 10,225 deadweight.
Dimensions: 143.41 (155.58 o.a.) x 19.87 x 13.11 m. 8.421 m draught.
Machinery: 10-cylinder 2 S.C.S.A. Burmeister & Wain oil engine of 9,300 b.h.p. by the shipbuilders. Service speed 17.5 knots.
735.10 cu. m. of refrigerated cargo space.
Passengers: 12.
21.7.1953: Launched by Eriksbergs Mekaniska Verkstads A/B, Gothenburg (Yard No. 440). *24.9.1953:* Completed. Price paid 18,852,466.43 kr. *3.3.1975:* Transferred to Arctic Shipping Singapore (Pte.) Ltd. (Torvan Shipping Ltd., managers), Singapore. *1976:* Managers became Barber Ship Management Ltd. *21.6.1977:* Sold to Pacific International Lines (Pte.) Ltd., Singapore and renamed KOTA MAS. *26.8.1980:* Arrived at Basrah and detained there as a result of the Iran-Iraq conflict. There has been no recent information about her, but she is regarded as a total loss.

TURCOMAN

210. TURCOMAN (I) (1954-1963) Tanker
Tonnages: 12,552 gross, 7,222 net, 18,610 deadweight.
Dimensions: 161.83 (169.53 o.a.) x 22.33 x 11.66 m. 9.392 m draught.
Machinery: 6-cylinder 2 S.C.S.A. Doxford oil engine of 8,500 b.h.p. by Barclay Curle & Co. Ltd., Glasgow. Service speed 15.5 knots.
26.10.1953: Launched by Charles Connell & Co. Ltd., Glasgow (Yard No. 474). *11.1.1954:* Completed. Price paid 17,331,928.09 kr. *31.12.1963:* Sold to Fairisle Investment Co. Inc., Liberia and renamed MERCANTILE PIONEER. *1968:* Renamed EDLA. *1970:* Sold to North Sea Barge Transportation Ltd., Liberia and renamed STOLT EDLA. *1970:* Sold to Aquarius Nav. Corp., Liberia. *1971:* Renamed TAKTIKOS. *1973:* Sold to Albemarle Shipping Corp., Liberia and renamed ASTIR. *1973:* Sold to Astir Shipping Co. S.A., Greece. *11.6.1975:* Arrived at Kaohsiung to be broken up by Huang Yung Steel & Iron Works. *4.8.1975:* Demolition commenced.

TABRIZ

211. TABRIZ (I) (1954-1967) Tanker

Tonnages: 11,747 gross, 6,824 net, 17,895 deadweight.
Dimensions: 160.33 (170.52 o.a.) x 21.34 x 11.97 m. 9.545 m draught.
Machinery: 8-cylinder 2 S.C.S.A. Burmeister & Wain oil engine of 10,000 b.h.p.
by the shipbuilders. Service speed 16.25 knots.
4.3.1954: Launched by Eriksbergs Mekaniska Verkstads A/B, Gothenburg
(Yard No. 480). *12.5.1954:* Completed. Price paid 22,499,669.36 kr.
10.8.1967: Sold to Astro Vencedor Cia. Naviera S.A., Liberia and renamed
DAMIANOS. *1975:* Sold to Dolphin Shipping Co. Ltd., Cyprus and renamed
TABRIZ. *1976:* Converted into a roll-on, roll-off vehicles carrier of 5,383 gross,
3,277 net, 8,941 deadweight and renamed DOLPHIN ELENA. *1979:* Sold
to Ciel Shipping Co. Ltd., Greece and renamed ELENA. *1981:* Sold to Aegis
Compania Naviera S.A. (John S. Latsis, manager), Greece and renamed
ADVENTURE I. *12.11.1983:* Laid up at Eleusis; managers subsequently became
Blinder Marine Corporation S.A. *1988:* Sold to Corpus S.A. (Intertrans
Shipping Ltd, managers), St. Vincent, renamed SPEEDO and *16.9.1988* re-
activated. *1988:* Renamed CHAMPION. *1.4.1989:* Arrived at Mangalore to
be broken up by Nathani Industrial Services. *15.5.1989:* Demolition
commenced.

TIBER in 8.1959

J. Y. Freeman

TIBER, now fitted with deck cranes, arriving at Hamburg, 3.8.1974   *Joachim Pein*

212. TIBER (1954-1976)
Tonnages: 6,355 gross, 3,794 net, 9,750 deadweight.
Dimensions: 143.52 (152.10 o.a.) x 19.56 x 13.09 m. 8.421 m draught.
Machinery: 10-cylinder 2 S.C.S.A. M.A.N. oil engine of 9,000 b.h.p. by the
shipbuilders. Service speed 17 knots.
805.33 cu. m. of refrigerated cargo space.
Passengers: 12.
29.1.1954: Launched by Kockums Mekaniska Verkstads A/B, Malmö (Yard
No. 369). *20.5.1954:* Completed. Price paid 23,029,010.68 kr. *15.12.1976:*
Sold to Pacific International Lines (Pte.) Ltd., Singapore and renamed KOTA
MOLEK. *3.11.1982:* Arrived at Gadani Beach to be broken up by Pak Mehran
Ltd. *16.4.1983:* Demolition commenced.

TROUBADOUR   *W.S.P.L.*

213. TROUBADOUR (II) (1954-1971)
Tonnages: 8,649 gross, 5,229 net, 9,720 deadweight.
Dimensions: 134.12 (143.80 o.a.) x 18.80 x 12.43 m. 8.109 m draught.
Machinery: 6-cylinder 2 S.C.S.A. Doxford oil engine of 7,500 b.h.p. by the
shipbuilders. Service speed 17 knots.
638.54 cu. m. of refrigerated cargo space.
Passengers: 12.

24.10.1953: Launched by Nederlandsche Dok en Scheepsbouw Maatschappij V.O.F., Amsterdam (Yard No. 456). *4.6.1954:* Completed. Price paid 19,533,191.09 kr. *13.11.1971:* Sold to John Swire & Sons Ltd., London and renamed SINKIANG. *1973:* Sold to Eggar Forrester (Holdings) Ltd., London. *1976:* Sold to China Mutual Steam Navigation Co. Ltd. (Blue Funnel Line Ltd., managers), Liverpool. *1.1977:* Sold to China Navigation Co. Ltd., Hong Kong. *7.1977:* Sold to Taikoo Nav. Co. Ltd. (China Navigation Co. Ltd., managers), Hong Kong. *26.7.1980:* Arrived at Kaohsiung to be broken up by Long Jong Industry Co. Ltd. *22.8.1980:* Demolition commenced.

TIBETAN

214. TIBETAN (I) (1954-1961) Tanker
Tonnages: 12,548 gross, 7,144 net, 18,610 deadweight.
Dimensions: 161.55 (169.53 o.a.) x 22.31 x 11.66 m. 9.380 m draught.
Machinery: 6-cylinder 2 S.C.S.A. Doxford oil engine of 8,500 b.h.p. by Barclay Curle & Co. Ltd., Glasgow. Service speed 15.5 knots.
7.5.1954: Launched by Charles Connell & Co., Ltd. Glasgow (Yard No. 476). *23.8.1954:* Completed. Price paid 17,192,045.61 kr. *2.6.1961:* Sold to Shell Canadian Tankers Ltd., Bermuda and renamed NORTHERN SHELL. *1964:* Owners became Shell Canada Ltd., Bermuda. *1972:* Owners became Shell Canadian Tankers (1964) Ltd., Bermuda. *5.12.1975:* Arrived at Bilbao and *20.1.1976* sold to Recuperaciones de Materiales S.A. for demolition there.

215. TARIM (I) (1954-1961) Tanker
Tonnages: 16,567 gross, 9,620 net, 25,145 deadweight.
Dimensions: 183.09 (192.13 o.a.) x 23.42 x 13.11 m. 10.484 m draught.
Machinery: Three steam turbines by the shipbuilders totalling 9,900 s.h.p. double reduction geared to a single screw shaft. Service speed 16 knots.
27.3.1954: Launched by Nederlandsche Dok en Scheepsbouw Maatschapij V.O.F., Amsterdam (Yard No. 463). *21.9.1954:* Completed. Price paid 28,012,559.93 kr. *7.7.1961:* Sold to Soc. Anon. de Navegacion Petrolera (Cia. Sudamericana de Vapores, managers), Chile and renamed MANANTIALES. *1964:* Sold to Poros Shipping Corporation (Stathatos & Co. Ltd., managers), Liberia and renamed MARNA. *11.10.1975:* Arrived at Hamburg to be scrapped by Eisen & Metall A.G.

TARIM

216. TUGELA (II) (1954-1976)
Tonnages: 9,947 gross, 6,101 net, 12,845 deadweight.
Dimensions: 143.67 (155.58 o.a.) x 19.87 x 13.11 m. 9.475 m draught.
Machinery: 8-cylinder 2 S.C.S.A. Burmeister & Wain oil engine of 10,000 b.h.p.
by the shipbuilders. Service speed 17.5 knots.
732.13 cu. m. of refrigerated cargo space.
Passengers: 12.
8.7.1954: Launched by Eriksbergs Mekaniska Verkstads A/B, Gothenburg
(Yard No. 449). *25.9.1954:* Completed. Price paid 21,007,166.72 kr.
14.5.1976: Sold to Pacific International Lines (Pte.) Ltd., Singapore and
renamed KOTA ALAM. *23.5.1982:* Left Hong Kong for Kaohsiung to be
scrapped by Nan Hor Steel Enterprise Co. Ltd. *8.6.1982:* Demolition
commenced.

TUGELA at Hong Kong in 3.1966   *Ambrose Greenway*

217. TOREADOR (1954-1973)
Tonnages: 8,607 gross, 5,200 net, 9,600 deadweight.
Dimensions: 134.12 (143.72 o.a.) x 18.80 x 12.43 m. 8.786 m draught.
Machinery: 6-cylinder 2 S.C.S.A. Doxford oil engine of 7,500 b.h.p. by the
shipbuilders. Service speed 17 knots.
638.54 cu. m. of refrigerated cargo space.
Passengers: 12.

TOREADOR

24.4.1954: Launched by Nederlandsche Dok en Scheepsbouw Maatschappij V.O.F., Amsterdam (Yard No. 457). *26.10.1954:* Completed. Price paid 19,644,317.10 kr. *28.3.1973:* Sold to Pacific International Lines (Pte.) Ltd., Singapore, and renamed KOTA MURNI. *1.5.1978:* Arrived at Karachi and about *16.5.1978* moved on to Gadani Beach for scrapping.

TERRIER

218. TERRIER (III) (1954-1973)
Tonnages: 8,125 gross, 4,682 net, 8,230 deadweight.
Dimensions: 128.02 (139.81 o.a.) x 18.32 x 12.20 m. 8.567 m draught.
Machinery: Two 7-cylinder 2 S.C.S.A. oil engines totalling 7,300 b.h.p. by N.V. "De Schelde", Flushing, geared to a single screw shaft. Service speed 16.5 knots.
776.72 cu. m. of refrigerated cargo space.
Passengers: 12.
3.7.1954: Launched by Kaldnes Mekaniske Verksted A/S, Tønsberg (Yard No. 139). *23.11.1954:* Completed. Price paid 21,520,218.89 kr. *21.3.1973:* Sold to Cia. Carica S.A., Greece and renamed TERRY. *1973:* Sold to Cia. Nav. Americana de Vapores S.r.l., Panama and renamed BASTIDAS. *1980:* Sold to Polyzynis Shipping Corporation, Panama and renamed BASTI. *22.10.1980:* Arrived at Karachi and later moved on to Gadani Beach for demolition by Shershah Industries Ltd. *17.12.1980:* Demolition commenced.

TANA

219. TANA (II) (1956-1969)
Tonnages: 6,553 gross, 3,796 net, 8,010 deadweight.
Dimensions: 122.03 (132.59 o.a.) x 17.71 x 10.90 m. 7.670 m draught.
Machinery: 6-cylinder 2 S.C.S.A. Götaverken oil engine of 4,500 b.h.p. by
the shipbuilders. Service speed 15.75 knots.
509.70 cu. m. of refrigerated cargo space.
Passengers: 12.
23.11.1955: Launched by A/S Fredriksstad Mekaniske Verksted, Fredrikstad
(Yard No. 352) as RINGFRED for Ringdals Rederi A/S (Olav Ringdal, manager),
Oslo. *4.2.1956:* Completed. *11.5.1956:* Purchased by Wilh. Wilhelmsen and
renamed TANA. Price paid 19,005,893.00 kr. *12.9.1969:* Sold to Johs.
Presthus Rederi A/S (Johs. Presthus, manager), Bergen and renamed JOHS.
PRESTHUS. *1970:* Transferred to Arne Presthus Rederi-A/S. *1971:* Sold to
Mares Neptunea S.A. (Bouboulina Shipping S.A., managers), Greece and
renamed JOHS. P. For a short period in *1971* she was renamed CONCORDIA
JOHS, and then reverted to JOHS. P. *18.3.1973:* Fire broke out on board when
she was nine miles east of Dungeness during a voyage from Sluiskil to
Guayaquil with a cargo of fertiliser. *20.3.1973:* Arrived in tow at Antwerp
and subsequently declared a constructive total loss. Repaired and in *1974*
renamed BOUBOULINA WAVE. *1978:* Sold to Al Khalifa & Mirchandani
Shipping Co. Ltd., Kuwait and renamed DALYAH. *1979:* Sold to South Korean
shipbreakers and *31.8.1979* arrived at Busan to be broken up. *15.9.1979:*
Demolition commenced.

220. TORONTO (II) (1956-1973)
Tonnages: 8,223 gross, 4,947 net, 9,560 deadweight.
Dimensions: 130.21 (141.99 o.a.) x 18.34 x 12.20 m. 8.865 m draught.
Machinery: 10-cylinder 2 S.C.S.A. Sulzer oil engine of 7,000 b.h.p. by N.V.
Werkspoor, Amsterdam. Service speed 16.5 knots.
954.27 cu. m. of refrigerated cargo space.
Passengers: 12.

TORONTO   *Norsk Sjøfartsmuseum*

12.5.1956: Launched by Kaldnes Mekaniske Verksted A/S, Tønsberg (Yard No. 143). *27.8.1956:* Completed. Price paid 23,958,941.00 kr. *17.1.1973:* Sold to Samudera Shipping (Liberia) Inc., Panama and renamed ASCARYA. *1978:* Transferred to P.T. Perusahaan Pelayaran Samudera ''Samudera Indonesia'', Indonesia. *9.10.1981:* Laid up at Djakarta. *9.4.1982:* Arrived in tow at Tandjong Priok for demolition at Marunda Scrapyard.

TEMERAIRE, as built   *Alex Duncan*

221. TEMERAIRE (III) (1957-1978)
Tonnages: *1957-1970:* 8,779 gross, 5,317 net, 10,080 deadweight. *1970-on:* 10,062 gross, 6,766 net, 12,337 deadweight.
Dimensions: *1957-1970:* 137.15 (149.31 o.a.) x 19.59 x 12.65 m. 9.169 m draught. *1970-on:* 159.54 (171.71 o.a.) x 19.59 x 12.65 m. 9.145 m draught.
Machinery: *1957-1970:* 6-cylinder 2 S.C.S.A. Doxford oil engine of 9,000 b.h.p. by Barclay Curle & Co. Ltd., Glasgow. Service speed 18 knots. *1970-on:*

6-cylinder 2 S.C.S.A. oil engine of 11,400 b.h.p. by Maschinenfabrik Augsburg-Nürnberg A.G., Augsburg. Service speed 18.25 knots.
956.39 cu. m. of refrigerated cargo space.
Passengers: 12.
1970-on: Container section with capacity for 84 containers under deck.
9.11.1956: Launched by Charles Connell & Co. Ltd., Glasgow (Yard No. 482).
9.2.1957: Completed. Price paid 26,958,166.06 kr. *19.1.1970:* Arrived at Sandefjord where she was lengthened by Framnæs Mekaniske Verksted A/S, who inserted a container-carrying section amidships and re-engined her with a new M.A.N. oil engine. *21.6.1970:* Reconstruction completed. *7.1.1978:* Sold to West Africa Navigation Co. S.A., Greece and renamed WARRI EXPRESS. *1979:* Sold to Sealine Maritime Inc. (Almouaket Shipping & Trading Agency Co. W.L.L., managers), Panama and renamed ALMONA. *1981:* Sold to Asia Marine Services Co. W.L.L., Kuwait. *18.6.1984:* Arrived at Kaohsiung to be scrapped by The Great Honor Steel Iron Works Co. Ltd. *27.6.1984:* Demolition commenced.

TYR

222. TYR (II) (1957-1967)
Tonnages: 5,208 gross, 2,886 net, 7,930 deadweight.
Dimensions: 118.88 (125.69 o.a.) x 18.32 x 11.46 m. 7.563 m draught.
Machinery: Two 6-cylinder 2 S.C.S.A. oil engines totalling 4,150 b.h.p. by Nordberg Manufacturing Co., Milwaukee geared to a single screw shaft. Service speed 14 knots.
2.4.1944: Launched by Pennsylvania Shipyards Inc., Beaumont, Texas (Yard No. 298) as CAPE DUCATO for the United States War Shipping Administration. *6.1944:* Completed. *1947:* Sold to Buries Markes Ltd., London and renamed LA ESTANCIA. *1951:* Sold to Canadian Shipowners Ltd. (Buries Markes Ltd., managers), Canada, re-registered at Liverpool and renamed MONTCALM. *1953:* Transferred to Montship Lines Ltd. (Buries Markes Ltd., managers), Canada, retaining Liverpool registry. *5.3.1957:* Purchased by Wilh. Wilhelmsen and renamed TYR. Price paid 13,008,768.00 kr. *19.4.1967:* Sold to Eastern Shipping Lines Inc., Philippine Islands and renamed EASTERN MARS. *21.4.1975:* Arrived at Hong Kong and *26.4.1975* delivered to Lee Sing Co. for scrapping. *29.5.1975:* Demolition commenced.

TURANDOT

223. TURANDOT (1957-1976)
Tonnages: 8,784 gross, 5,321 net, 10,200 deadweight.
Dimensions: 137.47 (149.36 o.a.) x 19.59 x 12.65 m. 9.170 m draught.
Machinery: 6-cylinder 2 S.C.S.A. Doxford oil engine of 9,000 b.h.p. by Barclay Curle & Co. Ltd., Glasgow. Service speed 18 knots.
766.25 cu. m. of refrigerated cargo space.
Passengers: 12.
15.8.1957: Launched by Charles Connell & Co. Ltd., Glasgow (Yard No. 486).
6.11.1957: Completed. Price paid 28,524,853.32 kr. *14.4.1976:* Sold to Bangladesh Shipping Corporation, Bangladesh and renamed BANGLAR PREETI. *27.6.1983:* Arrived at Chittagong to be broken up by H. Akbar Ali & Co., who commenced work the following month.

224. TEHERAN (I) (1958-1968) Tanker
Tonnages: 16,407 gross, 9,612 net, 27,075 deadweight.
Dimensions: 176.79 (187.46 o.a.) x 24.16 x 13.34 m. 10.478 m draught.
Machinery: 9-cylinder 2 S.C.S.A. Burmeister & Wain oil engine of 11,200 b.h.p. by the shipbuilders. Service speed 16.5 knots.
30.12.1957: Launched by Eriksbergs Mekaniska Verkstads A/B, Gothenburg (Yard No. 479). *27.3.1958:* Completed. Price paid 34,201,963.00 kr. *28.8.1968:* Sold to Norportex Inc., Jointship Inc., Fearnley Navigation Inc. and Suprema Cia. Nav. S.A., Panama and renamed PROSPECTOR. *28.2.1969:* Sold to Marathon Cia. Nav. S.A., Panama and renamed MARATHON. *1970:* Sold to Olliric Steamship Co.(Cirillo Bros. Sales Corp., managers), Panama and renamed CIBRO CARIBBEAN. *1970:* Transferred to Cia. Nav. Sirius S.A. (Cirillo Bros., managers), Panama. *1976:* Sold to Maroco Tankers S.A., Panama and renamed BARBARA MASSEY. *12.5.1977:* Arrived at Kaohsiung to be scrapped by Fubian Steel Enterprise Co. Ltd. *17.6.1977:* Demolition commenced.

TEHERAN

Alex Duncan

174

TAGAYTAY as built
W.S.P.L.

225. TAGAYTAY (1958-1979)

Tonnages: *1958-1970:* 9,450 gross, 5,704 net, 10,854 deadweight. *1970-on:* 11,744 gross, 8,125 net, 12,556 deadweight.
Dimensions: *1958-1970:* 146.96 (159.71 o.a.) x 20.05 x 11.89 m. 8.621 m draught. *1970-on:* 175.75 (188.73 o.a.) x 20.05 x 11.89 m. 8.621 m draught.
Machinery: 9-cylinder 2 S.C.S.A. oil engine of 11,200 b.h.p. by Burmeister & Wain's Maskin-og Skibsbyggeri A/S, Copenhagen. Service speed 18 knots. 941.81 cu. m. of refrigerated cargo space.
Passengers: 12.
1970-on: Container section with capacity for 120 containers under deck.
30.1.1958: Launched by Deutsche Werft A.G, Hamburg (Yard No. 718). *23.4.1958:* Completed. Price paid 24,576,944.00 kr. *11.6.1970:* Arrived at Nagasaki, where she was lengthened by Mitsubishi Heavy Industries Ltd., who inserted a container carrying section amidships. *14.7.1970:* Reconstruction completed. *13.9.1977:* Transferred to Arctic Shipping Singapore (Pte.) Ltd. (Barber Ship Management Ltd., managers), Singapore. *26.1.1979:* Sold to Hong Kong Ocean Shipping Co. Ltd. (Hong Kong Islands Shipping Co. Ltd., managers), Panama and renamed APLI CHAU. *29.6.1984:* Arrived at Kaohsiung to be broken up by Li Chong Steel & Iron Works Co. Ltd. *9.7.1984:* Demolition commenced.

TAGAYTAY after lengthening, in Barber Line colours
W.S.P.L.

175

TAI PING as built   *Alex Duncan*

226. TAI PING (II) (1958-1979)

Tonnages: *1958-1970:* 9,369 gross, 5,851 net, 10,854 deadweight. *1970-on:* 11,744 gross, 8,125 net, 12,597 deadweight.
Dimensions: *1958-1970:* 146.96 (159.71 o.a.) x 20.05 x 11.89 m. 8.621 m draught. *1970-on:* 175.75 (188.73 o.a.) x 20.05 x 11.89 m. 8.621 m draught.
Machinery: 9 cylinder 2 S.C.S.A. oil engine of 11,200 b.h.p. by Burmeister & Wain's Maskin-og Skibsbyggeri A/S, Copenhagen. Service speed 19 knots. 914.81 cu. m. ft. of refrigerated cargo space.
Passengers: 12.
1970-on: Container section with capacity for 120 containers under deck.
2.4.1958: Launched by Deutsche Werft A.G., Hamburg (Yard No. 719). *27.6.1958:* Completed. Price paid 24,770,638.00 kr. *30.7.1970:* Arrived at Yokohama where she was lengthened by Mitsubishi Heavy Industries Ltd., who inserted a container carrying section amidships. *3.9.1970:* Reconstruction completed. *1.10.1977:* Transferred to Arctic Shipping Singapore (Pte.) Ltd. (Barber Ship Management Ltd., managers), Singapore. *7.6.1979:* Sold to Compania Naviera Panagina S.A. (Mediterranean Shipping Co. S.A., managers), Panama and renamed GINA. *6.7.1984:* Arrived in Chittagong Roads to be broken up by National Foundry & Engineering Works (Pte.) Ltd. *12.7.1984:* Demolition commenced at Bhatiari.

TAI PING after lengthening, in Barber Line colours   *W.S.P.L.*

TITUS   W.S.P.L.

227. TITUS (I) (1959-1971) Tanker
Tonnages: 16,417 gross, 9,618 net, 26,975 deadweight.
Dimensions: 176.79 (187.71 o.a.) x 24.16 x 13.34 m. 10.478 m draught.
Machinery: 9-cylinder 2 S.C.S.A. Burmeister & Wain oil engine of 11,200 b.h.p.
by the shipbuilders. Service speed 16.5 knots.
14.11.1958: Launched by Eriksbergs Mekaniska Verkstads A/B, Gothenburg
(Yard No. 510). *7.2.1959:* Completed. Price paid 34,178,069.00 kr. *29.12.1971:*
Sold to Cleobulos Shipping Corp. Liberia and renamed CLEON. *1977:*
Transferred to Greek registry. *23.1.1982:* Delivered at Karachi to Ayaz
Corporation for scrapping. *28.2.1982:* Demolition commenced at Gadani
Beach.

228. TOLUMA (II) (1959-1972) Tanker
Tonnages: 16,417 gross, 9,617 net, 26,975 deadweight.
Dimensions: 176.79 (187.71 o.a.) x 24.16 x 13.34 m. 10.478 m draught.
Machinery: 9-cylinder 2 S.C.S.A. Burmeister & Wain oil engine of 11,200 b.h.p.
by the shipbuilders. Service speed 16.5 knots.
10.12.1958: Launched by Eriksbergs Mekaniska Verkstads A/B, Gothenburg
(Yard No. 511). *19.3.1959:* Completed. Price paid 33,787,783.00 kr. *28.1.1972:*
Sold to Antclizo Shipping Corp., Liberia and renamed ANTCLIZO. *18.11.1981:*
Arrived at Bombay and sold to Haryana Steel Company for demolition. *6.1982:*
Work commenced at Darukhana.

TOLUMA   Fotoflite incorporating Skyfotos

177

TIJUCA

229. TIJUCA (II) (1959-1977)
Tonnages: 8,831 gross, 5,341 net, 10,030 deadweight.
Dimensions: 137.47 (149.36 o.a.) x 19.59 x 12.65 m. 9.170 m draught.
Machinery: 6-cylinder 2 S.C.S.A. Doxford oil engine of 9,000 b.h.p. by Barclay Curle & Co. Ltd., Glasgow. Service speed 18 knots.
738.21 cu. m. of refrigerated cargo space.
Passengers: 12.
22.5.1959: Launched by Charles Connell & Co. Ltd., Glasgow (Yard No. 490). *4.9.1959:* Completed. Price paid 28,433,284.00 kr. *30.3.1977:* Sold to Vertigo Shipping Co. Ltd., Cyprus and renamed UZMA. *21.2.1979:* Arrived at Kaohsiung to be broken up by Kao Feng Iron & Steel Co. Ltd. *5.3.1979:* Demolition commenced.

TRAVIATA as built

230. TRAVIATA / TEMA (II) (1959-1979)
Tonnages: *1959-1970:* 9,297 gross, 5,629 net, 10,809 deadweight. *1970-on:* 11,744 gross, 8,125 net, 12,525 deadweight.
Dimensions: *1959-1970:* 146.96 (159.71 o.a.) x 20.05 x 11.89 m. 8.621 m draught. *1970-on:* 175.75 (188.73 o.a.) x 20.05 x 11.89 m. 8.621 m draught.
Machinery: 10-cylinder 2 S.C.S.A. Burmeister & Wain oil engine of 12,500 b.h.p. by Friedrich Krupp Dieselmotoren G.m.b.H., Essen. Service speed 18.5 knots.
878.10 cu. m. of refrigerated cargo space.
Passengers: 12.
1970-on: Container section with capacity for 120 containers under deck.

178

15.7.1959: Launched by Deutsche Werft A.G., Hamburg (Yard No. 748). *20.10.1959:* Completed. Price paid 28,305,902.00 kr. *25.6.1970:* Arrived at Yokohama where she was lengthened by Mitsubishi Heavy Industries Ltd., who inserted a container carrying section amidships. *31.7.1970:* Reconstruction completed. *29.7.1977:* Transferred to Arctic Shipping Singapore (Pte.) Ltd. (Barber Ship Management Ltd., managers), Singapore and renamed TEMA. *29.5.1979:* Sold to Hong Kong Orient Shipping Co. Ltd. S.A. (Hong Kong Islands Shipping Co. Ltd., managers), Panama and renamed SUNSHINE ISLAND. *1982:* Renamed LAMTONG CHAU. *29.5.1984:* In collision in the East China Sea with the Panamanian m. vehicle carrier VANTAGE, 20,610/76 during a voyage from San Francisco to Busan. Sold, unrepaired, to Taiwan shipbreakers and *22.6.1984* arrived at Kaohsiung for scrapping by Gwo Feng Steel Enterprise Co. Ltd. *7.7.1984:* Demolition commenced.

TRICOLOR

231. TRICOLOR (V) / TROJA (III) (1960-1979)
Tonnages: 9,997 gross, 5,924 net, 12,700 deadweight.
Dimensions: 143.90 (155.58 o.a.) x 20.81 x 12.65 m. 9.475 m draught.
Machinery: 10-cylinder 2 S.C.S.A. Burmeister & Wain oil engine of 12,500 b.h.p. by the shipbuilders. Service speed 19.5 knots.
953.28 cu. m. of refrigerated cargo space.
Passengers: 9.
24.9.1959: Launched by Eriksbergs Mekaniska Verkstads A/B, Gothenburg (Yard No. 526). *8.1.1960:* Completed. Price paid 30,000,000.00 kr. *18.10.1971:* Renamed TROJA. *29.1.1979:* Sold to Compania Naviera Americana de Vapores S.r.l., Panama and renamed BELALCAZAR. *1980:* Sold to Pacific International Lines (Pte.) Ltd, Singapore and renamed KOTA MAKMUR. *1.6.1985:* Arrived at Yantai for demolition by China National Metals & Minerals Import & Export Corporation.

TROJA

TOLEDO   *W.S.P.L.*

232. TOLEDO (II) (1960-1979)

Tonnages: 10,104 gross, 5,950 net, 12,600 deadweight.
Dimensions: 143.90 (155.58 o.a.) x 20.81 x 12.65 m. 9.475 m draught.
Machinery: 10-cylinder 2 S.C.S.A. Burmeister & Wain oil engine of 12,500
b.h.p. by the shipbuilders. Service speed 19.5 knots.
953.28 cu. m. of refrigerated cargo space.
Passengers: 9.
10.11.1959: Launched by Eriksbergs Mekaniska Verkstads A/B, Gothenburg
(Yard No. 523). *26.1.1960:* Completed. Price paid 30,000,000.00 kr.
16.7.1979: Sold to Nan Chiao Shipping (Pte.) Ltd. (Sin Chiao Shipping (Pte.)
Ltd., managers), Singapore and renamed NEW DOLPHIN. *19.3.1984:* Arrived
at Alang for scrapping by Rajesh Iron & Steel Works. *11.6.1984:* Demolition
commenced.

TARANTEL as built   *Alex Duncan*

233. TARANTEL (1960-1978)

Tonnages: *1960-1970:* 9,316 gross, 5,637 net, 10,665 deadweight. *1970-on:*
11,754 gross, 8,125 net, 12,512 deadweight.
Dimensions: *1960-1970:* 146.96 (159.71 o.a.) x 20.05 x 11.89 m. 8.621 m
draught. *1970-on:* 175.75 (188.73 o.a.) x 20.05 x 11.89 m. 8.621 m draught.
Machinery: 10-cylinder 2 S.C.S.A. Burmeister & Wain oil engine of 12,500
b.h.p. by Friedrich Krupp Dieselmotoren G.m.b.H., Essen. Service speed 18.5
knots.
878.10 cu. m. of refrigerated cargo space.
Passengers: 12.

TARANTEL after lengthening, in Barber Line colours   *W.S.P.L.*

1970-on: Container section with capacity for 120 containers under deck. *12.1.1960:* Launched by Deutsche Werft A.G., Hamburg (Yard No. 749). *2.4.1960:* Completed. Price paid 28,320,594.00 kr. *25.5.1970:* Arrived at Yokohama where she was lengthened by Mitsubishi Heavy Industries Ltd., who inserted a container carrying section amidships. *6.7.1970:* Reconstruction completed. *30.6.1977:* Transferred to Arctic Shipping Singapore (Pte.) Ltd. (Barber Ship Management Ltd., managers), Singapore. *13.12.1978:* Sold to Compania Naviera Regina S.A. (Mediterranean Shipping Co. S.A., managers), Panama and renamed REGINA S. *6.12.1984:* Sailed from Durban for Chittagong to be broken up. *17.4.1985:* National Shipbreakers commenced demolition at Madambibirhat.

234. TØNSBERG (II) (1960-1977)
Tonnage: 10,171 gross, 6,020 net, 12,430 deadweight.
Dimensions: 143.67 (155.58 o.a.) x 20.81 x 12.65 m. 9.475 m draught.
Machinery: 8-cylinder 2 S.C.S.A. Burmeister & Wain oil engine of 13,400 b.h.p. by Akers Mekaniske Verksted A/S, Oslo. Service speed 19.5 knots.
920.97 cu. m. of refrigerated cargo space.
Passengers: 9.

TØNSBERG at Sydney in 1.1964   *J. Y. Freeman*

21.3.1960: Launched by Kaldnes Mekaniske Verksted A/S, Tønsberg (Yard No. 145). *30.6.1960:* Completed. Price paid 34,335,688.00 kr. *8.12.1977:* Sold to Inversiones Navieras Imparca C.A., Venezuela and renamed TEREPAIMA. *1980:* Sold to Ocean Defiant Maritime Corporation, Liberia and renamed OCEAN DEFIANT. *1981:* Renamed DEFIANT. On *31.12.1984* her Liberian registry closed and at some date prior to *7.1985* she was sold by auction at Ho Chi Minh City to Vietnam Shipping Company and renamed TRUONG SON. She is believed to be still trading.

TAMPA   *Norsk Sjøfartsmuseum*

235. TAMPA (II) (1961-1967)
Tonnages: 5,221 gross, 3,012 net, 7,970 deadweight.
Dimensions: 118.88 (125.69 o.a.) x 18.32 x 11.46 m. 7.563 m draught.
Machinery: Two 6-cylinder 2 S.C.S.A. oil engines totalling 4,150 b.h.p. by Nordberg Manufacturing Co., Milwaukee, geared to a single screw shaft. Service speed 14 knots.
21.2.1943: Launched by Pennsylvania Shipyards Inc., Beaumont, Texas (Yard No. 271) as CAPE CONSTANTINE for the United States War Shipping Administration. *6.1943:* Completed. *1946:* Sold to Westfal-Larsen & Co. A/S, Bergen and renamed HINDANGER. *4.2.1961:* Purchased by Wilh. Wilhelmsen and renamed TAMPA. Price paid 4,200,000.00 kr. *9.6.1967:* Sold to Philippine President Lines Inc., Philippine Islands and renamed MANUEL QUEZON. *1968:* Renamed PRESIDENT QUIRINO. *1975:* Renamed LUCKY EIGHT. *10.3.1975:* Arrived at Kaohsiung to be broken up by Li Chong Steel & Iron Works Co. Ltd. *3.4.1975:* Demolition commenced.

TOSCANA

236. TOSCANA (I) (1961-1972) Tanker
Tonnages: 22,725 gross, 13,492 net, 38,450 deadweight.
Dimensions: 196.60 (208.03 o.a.) x 26.62 x 14.79 m. 11.564 m draught.
Machinery: 12-cylinder 2 S.C.S.A. Burmeister & Wain oil engine of 15,000 b.h.p. by the shipbuilders. Service speed 16.5 knots.

24.11.1960: Launched by Eriksbergs Mekaniska Verkstads A/B, Gothenburg (Yard No. 533). *16.2.1961:* Completed. Price paid 42,971,594.00 kr. *6.3.1972:* Sold to Lily Maritime Corp., Liberia and renamed MIRFAK. *1973:* Sold to Dido Shipping Co. S.A.. Greece and renamed SCAPMOUNT. *1982:* Sold to Emborios Compania Naviera S.A. (Alpha Managing & Financing Inc., managers), Greece. *18.12.1982:* Struck by an Iraqi missile about 25 miles off Bandar Khomeini during a voyage from Bushire to Bandar Khomeini and drifted aground on fire. Two members of her crew were killed.

TRIANON on the Kiel Canal, 22.2.1975   *Joachim Pein*

237. TRIANON (II) (1961-1978)
Tonnages: 10,120 gross, 5,892 net, 12,625 deadweight.
Dimensions: 143.90 (155.48 o.a.) x 20.81 x 12.65 m. 9.475 m draught.
Machinery: 10-cylinder 2 S.C.S.A. Burmeister & Wain oil engine of 12,500 b.h.p. by the shipbuilders. Service speed 19.5 knots.

TRIANON in winter conditions

953.28 cu. m. of refrigerated cargo space.
Passengers: 8.
30.12.1960: Launched by Eriksbergs Mekaniska Verkstads A/B, Gothenburg
(Yard No. 529). *29.3.1961:* Completed. Price paid 31,448,580.00 kr. *8.6.1977:*
Transferred to Arctic Shipping Singapore (Pte.) Ltd. (Barber Ship Management
Ltd., managers), Singapore. *26.5.1978:* Sold to Bluebell Shipping Inc. (Unique
Shipping Agencies Ltd., managers), Panama and renamed UNIQUE WINNER.
1983: Sold for scrapping to China Dismantled Vessels Trading Corporation.
26.8.1983: Arrived at Kaohsiung. *12.9.1983:* Yung Tai Steel & Iron Works
commenced demolition.

TARN   *W.S.P.L.*

238. TARN (II) (1961-1978)
Tonnages: 10,120 gross, 5,892 net, 12,500 deadweight.
Dimensions: 143.90 (155.48 o.a.) x 20.81 x 12.65 m. 9.468 m draught.
Machinery: 10-cylinder 2 S.C.S.A. Burmeister & Wain oil engine of 12,500
b.h.p. by the shipbuilders. Service speed 19.5 knots.
953.28 cu. m. of refrigerated cargo space.
Passengers: 8.
10.2.1961: Launched by Eriksbergs Mekaniska Verkstads A/B, Gothenburg
(Yard No. 530). *16.5.1961:* Completed. Price paid 31,457,123.00 kr. *8.3.1978:*
Sold to Hyundai International Inc., South Korea and renamed HALLA
PARTNER. *1979:* Transferred to Halla Maritime Corporation, South Korea.
1983: Sold to China Dismantled Vessels Trading Corporation. *15.9.1983:*
Arrived at Kaohsiung. *5.10.1983:* Kao Yung Steel Enterprise Co. Ltd.
commenced demolition.

239. TORO (I) (1961-1967)
Tonnages: 5,206 gross, 3,000 net, 7,970 deadweight.
Dimensions: 118.87 (125.70 o.a.) x 18.31 x 11.43 m. 7.569 m draught.
Machinery: Two 6-cylinder 2 S.C.S.A. oil engines totalling 4,150 b.h.p. by
Nordberg Manufacturing Co., Milwaukee, geared to a single screw shaft.
Service speed 14 knots.
7.2.1943: Launched by Pennsylvania Shipyards Inc., Beaumont, Texas (Yard
No. 270) as CAPE BLANCO for the United States War Shipping
Administration. *5.1943:* Completed. *1947:* Sold to A/S Ganger Rolf (Den
Norske Syd-Amerika Linje) (Fred Olsen & Co., managers), Oslo and renamed
BRA-KAR. *16.5.1961:* Purchased by Wilh. Wilhelmsen and renamed TORO.
Price paid 4,200,000.00 kr. *27.6.1967:* Sold to Eastern Shipping Lines Inc.,
Philippine Islands and renamed EASTERN SATURN. *1974:* Sold to Chi Shun
Hwa Steel Co. Ltd. for demolition at Kaohsiung. *5.4.1974:* Work commenced.

TORO

Norsk Sjøfartsmuseum

240. TYSLA (III) (1961-1964)

Tonnages: 5,163 gross, 2,760 net, 7,900 deadweight.
Dimensions: 119.12 (125.67 o.a.) x 18.34 x 11.43 m. 7.569 m draught.
Machinery: Two 6-cylinder 2 S.C.S.A. oil engines totalling 4,150 i.h.p. by Nordberg Manufacturing Co., Milwaukee, geared to a single screw shaft. Service speed 14 knots.
23.4.1944: Launched by Pennsylvania Shipyards Inc., Beaumont, Texas (Yard No. 299) as CAPE GASPE for the United States War Shipping Administration.
6.1944: Completed. *16.10.1947:* Sold to J. Lauritzen, Denmark and renamed GERDA DAN. *23.5.1961:* Purchased by Wilh. Wilhelmsen and renamed TYSLA. Price paid 4,054,000.00 kr. *11.5.1964:* Sold to Den Norske Amerikalinje A/S, Oslo and renamed VIKSFJORD. *1968:* Sold to Jens Hetland, Egersund and renamed RYTTERVIK. *31.1.1972:* Delivered at Shanghai to China National Machinery Import & Export Corporation and although possibly used for further trading, believed to have been broken up.

TYSLA

Norsk Sjøfartsmuseum

TROMS

241. TROMS (1961-1972) Tanker

Tonnages: 21,448 gross, 12,833 net, 36,000 deadweight.
Dimensions: 195.56 (202.70 o.a.) x 26.27 x 14.20 m. 11.151 m draught.
Machinery: 9-cylinder 2 S.C.S.A. Burmeister & Wain oil engine of 15,000 b.h.p.
by Akers Mekaniske Verksted A/S, Oslo. Service speed 16.9 knots.
16.9.1960: Hull launched by Stord Verft A/S, Leirvik (Yard No. 44) and
30.5.1961: Completed by Akers Mekaniske Verksted A/S, Oslo (Yard No. 523)
for Sameiet ''Troms'' in which Vesteraalens D/S and Wilh. Wilhelmsen each
had a 50 per cent holding, Wilhelmsen's share of the purchase price being
26,213,104.00 kr. *1.6.1966:* Wilh. Wilhelmsen bought the Vesteraalens D/S
interest in Sameiet ''Troms'' for 10,000,000.00 kr. and the ship became the
sole property of Wilh. Wilhelmsen. *23.3.1972:* Sold to Cia. Trafico Naviero
Sudcontinental S.A., Liberia. *1978:* Sold to Margaritis Marine Co. Ltd. (Tsakos
Shipping & Trading S.A., managers), Cyprus and renamed IRENES FIDELITY.
1979: Sold to Morfini S.p.A.- Trasporti Marittimi, Italy and renamed ARALDA.
1987: Sold to Afroditi Shipping Co. Ltd. (Tsakos Shipping & Trading S.A.,
managers), Malta and renamed LARGAVISTA. *20.7.1990:* Arrived off Alang.
7.8.1990: Beached for demolition by Arihant Shipbreakers.

TITANIA

242. TITANIA (IV) (1961-1971)
Tonnages: 5,443 gross, 3,015 net, 6,285 deadweight.
Dimensions: 111.38 (122.74 o.a.) x 16.49 x 10.03 m. 7.417 m draught.
Machinery: 6-cylinder 2 S.C.S.A. Burmeister & Wain oil engine of 4,700 b.h.p.
by the shipbuilders. Service speed 16 knots.
319.75 cu. m. of refrigerated cargo space.
Passengers: 12.
28.8.1958: Launched by Helsingör Skibsvaerft & Maskinbyggeri A/S,
Helsingör (Yard No. 343) as CRESTVILLE for Skibs A/S Goodwill (A.F.
Klaveness & Co. A/S, managers), Oslo. *11.1958:* Completed. *20.10.1961:*
Purchased by Wilh. Wilhelmsen and renamed TITANIA. Price paid
11,625,000.00 kr. *1.7.1971:* Sold to Ocean Tramping Co. Ltd., Somali Republic
and renamed PEIKIANG. *1974:* Sold to China Ocean Shipping Co., People's
Republic of China. Subsequently transferred to Shanghai Ocean Shipping
Company, and then to the Bureau of Maritime Transport Administration who
renamed her YU XIN. Later reverted to Shanghai Ocean Shipping Co. Believed
by now to have been broken up.

TORINO   *Norsk Sjøfartsmuseum*

243. TORINO (I) (1962-1969) Tanker
Tonnages: 25,465 gross, 15,269 net, 44,000 deadweight.
Dimensions: 202.70 (214.84 o.a.) x 29.01 x 14.94 m. 11.646 m draught.
Machinery: 12-cylinder 2 S.C.S.A. Burmeister & Wain oil engine of 15,000
b.h.p. by the shipbuilders. Service speed 16.5 knots.
30.10.1961: Launched by Eriksbergs Mekaniska Verkstads A/B, Gothenburg
(Yard No. 539). *2.2.1962:* Completed. Price paid 45,788,799.00 kr.
19.12.1969: Sold to Ina Tanker Corporation S.A., Liberia and renamed NOTO.
1974: Sold to Dana Shipping Corp., Liberia and renamed DANA. *1974:* Sold
to Nav. Maju S.A.(Ofer Brothers (Holdings) Ltd., managers), Panama and
renamed EUGENIA II. *1979:* Sold to Penelopi Shipping Co. (Allied Shipping
International Corporation, managers), Greece and renamed DESPINA
MICHALINOU. *1982:* Sold to Black Baronett Shipping Corporation, Greece
and renamed THEOSKEPASTI. *1983:* Renamed TRINITE. *1986:* Sold to
Maritime Transportation Ltd., Cayman Islands and renamed HOPE CREST.
(An earlier proposed sale to Breakaway Ltd., Guernsey, who intended to
rename her TRINITY A fell through.) *1987:* Sold to Tankers International Ltd.,
Cayman Islands and renamed BONARIA. *23.3.1992:* Indian Metal Traders
(proprietors Chawdhary & Chawdhary Ship Breakers Pvt. Ltd.) commenced
demolition at Bombay.

TEMPLAR

244. TEMPLAR (III) (1962-1965) Bulk Carrier
Tonnages: 12,153 gross, 6,643 net, 18,780 deadweight.
Dimensions: 148.28 (159.63 o.a.) x 21.13 x 13.59 m. 9.804 m draught.
Machinery: 5-cylinder 2 S.C.S.A. Burmeister & Wain oil engine of 9,400 i.h.p.
by the shipbuilders. Service speed 15 knots.
20.1.1962: Launched by Akers Mekaniske Verksted A/S, Oslo (Yard No. 524).
25.5.1962: Completed. Price paid 23,383,568.00 kr. *1.5.1965:* Broke in two
and sank about three miles N.W. of Point San Nicolas, Peru, whilst in tow
after striking a submerged rock the previous day during a voyage from San
Nicolas to Kokura with a cargo of iron ore pellets. Her Master was lost, but
the rest of the crew was saved.

TOULOUSE

245. TOULOUSE (II) (1962-1974)
Tonnages: 7,388 gross, 4,033 net, 10,025 deadweight.
Dimensions: 127.17 (136.75 o.a.) x 18.36 x 11.20 m. 8.661 m draught.
Machinery: 6-cylinder 2 S.C.S.A. Burmeister & Wain oil engine of 7,500 b.h.p.
by the shipbuilders. Service speed 16.5 knots.
460.99 cu. m. of refrigerated cargo space.
1.3.1962: Launched by Eriksbergs Mekaniska Verkstads A/B, Gothenburg (Yard
No. 547). *29.5.1962:* Completed. Price paid 23,959,020.00 kr. *15.6.1974:*
Transferred to Arctic Shipping (Pte.) Ltd. (Torvan Shipping Ltd., managers),

Singapore. *21.8.1974:* Foundered about 75 miles off Ishigaki in position 23.20 N, 123.23 E after encountering heavy seas during a voyage from Kobe to Khorramshahr with general cargo. 31 of her crew of 34 were lost.

TARIM at Rotterdam, 14.6.1968   *W.S.P.L. Slide Collection*

246. TARIM (II) (1962-1968) Tanker
Tonnages: 26,176 gross, 15,737 net, 44,370 deadweight.
Dimensions: 202.70 (214.84 o.a.) x 29.01 x 14.94 m. 11.646 m draught.
Machinery: 10-cylinder 2 S.C.S.A. Burmeister & Wain oil engine of 15,000 b.h.p. by the shipbuilders. Service speed 16.5 knots.
16.8.1962: Launched by Eriksbergs Mekaniska Verkstads A/B, Gothenburg (Yard No. 538). *22.11.1962:* Completed. Price paid 41,809,890.00 kr. *19.6.1968:* Sold to V.E.B. Deutsche Seereederei, East Germany and renamed WOLFEN. *1.1.1970:* Transferred to V.E.B. Deutfracht Internationale Befrachtung und Reederei Rostock, East Germany. *1.1.1974:* Owners became VEB Deutfracht/Seereederei, East Germany. *1984:* Sold to Interocean Shipping Co. Ltd., Jersey (Panama flag) and renamed TAUNUS. *1984:* Resold to Trasporti Marittimi Riuniti S.p.A., Italy and renamed NIAGARA. *1988:* Sold to West German interests for resale for scrapping, registered under the Antigua and Barbuda flag and renamed AGA. *30.7.1988:* Arrived at Alang for demolition by Goyal Traders.

247. TROJA (II) (1963-1970) Bulk Carrier
Tonnages: 12,289 gross, 7,089 net, 18,175 deadweight.
Dimensions: 155.71 (163.23 o.a.) x 21.65 x 12.73 m. 9.386 m draught.
Machinery: 6-cylinder 2 S.C.S.A. Burmeister & Wain oil engine of 7,500 b.h.p. by the shipbuilders. Service speed 15.5 knots.

TROJA

4.10.1962: Launched by Eriksbergs Mekaniska Verkstads A/B, Gothenburg (Yard No. 549). *4.1.1963:* Completed. Price paid 23,890,442.00 kr. *22.1.1970:* Sold to Cia. Mare Nostrum S.A. (Goulandris Brothers Ltd., managers), Liberia and renamed OCEAN TRITON. *1976:* Transferred to Greek registry. *1981:* Sold to Desna Shipping Corporation (Container & Cargo Services International Inc., managers), Greece and renamed EVELINE. *22.12.1983:* Laid up at Eleusis. *1986:* Sold to Maltese-flag owners (Flandermar Shipping Co. S.A., managers), Malta and renamed NORTH STAR. *29.4.1986:* Khanbhai Esoofbhai commenced demolition at Alang.

TIGRE

248. TIGRE (II) (1963-1969) Tanker
Tonnages: 26,419 gross, 14,071 net, 45,725 deadweight.
Dimensions: 202.70 (215.22 o.a.) x 29.01 x 15.40 m. 11.945 m draught.
Machinery: 10-cylinder 2 S.C.S.A. Burmeister & Wain oil engine of 15,000 b.h.p. by the shipbuilders. Service speed 16.5 knots.
20.12.1962: Launched by Eriksbergs Mekaniska Verkstads A/B, Gothenburg (Yard No. 546). *24.4.1963:* Completed. Price paid 42,213,313.00 kr. *26.6.1969:* Sold to Rederi A/S Mimer & Rederi A/S Norfart, later Rederi A/S Mimer, A/S Norfart & A/S Songa (Arne Blystad, manager), Oslo and renamed ANTILLA. *1973:* Sold to Nan Yang Shipping Co., Somali Republic and renamed WANYI. *1973:* Sold to China Ocean Shipping Co., Chinese People's Republic and renamed JIN HU. *1980:* Sold to Ocean Tramping Co. Ltd., Panama and renamed WAH FU. *1980:* Sold to Wah Fu Shipping Inc. (Hong Kong Ming Wah Shipping Co. Ltd., managers), Panama. *1982:* Sold to Philbro Transport S.A., Panama, renamed NIDO OIL and *25.6.1982* arrived at the Nido Terminal for use as a storage vessel. *1983:* Sold to Loadstar International Shipping Inc., Panama. *7.11.1984:* Arrived at Kaohsiung for scrapping by Lung Ching Steel Enterprise Co. Ltd. *15.11.1984:* Demolition commenced.

249. TEMA (I) (1963-1971)
Tonnages: 5,430 gross, 3,005 net, 6,275 deadweight.
Dimensions: 111.38 (122.74 o.a.) x 16.49 x 10.03 m. 7.417 m draught.
Machinery: 6-cylinder 2 S.C.S.A. Burmeister & Wain oil engine of 4,700 b.h.p. by the shipbuilders. Service speed 16 knots.
318.84 cu. m. of refrigerated cargo space.
Passengers: 12.
19.2.1960: Launched by Helsingör Skibsvaerft & Maskinbyggeri, Helsingör (Yard No. 348) as BROOKVILLE for Skibs A/S Solstad (A.F. Klaveness & Co. A/S, managers), Oslo. *5.1960:* Completed. *23.7.1963:* Purchased by Wilh. Wilhelmsen and renamed TEMA. Price paid 10,000,000.00 kr. *1.7.1971:* Sold

TEMA

to Ocean Tramping Co. Ltd., Somali Republic and renamed HANKIANG. *1973:*
Sold to Ceylon Shipping Corporation, Sri Lanka and renamed LANKA
KALYANI. *4.9.1985:* Arrived at Gadani Beach for demolition by Ahmed Steel
Ltd.

TIBETAN

250. TIBETAN (II) (1964-1968) Tanker
Tonnages: 35,824 gross, 19,334 net, 62,150 deadweight.
Dimensions: 226.07 (236.18 o.a.) x 32.19 x 16.62 m. 12.828 m draught.
Machinery: 9-cylinder 2 S.C.S.A. Burmeister & Wain oil engine of 18,900 b.h.p.
by the shipbuilders. Service speed 16.5 knots.
12.5.1964: Launched by Eriksbergs Mekaniska Verkstads A/B, Gothenburg
(Yard No. 563). *8.10.1964:* Completed. Price paid 47,384,101.00 kr. *16.4.1968:*
Sold to Jørgen P. Jensens Rederier, registered in the name of A/S Jensens
Rederi I, II, III & IV (Marlow Wangen, manager), Arendal and renamed CAPTO.
1975: Sold to Alltrans Shipping Ltd. (Allied Shipping International Corporation,
managers), Liberia and renamed ACTIUM. *1977:* Transferred to Greek registry.
1982: Sold to Sea Justice S.A., Greece and renamed HOPE. *1984:* Sold to
Hyundai Heavy Industries Co. Ltd. Offshore Construction Department, South
Korea and converted into the crane ship HHI 1200. She was shortened and
widened, her dimensions becoming 170.62 (177.86 o.a.) x 39.16 x 12.30
m., 7.033 m draught, and her tonnages 24,558 gross, 17,117 net. *1988:*
Transferred to Hyundai Engineering & Construction Co. Ltd. (managed by
the former owners). Still in service.

TARTAR

Fotoflite incorporating Skyfotos

251. TARTAR (II) (1965-1969) Tanker
Tonnages: 28,778 gross, 16,125 net, 50,150 deadweight.
Dimensions: 208.80 (216.36 o.a.) x 29.60 x 16.16 m. 12.161 m draught.
Machinery: 10-cylinder 2 S.C.S.A. Burmeister & Wain oil engine of 15,000 b.h.p. by Uddevallavarvet A/B, Uddevalla. Service speed 16.25 knots.
30.9.1964: Launched by Eriksbergs Mekaniska Verkstads A/B, Gothenburg (Yard No. 554). *1.1.1965:* Completed. Price paid 44,145,832.00 kr. *18.4.1969:* Sold to International Navigation Corporation (Tidewater Commercial Co. Inc., managers), Liberia and renamed LA FLECHE. *1981:* Sold to Octonia Trading Ltd., Liberia and renamed OCTONIA SUN. *1984:* Sold to Newbury Shipping Co. Ltd. (Nestor Pierakos, manager), Cyprus and renamed LYDIA P. *1987:* Sold to Springsea Maritime Corporation, Greece and renamed THEOMANA. *3.9.1991:* Suffered shell plating damage while loading at the terminal in the Albacora field, Campos Basin, Brazil and after repairs sold to Bangladesh shipbreakers. *5.5.1992:* Arrived at Chittagong to be broken up by Siddiqui Ltd.

TURCOMAN

252. TURCOMAN (II) (1965-1968) Tanker
Tonnages: 35,823 gross, 19,315 net, 59,050 deadweight.
Dimensions: 226.07 (236.18 o.a.) x 32.19 x 16.62 m. 12.828 m draught.
Machinery: 9-cylinder 2 S.C.S.A. Burmeister & Wain oil engine of 18,900 b.h.p. by the shipbuilders. Service speed 16.5 knots.
15.10.1964: Launched by Eriksbergs Mekaniska Verkstads A/B, Gothenburg (Yard No. 564). *19.1.1965:* Completed. Price paid 47,456,887.00 kr. *1.7.1968:* Sold to Hansen Tangens Rederi A/S and others (Yngvar Hansen-Tangen, later H.E. Hansen-Tangen, manager), Kristiansand S. and renamed KRISTINA. *1975:* Sold to K/S Kristina Joachim Grieg & Co. Holding A/S (H.E.Hansen-Tangen, manager), Kristiansand S. *1976:* Sold to Trident Maritime Co. S.A., Liberia and renamed ATLAS EXPLORER. *1980:* Sold to Empresa Naviera Santa S.A., Peru and renamed LUNAMAR. *7.8.1985:* Arrived at Kaohsiung to be broken up by Hsi Ying Enterprise Co. Ltd. *27.8.1985:* Demolition commenced.

TUAREG   *Fotoflite incorporating Skyfotos*

253. TUAREG (II) (1965-1973) Tanker
Tonnages: 43,572 gross, 24,394 net, 77,100 deadweight.
Dimensions: 233.76 (244.58 o.a.) x 37.24 x 16.84 m. 13.012 m draught.
Machinery: 10-cylinder 2 S.C.S.A. Burmeister & Wain oil engine of 21,000
b.h.p. by the shipbuilders. Service speed 16.75 knots.
11.5.1965: Launched by Eriksbergs Mekaniska Verkstads A/B, Gothenburg
(Yard No. 585). *5.10.1965:* Completed. Price paid 51,345,674.00 kr.
27.6.1973: Sold to I/S Mytilus A/S & Co. (Jørgen P. Jensen, manager), Arendal
and renamed CONDO. *1975:* Manager became Marlow Wangen. *1976:* Sold
to Rigdale Shipping Co. S.A. (Hunting & Son, Ltd., managers), Panama and
renamed KATO. *1978:* Sold to Nan Sin Steel Enterprise Co. Ltd., for scrapping.
10.8.1978: Demolition commenced at Kaohsiung.

254. TYSLA (IV) (1965-1972)
Tonnages: 8,735 gross, 4,974 net, 12,580 deadweight.
Dirnensions: 131.43 (142.45 o.a.) x 18.57 x 12.35 m. 9.049 m draught.
Machinery: 6-cylinder 2 S.C.S.A. Götaverken oil engine of 5,600 b.h.p. by
the shipbuilders. Service speed 15 knots.
9.11.1957: Launched by Uddevallavarvet A/B, Uddevalla (Yard No. 168) as
GOLDEN MASTER for Skibs A/S Golden West (Joh. H. Andresen, manager),
Oslo. *1960:* Sold to I/S Master (Skibs A/S Golden West, manager), Oslo and
renamed BAY MASTER. *11.10.1965:* Purchased by Wilh. Wilhelmsen and
renamed TYSLA. Price paid 11,070,600.00 kr. *3.11.1972:* Sold to Luen Yick
Shipping Co. (Yick Fung Shipping & Enterprises Co. Ltd., managers), Somali
Republic and renamed ARAFURA SEA. *1976:* Sold to China Ocean Shipping
Co., People's Republic of China and renamed TONG HUA. Subsequently
transferred to Tianjin Ocean Shipping Co. *1988:* Broken up, probably in China.

TYSLA   *W.S.P.L.*

255. TIBERIUS (1966-1976) Tanker

Tonnages: 43,572 gross, 24,389 net, 77,100 deadweight.
Dimensions: 233.48 (244.58 o.a.) x 37.24 x 16.84 m. 13.018 m draught.
Machinery: 10-cylinder 2 S.C.S.A. Burmeister & Wain oil engine of 21,000 b.h.p. by the shipbuilders. Service speed 16.75 knots.

TIBERIUS

13.9.1965: Launched by Eriksbergs Mekaniska Verkstads A/B, Gothenburg (Yard No. 586). *14.1.1966:* Completed. Price paid 51,274,200.00 kr. *21.3.1976:* Sold to Tonnevolds Tankrederi A/S (Olaf Tonnevold & Sonner A/S, managers), Grimstad and renamed THORHILD. *28.9.1978:* Arrived at Kaohsiung to be broken up by Chien Cheng Iron & Steel Co. Ltd. *26.10.1978:* Demolition commenced.

194

TULANE, 25.5.1968
J. Y. Freeman

256. TULANE (II) (1966-1977)
Tonnages: 9,189 gross, 5,299 net, 12,410 deadweight.
Dimensions: 137.45 (149.36 o.a.) x 19.21 x 11.87 m. 8.979 m draught.
Machinery: 6-cylinder 2 S.C.S.A. M.A.N. oil engine of 6,750 b.h.p. by the
shipbuilders. Service speed 15 knots.
9.6.1956: Launched by Howaldtswerke Hamburg A.G., Hamburg (Yard No.
909) as SKAUTROLL for A/S Brovanor and Salamis A/S (I. M. Skaugen,
manager), Oslo. *29.8.1956:* Completed and owner subsequently became A/S
Brovanor. *18.3.1966:* Purchased by Wilh. Wilhelmsen and renamed TULANE.
Price paid 11,850,000.00 kr. *8.10.1975:* Transferred to Arctic Shipping
Singapore (Pte.) Ltd. (Barber Ship Management Ltd., managers), Singapore.
12.4.1977: Sold to Pacific International Lines (Pte.) Ltd., Singapore, and
renamed KOTA MANIS. *4.6.1982:* Arrived at Gadani Beach to be broken up
by S.Z. Enterprises Ltd. *14.6.1982:* Demolition commenced.

TATRA at the Hook of Holland, 29.5.1971
Ambrose Greenway

257. TATRA (II) (1966-1977)
Tonnages: 8,781 gross, 4,874 net, 12,612 deadweight.
Dimensions: 135.34 (144.91 o.a.) x 18.80 x 12.04 m. 9.132 m draught.
Machinery: 7-cylinder 2 S.C.S.A. oil engine of 5,820 b.h.p. by Chantiers de
l'Atlantique, St. Nazaire. Service speed 14.5 knots.

195

13.9.1958: Launched by Ateliers et Chantiers de Bretagne, Nantes (Yard No. 11620) as SISTINA for Skibs-A/S Avanti, Skibs-A/S Glarona, Skibs-A/S Navalis, Skibs-A/S Ollimac & A/S Turicum (Tschudi & Eitzen, managers), Oslo. *5.1959:* Completed. *19.8.1966:* Purchased by Wilh. Wilhelmsen and renamed TATRA. Price paid 13,506,850.00 kr. *18.12.1973:* Transferred to Arctic Shipping Singapore (Pte.) Ltd. (Torvan Shipping Ltd., managers), Singapore. *21.6.1977:* Sold to Sincere Navigation Co. Ltd. (Far East Corporation Ltd., managers), Panama and renamed EASTERN PROSPERITY. *1979:* Sold to Marican Lines Pte. Ltd (Euro-Asia Ship Management Pte. Ltd, managers), Singapore and renamed ZULAIHA. *14.10.1982:* Arrived at Gadani Beach to be broken up by Ahmad Maritime Breakers Ltd. *6.11.1982:* Demolition commenced.

TOBRUK

258. TOBRUK (1966-1968) Tanker

Tonnages: 12,656 gross, 7,207 net, 19,665 deadweight.
Dimensions: 160.03 (172.78 o.a.) x 21.95 x 12.22 m. 9.716 m draught.
Machinery: 7-cylinder 2 S.C.S.A. Stork oil engine of 8,200 b.h.p. by Nederlandsche Dok en Scheepsbouw Maatschappij, Amsterdam. Service speed 15 knots.
3.5.1958: Launched by Bergens Mekaniske Verksteder A/S, Bergen (Yard No. 415) as NORDHAV for Skibs A/S Nordhav & Skibs A/S Sydhav (Per Lodding, manager), Oslo. *7.1958:* Completed. *1.9.1966:* Purchased by Wilh. Wilhelmsen and renamed TOBRUK. Price paid 11,638,685.00 kr. *1.11.1968:* Sold to Societa Internazionale di Navigazione per Azioni (d'Amico Soc. di Nav. S.p.A., managers), Italy and renamed CIELO AZZURRO. *1974:* Renamed MOLARA. *1975:* Sold to Cia. Trasporti Marittimi S.p.A., Italy (same managers). *1982:* Sold to d'Amico Societa di Navigazione S.p.A., Italy. *3.8.1985:* MEB Corporation Ltd. commenced demolition at Bhatiary, Chittagong.

259. TRIPOLI (1966-1968) Tanker
Tonnages: 16,025 gross, 9,074 net, 25,870 deadweight.
Dimensions: 175.57 (186.16 o.a.) x 23.25 x 13.19 m. 10.326 m draught.
Machinery: 9-cylinder 2 S.C.S.A. Götaverken oil engine of 8,150 b.h.p. by the
shipbuilders. Service speed 14.5 knots.
8.3.1961: Launched by Lindholmens Varv A/B, Gothenburg (Yard No. 1068)
as CARL LARSSON for A/B Transmarin (Erik Larsson, manager), Sweden.
10.1961: Completed. *21.10.1966:* Purchased by Wilh. Wilhelmsen and renamed
TRIPOLI. Price paid 13,404,705.00 kr. *6.11.1968:* Sold to Cia. Mar. Proti S.A.,
Greece and renamed KIMON. *11.11.1978:* Left Trieste for Vinaroz, where
Desguaces Maritimos commenced demolition later in the month.

TAURUS, with the tug **TARPAN** alongside   *M. R. Dippy*

260. TAURUS (V) (1966-1976) Tanker
Tonnages: 51,295 gross, 34,786 net, 93,520 deadweight.
Dimensions: 244.18 (255.91 o.a.) x 39.02 x 19.03 m. 14.034 m draught.
Machinery: 10-cylinder 2 S.C.S.A. Burmeister & Wain oil engine of 23,200
b.h.p. by Eriksbergs Mekaniska Verkstads A/B, Gothenburg . Service speed
16.25 knots.
16.6.1966: Launched by Uddevallavarvet A/B, Uddevalla (Yard No. 215).
2.12.1966: Completed. Price paid 60,847,157.00 kr. *3.5.1976:* Sold to the
U.S.S.R., placed in the ownership of U.S.S.R.-Novorossiysk Shipping Co., and
renamed ADYGEYA. *1979:* Sold to Compania Maritima Dana S.A. (Fadi
Maritime Corp., managers), Panama and renamed DANA B. *1982:* Fadi
Maritime Group ceased being managers; renamed DANA H. and became a
bunkering vessel at Jeddah. *1984:* Sold to Roymideast Ltd., Panama. *1985:*
Sold for scrapping to China National Metals & Minerals Import & Export
Corporation and having left Djibouti *14.11.1985,* arrived at Dongshan prior
to *3.1.1986* for demolition.

261. TORRENS (II) (1967-1983)
Tonnages: *1967-1971:* 10,510 gross, 6,213 net, 11,850 deadweight. *1971-on:*
12,435 gross, 7,810 net, 13,000 deadweight.
Dimensions: *1967-1971:* 143.73 (152.29 o.a.) x 20.81 x 13.26 m. 9.575 m
draught. *1971-on:* 165.67 (174.71 o.a.) x 20.81 x 13.26 m. 9.386 m draught.
Machinery: 8-cylinder 2 S.C.S.A. Burmeister & Wain oil engine of 12,000 b.h.p.
by the shipbuilders. Service speed 19 knots.
1,201.90 cu. m. of refrigerated cargo space.
Passengers: 12.
1971-on: Container section with capacity for 90 containers under deck.

TORRENS after lengthening

J. K. Byass

21.10.1966: Launched by Uddevallavarvet A/B. Uddevalla (Yard No. 276). *26.2.1967:* Completed. Price paid 33,891,444.00 kr. *14.2.1971:* Arrived at Yokohama to be lengthened by Mitsubishi Heavy Industries Ltd., who inserted a container carrying section amidships. *20.3.1971:* Reconstruction completed. *13.10.1979:* Transferred to Arctic Shipping Singapore (Pte.) Ltd (Barber Ship Management Ltd., managers), Singapore. *4.2.1983:* Sold to Novelda S.A., Panama and renamed TORRE-S. *1983:* Sold to Gasmar S.A. (Bottacchi S.A. de Navegacion, managers), Uruguay and renamed YAGUARI. *1985:* Sold to Acualin S.A. (same managers), Uruguay. *1987:* Sold to Novelda S.A. (same managers), Panama and renamed YAGUAR. *1993:* Sold to Indian shipbreakers. *29.7.1993:* Left New Mangalore for the breakers' yard.

TEMPLAR

262. TEMPLAR (IV) (1967-1978) Tanker

Tonnages: 45,810 gross, 29,756 net, 82,200 deadweight.
Dimensions: 233.99 (244.97 o.a.) x 37.24 x 17.76m. 13.780 m draught.
Machinery: 10-cylinder 2 S.C.S.A. Burmeister & Wain oil engine of 21,000 b.h.p. by the shipbuilders. Service speed 16.75 knots.
26.10.1966: Launched by Eriksbergs Mekaniska Verkstads A/B, Gothenburg (Yard No. 604). *22.3.1967:* Completed. Price paid 53,920,705.00 kr. *5.4.1978:* Arrived at Kaohsiung to be broken up by Long Jong Industry Co. Ltd. *11.5.1978:* Demolition commenced.

TARONGA as built   *Fotoflite incorporating Skyfotos*

263. TARONGA (III) (1967-1982)

Tonnages: *1967-1971:* 10,510 gross, 6,203 net, 11,850 deadweight. *1977 -on:* 12,407 gross, 7,619 net, 13,046 deadweight.
Dimensions: *1967-1977:* 143.73 (152.29 o.a.) x 20.81 x 13.26 m. 9.575 m draught. *1971-on:* 165.67 (172.19 o.a.) x 20.81 x 13.26 m. 9.386 m draught.
Machinery: 8-cylinder 2 S.C.S.A. Burmeister & Wain oil engine of 12,000 b.h.p. by the shipbuilders. Service speed 19 knots.
1,201.90 cu. m. of refrigerated cargo space.
Passengers: 12.
1971-on: Container section with capacity for 90 containers under deck.

TARONGA after lengthening   *Ambrose Greenway*

18.11.1966: Launched by Uddevallavarvet A/B, Uddevalla (Yard No. 277). *6.4.1967:* Completed. Price paid 34,069,692.00 kr. *23.1.1971:* Arrived at Yokohama to be lengthened by Mitsubishi Heavy Industries Ltd., who inserted a container carrying section amidships. *24.4.1971:* Reconstruction completed. *20.7.1979:* Transferred to Arctic Shipping Singapore (Pte.) Ltd. (Barber Ship Management Ltd., managers), Singapore. *21.12.1982:* Sold to Estela Oceanica S.A. (A. Bottacchi S.A. de Navegacion, managers), Panama and renamed SEA MOON. *1984:* Sold to A. Bottacchi S.A. de Navegacion, Argentina and renamed PUNTA ANCLA. Still in service, but laid up since *4.2.1993* at Buenos Aires.

TAMERLANE

264. TAMERLANE (II) (1967-1978)

Tonnages: *1967-1970:* 10,184 gross, 6,463 net, 12,830 deadweight. *1971-on:* 12,124 gross, 8,161 net, 14,500 deadweight.
Dimensions: *1967-1970:* 143.73 (152.20 o.a.) x 20.81 x 13.26 m. 9.575 m draught. *1971-on:* 165.67 (172.19 o.a.) x 20.81 x 13.26 m. 9.380 m draught.
Machinery: Two 16-cylinder 4 S.C.S.A. Pielstick oil engines totalling 13,000 b.h.p. by Lindholmens Varv A/B., Gothenburg, geared to a single screw shaft. Service speed 19 knots.

TAMERLANE after lengthening, in Barber Line colours   *W.S.P.L.*

1,314.03 cu. m. of refrigerated cargo space.
Passengers: 12.
1971-on: Container section with capacity for 90 containers under deck.
28.12.1966: Launched by Uddevallavarvet A/B, Uddevalla (Yard No. 278).
10.5.1967: Completed. Price paid 35,917,728.00 kr. *1.12.1970:* Arrived at
Oslo to be lengthened by Akers Mekaniske Verksted, who inserted a container
carrying section amidships. *16.1.1971:* Reconstruction completed. *15.12.1978:*
Sold to Telendos Shipping Corporation (World Wide Liner Services Inc.,
managers), Greece and renamed TELENDOS. *1980:* Sold to Soc. Navale de
l'Ouest, France and renamed SAINT BERNARD. *1984:* Sold to Pelton Shipping
Ltd. (Anglomar Shipping Services Ltd., managers), Gibraltar and renamed
BERN. *1984:* Sold to Chinese shipbreakers and during *12.1984* delivered at
Dalian for scrapping.

TIRRANNA as built   *Alex Duncan*

265. TIRRANNA (III) (1967-1978)
Tonnages: *1967-1971:* 10,060 gross, 6,346 net, 12,830 deadweight. *1971-on:*
12,142 gross, 8,164 net, 14,500 deadweight.
Dimensions: *1967-1971:* 143.73 (151.78 o.a.) x 20.81 x 13.26 m. 9.575m
draught. *1971-on:* 165.67 (172.19 o.a.) x 20.81 x 13.26 m. 9.351 m draught.
Machinery: Two 16-cylinder 4 S.C.S.A. Pielstick oil engines totalling 13,000
b.h.p. by Lindholmens Varv A/B, Gothenburg, geared to a single screw shaft.
Service speed 19 knots.
1,314.03 cu. m. of refrigerated cargo space.
Passengers: 12.
1971-on: Container section with capacity for 90 containers under deck.
17.3.1967: Launched by Uddevallavarvet A/B, Uddevalla (Yard No. 279).
30.6.1967: Completed. Price paid 35,935,045.00 kr. *31.12.1970:* Arrived at
Oslo to be lengthened by Akers Mekaniske Verksted, who inserted a container
carrying section amidships. *10.2.1971:* Reconstruction completed. *21.9.1978:*
Sold to Tilos Shipping Corporation (World Wide Liner Services Inc., managers),
Greece and renamed TILOS. *1980:* Sold to Societe Navale de l'Ouest, France
and renamed SAINT BERTRAND. *1984:* Sold to Vigour Investments Inc.

(Bruusgaard Kiosteruds Skibs-A/S, managers), Panama and renamed HERMION. *1986:* Sold to Thoresen & Co. (Bangkok) Ltd., Panama. *4.8.1986:* Arrived at Kaohsiung to be scrapped by Chien Yu Steel Industrial Co. Ltd. *2.9.1986:* Demolition commenced.

TALABOT off Cape St. Vincent in 3.1969   *Ambrose Greenway*

266. TALABOT (IV) (1967-1979)
Tonnages: 12,545 gross, 7,303 net, 15,612 deadweight.
Dimensions: 159.42 (168.26 o.a.) x 24.36 x 14.08 m. 9.075 m draught.
Machinery: 7-cylinder 2 S.C.S.A. Burmeister & Wain oil engine of 16,100 b.h.p. by the shipbuilders. Service speed 21.5 knots.
1,989 cu. m. of refrigerated cargo space.
Passengers: 12.
20.3.1967: Launched by Mitsui Zosen K.K., Tamano (Yard No. 774). *26.9.1967:* Completed. Price paid 43,426,500.00 kr. *29.5.1979:* Sold to New Dawn Shipping Co. S.A. (Wallem Shipmanagement Ltd., managers), Liberia and renamed NEW DAWN. *1980:* Sold to Compania Sud-Americana de Vapores, Chile and renamed MALLECO. *1983:* Transferred to Panamanian registry. *1986:* Reverted to Chilean registry. *1992:* Sold to Bangladesh shipbreakers. *9.4.1992:* Arrived at Chittagong to be broken up by H.Steel. *19.4.1992:* Demolition commenced.

267. TAIKO (1968-1985)
Tonnages: 12,546 gross, 7,304 net, 15,612 deadweight.
Dimensions: 159.42 (168.26 o.a.) x 24.36 x 14.08 m. 9.932 m draught.
Machinery: 7-cylinder 2 S.C.S.A. Burmeister & Wain oil engine of 16,100 b.h.p. by the shipbuilders. Service speed 21.5 knots.
1,976 cu. m. of refrigerated cargo space.
Passengers: 12.

TAIKO   *Fotoflite incorporating Skyfotos*

18.9.1967: Launched by Mitsui Zosen K.K., Tamano (Yard No. 775). *22.1.1968:* Completed. Price paid 42,804,342.00 kr. *20.5.1985:* Sold to Thoresen & Co. (Bangkok), Ltd. (Bruusgaard Kiosteruds Skibs-A/S, managers), Thailand and renamed HAI LEE. *1986:* Bruusgaard Kiosterud management ceased. *1993:* Sold to Indian shipbreakers and *17.2.1993* anchored off Alang. *22.2.1993:* Beached for demolition.

TONGA

268. TONGA / TOLGA / TAKACHIHO (II) (1968-1984) Bulk Carrier

Tonnages: 35,955 gross, 23,406 net, 56,939 deadweight.
Dimensions: 211.03 (224.01 o.a.) x 31.86 x 18.37 m. 12.243 m draught.
Machinery: 6-cylinder 2 S.C.S.A. Sulzer oil engine of 13,800 b.h.p. by
Mitsubishi Heavy Industries Ltd., Hiroshima. Service speed 15 knots.
22.11.1967: Launched by Mitsubishi Heavy Industries Ltd., Yokohama (Yard
No. 891). *24.2.1968:* Completed. Price paid 40,757,640,00 kr. *30.9.1969:*
Transferred to Arctic Shipping Co. Ltd., Hong Kong, registered at Melbourne,
renamed TOLGA and bareboat chartered to Australian National Line. *2.1983:*
Transferred to Hong Kong registry and renamed TAKACHIHO. *14.11.1984:* Sold
to Eurolane Maritime Ltd. (H. Glahr & Co. G.m.b.H & Co. K.G., managers),
Cyprus and renamed ORANGE CORAL. *1988:* Sold to Utopia Maritime Co.
Ltd., Cyprus and renamed SORAL. *1991:* Renamed SAN MARCO. Still in
service.

TANABATA

269. TANABATA (1968-1983) Bulk Carrier, later Car Carrier

Tonnages: 35,955 gross, 22,796 net, 56,768 deadweight.
Dimensions: 211.03 (224.01 o.a.) x 31.86 x 18.37 m. 12.243 m draught.
Machinery: 6-cylinder 2 S.C.S.A. Sulzer oil engine of 13,800 b.h.p. by
Mitsubishi Heavy Industries Ltd., Nagasaki. Service speed 15 knots.
1977-on: Capacity for 3,450 cars.

204

20.1.1968: Launched by Mitsubishi Heavy Industries Ltd., Yokohama (Yard No. 892). *24.4.1968:* Completed. Price paid 40,672,593.00 kr. *23.12.1977:* Completed conversion by Hyundai Mipo Dockyard Co. Ltd, Ulsan into a Car Carrier with a capacity of 3,450 cars. *30.3.1983:* Sold to Nicola Shipping Ltd., Panama and renamed NICOLA JILL. *16.3.1986:* Arrived at Aliaga to be broken up by Gemi Sokum Ticaret A.S. *25.3.1986:* Demolition commenced.

TAMANO

270. TAMANO (I) (1968-1976) Tanker
Tonnages: 46,988 gross, 30,052 net, 88,072 deadweight.
Dimensions: 238.82 (246.90 o.a.) x 39.02 x 17.68 m. 13.545 m draught.
Machinery: 9-cylinder 2 S.C.S.A. Burmeister & Wain oil engine of 20,700 b.h.p. by the shipbuilders. Service speed 16 knots.
27.1.1968: Launched by Mitsui Zosen K.K., Tamano (Yard No. 763). *26.4.1968:* Completed. Price paid 56,948,463.00 kr. *15.7.1976:* Sold to Hancock Shipping Co. Ltd. (Anglo Nordic Bulkships (Management) Ltd., managers), Liberia, and renamed BURGHAUSEN. *1980:* Managers became Marathon International Petroleum (G.B.) Ltd. *1980:* Sold to Eagle Marine Ltd., Liberia and renamed SEA EAGLE. *1982:* Sold to Comert Denizcilik ve Ticaret Anonim Sirketi, Turkey and renamed FAHIRE GUNERI. *14.3.1985:* Left Valletta for Aliaga where she arrived later in the month to be broken up by Kalkavan Ticaret Sadan Kalkavan. *15.8.1985:* Demolition commenced.

TAKARA, as a bulk carrier, at Hamburg 28.1.1977   *Joachim Pein*

271. TAKARA (1968-1983) Bulk Carrier, later Car Carrier
Tonnages: 35,955 gross, 22,796 net, 56,896 deadweight.
Dimensions: 211.03 (224.01 o.a.) x 31.86 x 18.37 m. 12.243 m draught.
Machinery: 6-cylinder 2 S.C.S.A. Sulzer oil engine of 13,800 b.h.p. by Mitsubishi Heavy Industries Ltd., Nagasaki. Service speed 15 knots.
1978-on: Capacity for 3,450 cars.

TAKARA as a car carrier

12.3.1968: Launched by Mitsubishi Heavy Industries Ltd., Yokohama (Yard No. 896). *15.6.1968:* Completed. Price paid 41,109,000.00 kr. *3.1978:* Completed conversion by Hyundai Mipo Dockyard Co. Ltd., Ulsan, into a Car Carrier with a capacity of 3,450 cars. *17.10.1983:* Sold to Efway Shipping Co. S.A., Greece and renamed ARISTIDIS. *1984:* Converted back into a bulk carrier. *30.12.1986:* Arrived at Kaohsiung to be broken up by Gwo Feng Steel Enterprise Co. Ltd. *7.1.1987:* Demolition commenced.

TYR leaving Hamburg, 22.7.1971   *Joachim Pein*

272. TYR (III) (1968-1978)
Tonnages: 8,255 gross, 5,238 net, 10,610 deadweight.
Dimensions: 130.26 (138.06 o.a.) x 20.07 x 11.82 m. 8.421 m draught.
Machinery: Two 10-cylinder 4 S.C.S.A. Pielstick oil engines totalling 8,000 b.h.p. by Nippon Kokan K.K. Tsurumi, Yokohama, geared to a single screw shaft. Service speed 16.25 knots.
1,382.50 cu. m. of refrigerated cargo space.
27.4.1968: Launched by Sasebo Heavy Industries Co. Ltd., Sasebo (Yard No. 188). *12.8.1968:* Completed. Price paid 26,489,000.00 kr. *12.6.1978:* Sold to Seawind Maritime Inc. (Universal Glow Inc., managers), Greece. *1980:* Sold to Bruusgaard Kiosteruds Skibs-A/S (Thoresen Trading Ltd., managers), Panama and renamed HALLDOR. *1986:* Sold to Thoresen & Co. (Bangkok), Ltd., Thailand. *1993:* Sold to Indian shipbreakers. *14.10.1993:* Arrived at Alang to be broken up.

TEHERAN

273. TEHERAN (II) (1968-1973) Ore/Bulk/Oil Carrier

Tonnages: 56,709 gross, 37,713 net, 89,529 deadweight.
Dimensions: 251.01 (261.53 o.a.) x 38.99 x 19.99 m. 13.329 m draught.
Machinery: 9-cylinder 2 S.C.S.A. Burmeister & Wain oil engine of 20,700 b.h.p.
by Hitachi Zosen, Osaka. Service speed 16 knots.
10.6.1968: Launched by Hitachi Zosen, Innoshima (Yard No. 4125). *4.9.1968:*
Completed. Price paid 64,239,000.00 kr. *25.3.1973:* Sold to Lafumina
Shipping Inc., Liberia, and renamed LAFUMINA. *1983:* Sold to Seawasp
Maritime Inc., Liberia and renamed BRISTOL LAKE. *26.11.1986:* Arrived at
Inchon to be broken up by Han Sung Salvage Co. Ltd. *8.12.1986:* Demolition
commenced.

TRINIDAD   *Fotoflite incorporating Skyfotos*

274. TRINIDAD (II) / TAMANO (II) (1968-1979)

Tonnages: 12,564 gross, 7,307 net, 15,612 deadweight.
Dimensions: 159.42 (168.26 o.a.) x 24.36 x 14.08 m. 10.180 m draught.
Machinery: 7-cylinder 2 S.C.S.A. Burmeister & Wain oil engine of 16,100 b.h.p.
by the shipbuilders. Service speed 21.5 knots.
1,976 cu. m. of refrigerated cargo space.
Passengers: 12.

207

TAMANO   *Ambrose Greenway*

20.6.1968: Launched by Mitsui Zosen K.K., Tamano (Yard No. 776). *28.9.1968:* Completed. Price paid 42,730,000.00 kr. *1.6.1978:* Transferred to Arctic Shipping Singapore (Pte.) Ltd (Barber Ship Management Ltd., managers), Singapore and renamed TAMANO. *13.6.1979:* Sold to New Sun Shipping Co. S.A. (Wallem Shipmanagement Ltd., managers), Liberia and renamed NEW SUN. *1980:* Sold to Compania Sud-Americana de Vapores, Chile and renamed MAULE. *1987:* Sold to China National Metals & Minerals Import & Export Corporation. *12.5.1987:* Arrived at Beihai for demolition.

TAIMYR   *Ambrose Greenway*

275. TAIMYR (1968-1980)

Tonnages: 12,565 gross, 7,308 net, 15,612 deadweight.
Dimensions: 159.42 (168.26 o.a.) x 24.36 x 14.08 m. 10.180 m draught.
Machinery: 7-cylinder 2 S.C.S.A. Burmeister & Wain oil engine of 16,100 b.h.p.
by the shipbuilders. Service speed 21.5 knots.
1,976 cu. m. of refrigerated cargo space.
Passengers: 12.
9.9.1968: Launched by Mitsui Zosen K.K., Tamano (Yard No. 777). *14.12.1968:*
Completed. Price paid 42,939,000.00 kr. *16.12.1980:* Sold to New Dawn
Shipping Co. S.A. (Wallem Shipmanagement S.A., managers), Liberia and
renamed SOUTHERN DIAMOND. *1983:* Southern Shipmanagement (Chile)
Ltd. became managers. *1987:* Sold to Compania Sud-Americana de Vapores
(same managers), Chile and renamed MAULLIN. *23.6.1992:* Arrived at
Chittagong to be broken up. *18.9.1992:* H. Steel commenced demolition at
Fouzderhat.

TORO at Cape Town   *W.S.P.L.*

276. TORO (II) (1969-1978)

Tonnages: 8,256 gross, 5,238 net, 10,445 deadweight.
Dimensions: 130.26 (138.06 o.a.) x 20.07 x 11.79 m. 8.344 m draught.
Machinery: Two 10-cylinder 4 S.C.S.A. Pielstick oil engines totalling 8,000
b.h.p. by Nippon Kokan K.K., Tsurumi, Yokohama, geared to a single screw
shaft. Service speed 16.25 knots.
1,331.53 cu. m. of refrigerated cargo space.
8.4.1969: Launched by Sasebo Heavy Industries Co. Ltd., Sasebo (Yard No.
199). *15.7.1969:* Completed. Price paid 25,512,554.00 kr. *13.7.1978:* Sold
to Stella Maritime Inc. (Universal Glow Inc., managers), Greece. *1980:* Sold
to Bruusgaard Kiosteruds Skibs-A/S, Panama and renamed HALLVARD. *1986:*
Sold to Thoresen & Co. (Bangkok) Ltd., Thailand. *1.1.1991:* Sailed from Dubai
bound for Thailand for demolition.

277. TAMPA (III) (1969-1973)

Tonnages: 6,115 gross, 3,167 net, 9,606 deadweight.
Dimensions: 138.69 (151.16 o.a.) x 19.26 x 11.66 m. 7.992 m draught.
Machinery: 6-cylinder 2 S.C.S.A. oil engine of 7,200 b.h.p. by Gebr. Stork
& Co. N.V., Hengelo. Service speed 15.5 knots.
292.23 cu. m. of refrigerated cargo space.

TAMPA, shortly after being purchased   *Norsk Sjøfartsmuseum*

3.1.1959: Launched by Boele's Scheepswerven en Machinefabriek N.V., Bolnes (Yard No. 963) as ALAMAK for van Nievelt, Goudriaan & Co's Stoomvaart Maatschappij N.V., Netherlands. *16.7.1959:* Completed. *8.8.1969:* Purchased by Wilh. Wilhelmsen and renamed TAMPA. Price paid 10,590,140.00 kr. *26.6.1973:* Sold to China Ocean Shipping Company, Chinese People's Republic and renamed WEN SHUI. Later transferred to Guangzhou Ocean Shipping Company. *1987:* Sold to Chinese shipbreakers and arrived at Huangpu *26.6.1987* for demolition.

TAMPA, 1.11.1969, after being fitted with deck cranes   *J. Y. Freeman*

278. TORTUGAS (III) (1969-1973)
Tonnages: 6,116 gross, 3,167 net, 9,584 deadweight.
Dimensions: 138.69 (151.16 o.a.) x 19.26 x 11.66 m. 7.992 m draught.
Machinery: 6-cylinder 2 S.C.S.A. oil engine of 7,200 b.h.p. by Gebr. Stork & Co., Hengelo. Service speed 15.5 knots.
292.23 cu. m. of refrigerated cargo space.
21.7.1959: Launched by N.V. Werf "Gusto", Schiedam (Yard No. 121) as ALCHIBA for van Nievelt, Goudriaan & Co's. Stoomvaart Maatschappij N.V., Netherlands. *30.12.1959:* Completed. *19.9.1969:* Purchased by Wilh. Wilhelmsen and renamed TORTUGAS. Price paid 10,599,598.00 kr.

TORTUGAS   *Norsk Sjøfartsmuseum*

20.8.1973: Sold to China Ocean Shipping Company, Chinese People's
Republic and renamed GUANG SHUI. Later transferred to Guangzhou Ocean
Shipping Company and then to Guangzhou Shipping & Enterprises Co. Ltd.
Possibly still in service.

TEXAS   *Norsk Sjøfartsmuseum*

279. TEXAS (II) (1969-1973)
Tonnages: 6,723 gross, 3,897 net, 9,606 deadweight.
Dimensions: 138.69 (151.16 o.a.) x 19.26 x 11.66 m. 7.989 m draught.
Machinery: 6-cylinder 2 S.C.S.A. oil engine of 7,200 b.h.p. by Gebr. Stork
& Co. N.V., Hengelo. Service speed 15.5 knots.
292.23 cu. m. of refrigerated cargo space.
10.5.1960: Launched by Werf De Noord N.V., Alblasserdam (Yard No. 649)
as ALUDRA for van Nievelt, Goudriaan & Co's. Stoomvaart Maatschappij N.V.,
Netherlands. *15.9.1960:* Completed. *6.11.1969:* Purchased by Wilh.
Wilhelmsen and renamed TEXAS. Price paid 10,599,598.00 kr. *10.9.1973:*
Sold to China Ocean Shipping Company, People's Republic of China and
renamed LI SHUI. Later transferred to Guangzhou Ocean Shipping Company
and then to Guangzhou Shipping & Enterprises Co. Ltd. Possibly still in service,
but no movements reported since 9.1991.

280. TENNESSEE (III) (1969-1973)
Tonnages: 6,723 gross, 3,897 net, 9,606 deadweight.
Dimensions: 138.69 (151.16 o.a.) x 19.26 x 11.66 m. 7.992 m draught.
Machinery: 6-cylinder 2 S.C.S.A. oil engine of 7,200 b.h.p. by Gebr. Stork
& Co. N.V., Hengelo. Service speed 15.5 knots.
292.23 cu. m. of refrigerated cargo space.
4.6.1960: Launched by Boele's Scheepswerven en Machinefabriek N.V.,
Bolnes (Yard No. 964) as ALNITAK for van Nievelt, Goudriaan & Co's.
Stoomvaart Maatschappij N.V., Netherlands. *14.10.1960:* Completed.
12.11.1969: Purchased by Wilh. Wilhelmsen and renamed TENNESSEE. Price
paid 10,619,773.00 kr. *23.7.1973:* Sold to China Ocean Shipping Company,
Chinese People's Republic and renamed JIAN SHUI. Later transferred to
Guangzhou Ocean Shipping Company. *1987:* Sold to Chinese shipbreakers.
14.5.1987: Demolition commenced at Huangpu.

TARIM

281. TARIM (III) (1970-1972) Ore/Bulk/Oil Carrier
Tonnages: 84,629 gross, 62,319 net, 149,900 deadweight.
Dimensions: 281.69 (293.20 o.a.) x 42.58 x 24.74 m. 17.457 m draught.
Machinery: 8-cylinder 2 S.C.S.A Burmeister & Wain oil engine of 30,600 b.h.p.
by Friedrich Krupp Maschinenfabriken G.m.b.H., Essen. Service speed 16
knots.
Ordered from A.G. Weser, Bremen (Yard No. 1373) by Hvalfanger A/S
Rosshavet, Sandefjord. Purchased by Wilh. Wilhelmsen whilst under
construction and *5.2.1970* launched as TARIM. *28.3.1970:* Completed. Price
paid 123,525,946.00 kr. *22.9.1972:* Sold to Fernavi S.p.A., Italy and renamed
MARCUS LOLLI-GHETTI. *1974:* Sold to Navigazione Alta Italia S.p.A
(Sidermar S.p.A., managers), Italy and renamed NAI MARCUS. *1980:* Sold
to Italsider S.p.A. (same managers), Italy and renamed LYRA. *1981:* Transferred
to Nuova Italsider S.p.A. (same managers), Italy. *1990:* Sold to Quorate
International Inc., Liberia and renamed TIBER ORE. *1993:* Sold to China
National Metals and Minerals Import & Export Corporation. *8.5.1993:* Arrived
at Beilun for demolition.

282. TROLL FOREST (I) / WILLINE TARO (1970-1986) Car/Paper/Bulk Carrier, later Container Ship
Tonnages: 20,222 gross, 13,083 net, 29,000 deadweight.
Dimensions: 179.71 (187.43 o.a.) x 26.45 x 15.24 m. 10.764 m draught.
Machinery: 6-cylinder 2 S.C.S.A. Sulzer oil engine of 13,800 i.h.p. by Horten
Verft, Horten. Service speed 16.5 knots.
1977-on: Container capacity 1,093 TEU.

TROLL FOREST   *W.S.P.L.*

18.2.1970: Launched by Kaldnes Mekaniske Verksted A/S, Tønsberg (Yard No. 184). *9.7.1970:* Completed. Price paid 51,509,083.00 kr. *8.1977:* Completed conversion by Nylands Verksted, Oslo, into a container ship. *21.2.1980:* Renamed WILLINE TARO. *6.12.1980:* Transferred to Arctic Shipping Singapore (Pte.) Ltd. (Barber Ship Management Ltd., later Barber Ship Management Singapore (Pte.) Ltd., managers), Singapore. *8.4.1986:* Arrived at Dongshan and sold for demolition there to China National Metals & Minerals Import & Export Corporation.

WILLINE TARO

283. TABRIZ (II) (1970-1979) Tanker
Tonnages: 106,970 gross, 80,859 net, 210,650 deadweight.
Dimensions: 305.62 (316.09 o.a.) x 48.82 x 24.52 m. 19.010 m draught.
Machinery: Two steam turbines totalling 32,000 s.h.p by the shipbuilders geared to a single screw shaft. Service speed 16 knots.

TABRIZ

7.9.1970: Launched by Kockums Mekaniska Verkstads A/B, Malmö (Yard No. 528). *28.10.1970:* Completed. Price paid 130,236,696.00 kr. *5.2.1979:* Sold to Arapaho Shipping Corporation, Greece and renamed SIRIUS. *1979:* Sold to Union Energy Co. Ltd., Liberia and renamed UNION ENERGY. *1980:* Sold to Kuo Dar Steel & Iron Enterprise Co. Ltd for scrapping. *31.7.1980:* Demolition commenced at Kaohsiung.

TIBETAN

284. TIBETAN (III) (1970-1972) Ore/Bulk/Oil Carrier
Tonnages: 82,793 gross, 59,680 net, 150,835 deadweight.
Dimensions: 290.05 (302.98 o.a.) x 42.78 x 22.94 m. 16.942 m draught.
Machinery: 8-cylinder 2 S.C.S.A. Burmeister & Wain oil engine of 30,600 b.h.p. by the shipbuilders. Service speed 16 knots.
8.8.1970: Launched by by Eriksbergs Mekaniska Verkstads A/B, Gothenburg (Yard No. 637). *6.11.1970:* Completed. Price paid 94,811,248.00 kr. *25.10.1972:* Sold to Barclays Export & Finance Co. Ltd. (Denholm Ship Management Ltd., managers), Glasgow and renamed MUIRFIELD. *1978:* Sold to South Pacific Tankers Transport Ltd. (Golden Peak Maritime Agencies Ltd., managers), Hong Kong and renamed ATLANTIC SPLENDOUR. *1980:* Managers became Furness Withy (Shipping) Ltd. *1982:* Sold to Korea Line Corporation, South Korea and renamed SALVIA. *9.2.1991:* Suffered a crack in her hull when in a position 26.20 N, 155.12 E during a voyage from Guayacan and Huasco with a cargo of iron ore. *10.2.1991:* Abandoned by her crew and sank in a position 24.15 N, 154.33 E.

TROLL PARK

285. TROLL PARK (1971-1984) Open Type Bulk Carrier with Car Decks
Tonnages: 22,160 gross, 13,651 net, 32,300 deadweight.
Dimensions: 173.11 (183.47 o.a.) x 26.88 x 16.01 m. 11.367 m draught.
Machinery: 7-cylinder 2 S.C.S.A. Sulzer oil engine of 14,000 b.h.p. by R.O.
Tvornica Dizel Motora ''Treci Maj'', Rijeka. Service speed 16 knots.
Car capacity: About 2,000 cars.
12.7.1970: Launched by Brodogradiliste ''Treci Maj'', Rijeka (Yard No. 529)
as TROLL PARK for Norpark Shipping Co. Ltd. (Denholm Ship Management
Ltd., managers), London. *19.1.1971:* Completed. *24.8.1982:* Sold to Cannor
Shipping Ltd., London. *1982:* Wilh. Wilhelmsen took over her management.
29.11.1984: Sold to Belgravia Navigation Co. S.A. (Transoceanic (U.B.A.)
Maritime S.A., managers), Greece and renamed JASMINE. *1986:* Sold to
Moonlight Shipping Co. Ltd (Sea Justice S.A., managers), Cyprus and
renamed IVY. *1988:* Sold to Cia. Naviera Panachiara S.A. (Mediterranean
Shipping Co., managers), Panama and renamed CHIARA S. *1989:* Renamed
DA MOSTO A. *1992:* Renamed MSC LAURA. Still in service.

TURCOMAN   *Michael Cassar*

286. TURCOMAN (III) (1971-1978) Ore/Bulk/Oil Carrier
Tonnages: 82,791 gross, 59,682 net, 150,900 deadweight.
Dimensions: 290.05 (302.98 o.a.) x 42.78 x 22.94 m. 16.942 m draught.
Machinery: 8-cylinder 2 S.C.S.A. Burmeister & Wain oil engine of 30,600 b.h.p.
by the shipbuilders. Service speed 16 knots.

30.7.1971: Launched by Eriksbergs Mekaniska Verkstads A/B, Gothenburg (Yard No. 638). *18.11.1971:* Completed. Price paid 94,700,000.00 kr. *2.6.1978:* Sold to Resolute Maritime Inc., Liberia and renamed RESOLUTE. *1979:* Sold to Marber Two Ltd., Bermuda, registered at London in the name of Dashwood Co. Ltd and renamed DASHWOOD. *1981:* Sold to Tricolor Shipping Corporation, Liberia and renamed TIFFANY. *1989:* Sold to Liberty Alliance S.A., Panama and renamed ROKKO SAN. Still in service.

TROLL LAKE   *W.S.P.L.*

287. TROLL LAKE (1971-1985) Open Type Bulk Carrier with Car Decks
Tonnages: 22,160 gross, 13,651 net, 32,300 deadweight.
Dimensions: 173.11 (183.32 o.a.) x 26.88 x 16.01 m. 11.373 m draught.
Machinery: 7-cylinder 2 S.C.S.A. Sulzer oil engine of 14,000 b.h.p. by R.O. Tvornica Dizel Motora ''Treci Maj'', Rijeka. Service speed 16 knots.
Car capacity: About 2,000 cars.
24.7.1971: Launched by Brodogradiliste ''Treci Maj'', Rijeka (Yard No. 542) for Twopark Shipping Co. Ltd. (Denholm Ship Management Ltd., managers), London. *20.12.1971:* Completed. *1982:* Wilh. Wilhelmsen took over her management. *25.10.1984:* Transferred to Troll Lake Shipping Ltd. (Ocean Fleets Ltd., managers), London. *23.9.1985:* Sold to d'Amico Societa di Navigazione S.p.A., Italy and renamed CIELO DI AMALFI. Still in service.

288. TAKASAGO / TAMBO RIVER / TAKASAGO (1972-1985) Bulk Carrier
Tonnages: 36,265 gross, 23,302 net, 63,479 deadweight.
Dimensions: 212.63 (223.96 o.a.) x 31.83 x 18.37 m. 13.348 m draught.
Machinery: 7-cylinder 2 S.C.S.A. Sulzer oil engine of 14,000 b.h.p. by the shipbuilders. Service speed 15.5 knots.
15.2.1972: Launched by Mitsubishi Heavy Industries Ltd., Kobe (Yard No. 1034). *14.6.1972:* Completed. Price paid 93,500,000.00 kr. *26.9.1975:* Transferred to the subsidiary company, Northern Bulk Carriers Ltd., Hong Kong and renamed TAMBO RIVER, as the name ''Takasago'' was already registered in Hong Kong. *22.12.1979:* Renamed TAKASAGO. *1982:* Barber Ship Management Ltd became managers. *16.7.1985:* Sold to Oceanlight Marine Ltd., Cyprus and renamed GESALINA. *1988:* Sold to Pontus Shipping Co. Ltd (Baltic Shipping Co. Ltd., managers), Liberia and renamed PONTUS. Still in service.

TAKASAGO

289. TARTAR (III) (1972-1978) Ore/Oil Carrier
Tonnages: 116,270 gross, 95,058 net, 215,621 deadweight.
Dimensions: 310.02 (327.82 o.a.) x 50.09 x 25.51 m. 19.159 m draught.
Machinery: Two steam turbines totalling 32,000 s.h.p. by Mitsubishi Heavy Industries Ltd., Nagasaki double reduction geared to a single screw shaft.
Service speed 16.25 knots.

TARTAR, 18.8.1974, after drydocking at Hamburg   *Silke Pein*

30.5.1972: Launched by Nippon Kokan K.K., Tsu (Yard No. 10). *29.8.1972:* Completed. Price paid 134,778,000.00 kr. *12.10.1978:* Sold to Liberian Pristella Transports Inc. (World-Wide Shipping Agency, Ltd., managers), Liberia and renamed WORLD LADY. *4.4.1985:* Arrived at Ulsan to be broken up by Hyundai Precision Industry Co. Ltd. *27.4.1985:* Demolition commenced.

TRICOLOR in ScanCarriers livery at Rotterdam, 23.6.1979 *W.S.P.L. Slide Collection*

290. TRICOLOR (VI) (1972-1985) Ro-Ro Vessel
Tonnages: 13,874 gross, 7,108 net, 21,810 deadweight.
Dimensions: 193.71 (207.40 o.a.) x 29.62 x 16.87 m. 9.907 m draught.
Machinery: Three 18-cylinder 4 S.C.S.A. Pielstick oil engines totalling 28,890 b.h.p. by Chantiers de l'Atlantique, St. Nazaire, geared to a single screw shaft. Service speed 21.5 knots.
Container capacity: 1,319 TEU. Quarter stern door and ramp.
The first roll-on, roll-off vessel in the Wilhelmsen fleet.
18.3.1972: Launched by Chantiers de France-Dunkerque, Dunkirk (Yard No. 281). *1.9.1972:* Completed. Price paid 93,000,000.00 kr. *23.9.1985:* Sold to the United States Department of Transportation for service with the Ready Reserve Force of the U.S. Reserve Fleet and renamed CAPE DIAMOND. Still in service.

291. TENDER TROUT (I) (1972-1977) Tug/Supply Ship
Tonnages: 497 gross, 150 net, 832 deadweight.
Dimensions: 53.65 (57.46 o.a.) x 11.61 x 4.88 m. 4.131 m draught.
Machinery: Two 16-cylinder 2 S.C.S.A. oil engines totalling 4,700 b.h.p. by General Motors Corporation Electro-Motive Division, La Grange, driving twin controllable pitch propellers. Service speed 14.5 knots.
Passengers: 12.
26.5.1972: Launched by Mangone Shipbuilding Corporation, Houston, Texas (Yard No. 105) for Wilhelmsen Offshore Services, of which Wilh. Wilhelmsen were managers. *8.9.1972:* Completed. Price paid 12,530,000.00 kr. *9.11.1977:* Sold to Compagnie Surf S.A., France. *1978:* Owners became Compagnie des Moyens de Surface (SURF), later Cie. des Moyens de Surface adaptes à

TENDER TROUT

l'Exploitation des Oceans (SURF), France and renamed ALADIN. *1987:* Sold to Ulyssis Shipping Co. Ltd., Malta and renamed ALAD. *6.2.1988:* Arrived at Gadani Beach to be broken up by Chiltan (Pvt.) Ltd. *10.2.1988:* Demolition commenced.

292. TOYAMA (1972-1991) Container Vessel
Tonnages: *1972-1984:* 52,196 gross, 30,967 net, 33,496 deadweight. *1984-on:* 57,123 gross, 17,137 net, 34,033 deadweight.
Dimensions: *1972-1984:* 259.09 (275.09 o.a.) x 32.31 x 24.01 m. 11.059

TOYAMA arriving at Rotterdam, 12.6.1987   *Joachim Pein*

m draught. *1984-on:* 274.96 (289.49 o.a.) x 32.31 x 24.01 m. 11.610 m draught.
Machinery: *1972-1984:* One 12-cylinder and two 9-cylinder Burmeister & Wain oil engines totalling 78,200 b.h.p. by the shipbuilders driving triple screws. Service speed 27.75 knots. *1984-on:* One 6-cylinder and two 9-cylinder Burmeister & Wain oil engines totalling 62,900 b.h.p. by the shipbuilders driving the triple screws. Service speed 26.25 knots.
Container capacity: *1972-1984:* 2,208 TEU. *1984-on:* 2,666 TEU.
2.6.1972: Launched by Mitsui Zosen, Tamano (Yard No. 900). *27.11.1972:* Completed. Price paid 143,500,000.00 kr. *1984:* Lengthened by Hyundai Mipo Dockyard Co. Ltd., Ulsan, thereby increasing her capacity from 2,208 to 2,666 containers. Her 9-cylinder engines were removed and reconditioned and the 12-cylinder engine driving the centre shaft was replaced by a new one with 6 cylinders, reducing the horse power and her speed to 26.25 knots.
25.4.1991: Sold to Det Ostasiatiske Kompagni, Denmark and registered under the Bahamas flag. *1993:* Sold to A.P. Moller, Denmark and renamed MAERSK NANHAI. Still in service.

TENDER TUNA   *Ken Turrell*

293. TENDER TUNA (1972-1974) Tug/Supply Ship
Tonnages: 498 gross, 150 net, 832 deadweight.
Dimensions: 53.65 (57.46 o.a.) x 11.61 x 4.88 m. 4.131 m draught.
Machinery: Two 16-cylinder 2 S.C.S.A. oil engines totalling 4,700 b.h.p. by General Motors Corporation Electro-Motive Division, La Grange, driving twin controllable pitch propellers. Service speed 14.5 knots.
Passengers: 12.
29.7.1972: Launched by Mangone Shipbuilding Corporation, Houston, Texas (Yard No. 106) for Wilhelmsen Offshore Services, of which Wilh. Wilhelmsen were managers. *28.11.1972:* Completed. Price paid 12,632,000.00 kr. *27.3.1974:* Sold to City Leasing Ltd. (Star Offshore Services (Supply Boats) Ltd., managers), Aberdeen and renamed STAR ORION. *1980:* Renamed STAR SERVICE. *1982:* Sold to Zapata Marine Service Ltd., Panama. *1983:* Transferred to Zapata Marine Service Italia S.p.A., Italy and renamed AQUILA. Still in service.

TAKAMINE   *Fotoflite incorporating Skyfotos*

294. TAKAMINE (1973-1975) Bulk Carrier
Tonnages: 36,265 gross, 23,302 net, 63,423 deadweight.
Dimensions: 212.63 (224.01 o.a.) x 31.81 x 18.37 m. 13.342 m draught.
Machinery: 7-cylinder 2 S.C.S.A. Sulzer oil engine of 14,000 b.h.p. by the
shipbuilders. Service speed 15.5 knots.
29.9.1972: Launched by Mitsubishi Heavy Industries Ltd., Kobe (Yard No.
1035). *27.1.1973:* Completed. Price paid 75,200,000.00 kr. *1.1.1975:*
Transferred to Morten Werring's Rederi (Skips A/S Triton). *27.1.1984:*
Transferred to Arctic Shipping Co. Ltd., Hong Kong. *21.12.1984:* Sold to Space
Shipping Inc. (Semih Sohtorik Deniz Isletmeciligi ve Agentelik A.S., managers),
Liberia and renamed BULK SPACE. *1985:* Sold to Setal Denizcilik A.S. (same
managers), Turkey and renamed BULK TRANSPORTER. *1991:* Sold to Result
Shipping Co. Ltd. (Medsea S.A.M. Aigue Marine, managers), Cyprus and
renamed SEA TRANSPORTER. Still in service.

295. TARAGO (1973-1985) Ro-Ro Vessel
Tonnages: 13,874 gross, 7,104 net, 21,774 deadweight.
Dimensions: 193.71 (207.40 o.a.) x 29.62 x 16.87 m. 9.576 m draught.
Machinery: Three 18-cylinder 4 S.C.S.A. Pielstick oil engines totalling 28,980
b.h.p. by Chantiers de l'Atlantique, St. Nazaire, geared to a single screw shaft.
Service speed 21.5 knots.
Container capacity: 1,319 TEU. Quarter stern door and ramp.

TARAGO, 25.3.1973   *J. Y. Freeman*

7.10.1972: Launched by Chantiers de France-Dunkerque, Dunkirk (Yard No. 282). *20.2.1973:* Completed. Price paid 93,000,000.00 kr. *16.10.1985:* Sold to the United States Department of Transportation for service with the Ready Reserve Force of the U.S.Reserve Fleet and renamed CAPE DOMINGO. Still in service.

TENDER TURBOT

296. TENDER TURBOT (I) (1973-1977) Tug/Supply Ship
Tonnages: 499 gross, 149 net, 845 deadweight.
Dimensions: 53.65 (57.46 o.a.) x 11.61 x 5.03 m. 4.131 m draught.
Machinery: Two 16-cylinder 2 S.C.S.A oil engines totalling 4,700 b.h.p. by General Motors Corporation Electro-Motive Division, La Grange, driving twin controllable pitch propellers. Service speed 14.5 knots.
Passengers: 12.
1.1973: Launched by Mangone Shipbuilding Corporation, Houston, Texas (Yard No. 108) for Wilhelmsen Offshore Services, of which Wilh. Wilhelmsen were managers. *17.4.1973:* Completed. Price paid 11,844,000.00 kr. *10.10.1977:* Sold to Compagnie des Moyens de Surface (SURF), later Cie. des Moyens de Surface adaptes à l'Exploitation des Oceans (SURF), France and renamed APSARA. *1987:* Renamed ASTERIAS. *1988:* Sold to Smalto Shipping Co. Ltd. (Martontree Shipping Co. S.A., managers). Cyprus and renamed ALADIN SEA. *1991:* Sold to Caribbean Operators Ltd., Trinidad and Tobago and renamed JULIA EDWARDS. Still in service.

297. TOMBARRA (1973-1985) Ro-Ro Vessel
Tonnages: 13,887 gross, 7,115 net, 22,000 deadweight.
Dimensions: 193.66 (207.40 o.a.) x 29.62 x 16.87 m. 9.938 m draught.
Machinery: Three 18-cylinder 4 S.C.S.A. Pielstick oil engines totalling 27,000 b.h.p. by Lindholmen Motor A/B, Gothenburg, geared to a single screw shaft. Service speed 21.5 knots.
Container capacity: 1,319 TEU. Quarter stern door and ramp.
29.3.1973: Launched by Eriksbergs Mekaniska Verkstads A/B (Lindholmen Division), Gothenburg (Yard No. 664). *30.8.1973:* Completed. Price paid 93,000,000.00 kr. *23.9.1985:* Sold to the United States Department of Transportation for service with the Ready Reserve Force of the U.S. Reserve Fleet and renamed CAPE DECISION. Still in service.

TOMBARRA

298. TENDER TARPON (I) (1973-1979) Tug/Supply Ship
Tonnages: 498 gross, 150 net, 813 deadweight.
Dimensions: 53.65 (57.46 o.a.) x 11.61 x 5.03 m. 4.134 m draught.
Machinery: Two 16-cylinder 2 S.C.S.A. oil engines totalling 3,800 b.h.p. by General Motors Corporation Electro-Motive Division, La Grange, driving twin controllable pitch propellers. Service speed 14.5 knots.
Passengers: 12.
22.5.1973: Launched by Mangone Shipbuilding Corporation, Houston, Texas (Yard No. 109) for Wilhelmsen Offshore Services, of which Wilh. Wilhelmsen were managers. *24.9.1973:* Completed. Price paid 12,959,000.00 kr. *11.6.1979:* Sold to Zapata Marine Service Inc., Panama and renamed CHALLENGER SERVICE. Later transferred to Zapata Gulf Marine Service Ltd (Zapata Gulf Marine Corporation, managers), Panama, and then to Offshore Marine International Ltd. (same managers), Vanuatu. *1993:* Managers became Tidewater Marine Inc. *1993:* Sold to Selat Marine Services Co. Ltd., United Arab Emirates and renamed SELAT ARJUNA. Still in service.

TENDER TARPON

223

TAKACHIHO

299. TAKACHIHO (I) (1973-1978) Bulk Carrier
Tonnages: 36,264 gross, 23,302 net, 63,533 deadweight.
Dimensions: 212.63 (224.01 o.a.) x 31.81 x 18.37 m. 13.348 m draught.
Machinery: 7-cylinder 2 S.C.S.A. Sulzer oil engine of 14,000 b.h.p. by
Mitsubishi Heavy Industries Ltd., Nagasaki. Service speed 15.5 knots.
22.8.1973: Launched by Mitsubishi Heavy Industries Ltd., Kobe (Yard No.
1036). *27.11.1973:* Completed. Price paid 78,700,000.00 kr. *24.7.1978:* Sold
to Metropolitan World Shipping Corporation, Greece and renamed MOUNT
PARNASSOS. *1984:* Sold to Anko Anadolu Koparan Denizcilik ve Ticaret A.S.
(Anadolu Denizcilik ve Ticaret A.S., managers), Turkey and renamed
ANADOLU KOPARAN. *1990:* Sold to Istanbul Shipping & Trading S.A. (Zihni
Gemi Isletmeleri A.S., managers), Turkey and renamed ISTANBUL Z. *1991:*
Sold to Trust Ships Management (Entrust Maritime Co. Ltd., managers),
Greece and renamed ENTRUST FAITH. *27.11.1991:* Arrived at Ponta Delgada
with damage to her shell plating sustained during bad weather whilst on
her voyage from Puerto Ordaz to Bremen with iron ore. *6.12.1991:* Abandoned
by her crew after water had been found in her holds and towed out to sea.
7.12.1991: Sank in a position 37.16 N, 25.31 W.

300. TIGRE (III) (1974-1984) Tanker
Tonnages: 140,277 gross, 108,861 net, 286,170 deadweight.
Dimensions: 331.45 (347.84 o.a.) x 51.85 x 28.40 m. 22.143 m draught.
Machinery: Two steam turbines totalling 34,472 s.h.p. by STAL-LAVAL Turbin
AB, Finspong. Service speed 15.5 knots.
Constructed by Stord Verft A/S, Stord in two sections, the after part being
launched in *1.1974* as Yard No 677. *28.2.1974:* Completed. Price paid
200,039,000.00 kr. *26.11.1984:* Sold to Elmini Limit Inc. (Ceres Hellenic
Shipping Enterprises Ltd., managers) and renamed FREESHIP L. *1986:* Sold
to K/S Tank-Invest A/S (Barber International A/S, managers), Oslo and
renamed HAPPY KARI. *18.12.1987:* Attacked and set on fire by Iranian
gunboats when outward bound from Kuwait in the Strait of Hormuz in a

TIGRE

position 26.15 N, 56.12 E. She was, however, able to continue her voyage. *11.2.1988:* Attacked again by Iranian gunboats when about 20 miles off Dubai in a position 25.52 N, 55.36 E during a voyage from Kuwait to Rotterdam. A major fire broke out aft but she was able to reach Fujairah Anchorage *12.2.1988* under her own power. She was subsequently repaired and sold to K/S Finans-Invest VI A/S Konsortie (Norman International A/S, managers), Oslo and renamed IGRE. Later in *1988* she was renamed HAPPY MARIANNE. *1989:* Sold to Nor Explorer Ltd. (same managers), Liberia (Norwegian flag) and renamed NOR EXPLORER. *1992:* Sold to Chinese shipbreakers. *19.5.1992:* Arrived at Huangpu to be broken up.

TENDER CARRIER as a Diving Support Ship

301. TENDER CARRIER (1974-1986) Multi-purpose Supply Ship, later Diving Support Ship

Tonnages: *1974-1977:* 1,421 gross, 655 net, 2,667 deadweight. *1977-on:* 1,764 gross, 506 net, 2,667 deadweight.
Dimensions: 76.21 (81.08 o.a.) x 18.04 x 7.32 m. 4.026 m draught.
Machinery: Two 6-cylinder 4 S.C.S.A. oil engines totalling 4,000 b.h.p. by Atlas-MaK Maschinenbau G.m.b.H., Kiel, driving twin controllable pitch propellers. Service speed 14 knots.
9.3.1974: Launched by Ulstein Hatlo A/S, Ulsteinvik (Yard No. 125) for Wilhelmsen Offshore Services, of which Wilh. Wilhelmsen were managers. *29.4.1974:* Completed. Price paid 24,484,000.00 kr. *1977:* Converted by Schichau Unterweser A.G., Bremerhaven into a Diving Support Ship. *19.11.1984:* Transferred to Wilcarrier Inc., Liberia. *1986:* Sold to K/S Far Venture A/S (Sverre Farstad & Co., managers), Liberia and renamed SCAN CARRIER.

(The name FAR CARRIER was originally intended but was not borne.) *1989:* Sold to Heswall International Ltd., Liberia. *1990:* Sold to Harvard Enterprises S.A., Liberia. *1992:* Sold to Scan Carrier N.V. (Workships Contractors B.V., managers), Liberia. Still in service.

TENDER TRIGGER

302. TENDER TRIGGER (1974-1979) Tug/Supply Ship
Tonnages: 495 gross, 153 net, 815 deadweight.
Dimensions: 53.65 (57.46 o.a.) x 11.61 x 5.03 m. 4.134 m draught.
Machinery: Two 16-cylinder 2 S.C.S.A. oil engines totalling 3,800 b.h.p. by General Motors Corporation Electro-Motive Division, La Grange, driving twin controllable pitch propellers. Service speed 15 knots.
Passengers: 2.
22.12.1973: Launched by Mangone Shipbuilding Corporation, Houston, Texas (Yard No. 112) for Wilhelmsen Offshore Services, of which Wilh. Wilhelmsen were managers. *14.5.1974:* Completed. Price paid 12,238,000.00 kr. *1979:* Sold to Offshore Italia S.p.A., Italy and renamed ORSA MAGGIORE. *1990:* Sold to Navigazione Alta Italia S.p.A., Italy. *1991:* Sold to Nai Offshore S.p.A., Italy. Still in service.

303. TENDER CLIPPER (1974-1986) Multi-purpose Supply Ship, later Fire Fighting Standby and Rescue Vessel
Tonnages: *1974-1978:* 1,376 gross, 670 net, 2,667 deadweight. *1978-on:* 1,562 gross, 812 net, 2,667 deadweight.
Dimensions: 76.21 (81.08 o.a.) x 18.04 x 7.32 m. 4.026 m draught.
Machinery: Two 6-cylinder 4 S.C.S.A. oil engines totalling 4,000 b.h.p. by Atlas-MaK Maschinenbau G.m.b.H., Kiel, driving twin controllable pitch propellers. Service speed 14 knots.
6.4.1974: Launched by Ulstein Hatlo A/S, Ulsteinvik (Yard No. 126) for Wilhelmsen Offshore Services, of which Wilh. Wilhelmsen were managers. *19.6.1974:* Completed. Price paid 24,330,000.00 kr. *1978:* Converted by Kristiansands Mekaniske Verksted A/S into a Fire Fighting Rescue and Standby Rescue Vessel of 1,562 gross. *17.12.1986:* Sold to K/S Far Venture A/S (Sverre Farstad & Co., managers), Aalesund and renamed FAR CLIPPER.

TENDER CLIPPER   *Ken Turrell*

1987: Sold to Edison Chouest Boat Rentals, U.S.A. and later in *1987* renamed
CORY CHOUEST. *1988:* Transferred to Alpha Marine Services Inc., Bahamas.
1989: Transferred to United States registry. Still in service.

TACHIBANA

304. TACHIBANA (1974-1975) Bulk Carrier
Tonnages: 36,243 gross, 23,325 net, 3,550 deadweight.
Dimensions: 212.68 (224.01 o.a.) x 31.86 x 18.37 m. 13.348 m draught.
Machinery: 7-cylinder 2 S.C.S.A. Sulzer oil engine of 14,000 b.h.p. by the
shipbuilders. Service speed 15.5 knots.
14.3.1974: Launched by Mitsubishi Heavy Industries Ltd., Kobe (Yard No.
1044). *12.7.1974:* Completed. Price paid 67,800,000.00 kr. *1.1.1975:*
Transferred to Morten Werring's Rederi (Skips A/S Triton). *1984:* Transferred
to Talas Shipping Ltd., Hong Kong. *1986:* Sold to Jakato Shipping Ltd. (Ugland
Brothers Ltd, managers), Hong Kong and renamed CHIBA. *1987:* Sold to
Alexandrite Shipping Corporation, Liberia and renamed CORNILIOS. Still in
service.

TENDER TRUMPET   *W. J. Harvey*

305. TENDER TRUMPET (1974-1979) Tug/Supply Ship

Tonnages: 495 gross, 153 net, 815 deadweight.
Dimensions: 53.65 (57.46 o.a.) x 11.61 x 5.03 m. 4.134 m draught.
Machinery: Two 16-cylinder 2 S.C.S.A. oil engines totalling 5,800 b.h.p. by
General Motors Corporation Electro-Motive Division, La Grange, driving twin
controllable pitch propellers. Service speed 15 knots.
Passengers: 12.
20.4.1974: Launched by Mangone Shipbuilding Corporation, Houston, Texas
(Yard No. 113) for Wilhelmsen Offshore Services, of which Wilh. Wilhelmsen
were managers. *12.8.1974:* Completed. Price paid 12,263,000.00 kr.
13.6.1979: Sold to Zapata Marine Service Ltd. S.A., Panama and renamed
CHARGER SERVICE. Later transferred to Zapata Gulf Marine Operators Inc.,
Panama. *1993:* Managers became Tidewater Marine Service Inc. Still in
service.

TENDER CAPTAIN

306. TENDER CAPTAIN (I) (1975-1979) Multi-purpose Supply Ship, later Standby Rescue Vessel
Tonnages: 1,376 gross, 670 net, 2,667 deadweight.
Dimensions: 76.21 (81.08 o.a.) x 18.04 x 7.32 m. 4 026 m draught.
Machinery: Two 6-cylinder 4 S.C.S.A. oil engines totalling 4,000 b.h.p. by MaK Maschinenbau G.m.b.H., Kiel, driving twin controllable pitch propellers. Service speed 14 knots.
15.2.1975: Launched by Ulstein Hatlo A/S, Ulsteinvik (Yard No. 130) for Wilhelmsen Offshore Service's, of which Wilh. Wilhelmsen were managers. *11.4.1975:* Completed. Price paid 36,900,000.00 kr. *1977:* Converted by Tyne Shiprepair, Newcastle, into a Standby Rescue Vessel with a hospital with 100 beds. *31.1.1979:* Sold to Societa Azionaria Italiana Perforazioni e Montaggi S.p.A., Italy and renamed SAIPEM RAGNO DUE. Still in service.

TENDER SENIOR

307. TENDER SENIOR / MAERSK SENIOR / TENDER SENIOR (1975-1986) Anchor Handling Tug/Supply Ship
Tonnages: 498 gross, 186 net, 1,072 deadweight.
Dimensions: 56.42 (64.39 o.a.) x 13.85 x 6.91 m. 4.717 m draught.
Machinery: Two 12-cylinder 4 S.C.S.A. oil engines totalling 9,000 b.h.p. by MaK Maschinenbau G.m.b.H., Kiel, driving twin controllable pitch propellers. Service speed 16 knots.
Passengers: 12.
1.2.1975: Launched by Hermann Sürken G.m.b.H. & Co. K.G., Papenburg (Yard No. 282) for Wilhelmsen Offshore Services, of which Wilh. Wilhelmsen were managers. *25.4.1975:* Completed. Price paid 22,580,000.00 kr. *18.2.1985:* Transferred to Wilsenior Inc., Liberia and briefly renamed MAERSK SENIOR, but soon reverted to TENDER SENIOR. *3.10.1986:* Sold to K/S Far Venture A/S (Sverre Farstad & Co., managers), Aalesund, retaining Liberian registry, and renamed FAR SOUTH. (The name FAR SENIOR was initially intended.) *1987:* Reverted to Wilsenior Inc. (Sverre Farstad & Co. A/S, managers), Liberia. *1988:* Renamed RED ROBIN, transferred to St. Vincent registry and placed under the management of Care Offshore S.A. *1993:* Sold to Red Robin Shipping Corporation (same managers), St. Vincent. Still in service.

229

TENDER SEARCHER

308. TENDER SEARCHER (1975-1986) Anchor Handling Tug/Supply Ship
Tonnages: 498 gross, 186 net, 1,110 deadweight.
Dimensions: 56.42 (64.52 o.a.) x 13.85 x 6.91 m. 4.719 m draught.
Machinery: Two 12-cylinder 4 S.C.S.A. oil engines totalling 8,000 b.h.p. by Atlas-MaK Maschinenbau G.m.b.H., Kiel, driving twin controllable pitch propellers. Service speed 16 knots.
Passengers: 12.
30.5.1975: Launched by Hermann Sürken G.m.b.H. & Co. K.G., Papenburg (Yard No. 283) for Wilhelmsen Offshore Services, of which Wilh. Wilhelmsen were managers. *21.8.1975:* Completed. Price paid 23,000,000.00 kr. *23.2.1984:* Transferred to Wilsupply Inc. (Wilhelmsen Offshore Services, managers), Liberia. *13.10.1986:* Sold to K/S Far Venture A/S (Sverre Farstad & Co., managers), Aalesund, retaining Liberian registry, and renamed FAR SEARCHER. *1990:* Sold to K/S Pan Searcher, Liberia and renamed PAN SEARCHER. *1992:* Sold to Norway Offshore Ltd. A/S, Liberia. Still in service.

TREASURE HUNTER as a Support Vessel

230

TREASURE HUNTER as an Oil Drilling Rig

309. TREASURE HUNTER (1975-1988) Semi-Submersible Oil Drilling Rig, later Support Vessel, then Semi-Submersible Oil Drilling Rig
1975-1976 and *1985-on:* Drilling Rig. *1976-1983:* Construction Support Vessel. *1983-1985:* Drilling Tender Support Vessel.
Details as a Drilling Tender Support Vessel:
Operating displacement 24,900 tonnes.
Dimensions: 108.20 x 67.36 m. Operating draught 21.40 m. Height of main deck above keel 36.60 m.
Diesel generator sets: Four x 2,200 h.p. Bergen. Propulsion: Two 3,400 h.p. Kort nozzles. Transit speed 7 knots.
Maximum water depth capability 460 m.
Operating deck load capacity 2,550 tonnes. Storage area 1,600 sq. m. Workshop area 240 sq. m.
Accommodation: 140 beds.
Cranes: One 40 tonnes capacity, with 47 m boom, one 40 tonnes capacity, with 36.5 m boom.

Heliport for Sikorski 61 or similar helicopter.
Gangway: One fixed gangway of 30 m length.
15.12.1975: Completed by Nylands Verksted (Aker Group), Oslo (Yard No. 722) as a Semi-Submersible Oil Drilling Rig of Aker H-3 design. Price paid 205,000,000.00 kr. Employed in the Mediterranean and the Baltic. *1976:* Converted by Nylands Verksted into a Construction Support Vessel. *1983:* Converted by Götaverken Arendal A/B, Gothenburg into a Drilling Tender Support Vessel. *1985:* Converted back to a Semi-Submersible Oil Drilling Rig by Blohm + Voss A.G., Hamburg. *20.4.1988:* Sold to K/S Hunter Drilling, Oslo, registered in the Bahamas and in *1989* renamed HUNTER. *1990:* Stena Offshore Ltd., became managers. *4.1992:* Sold to Lauritzen Shipping (Bahamas) Ltd. (Lauritzen Offshore A/S, managers), Bahamas and renamed DAN PRINCESS. Still in service.

TENDER POWER on trials prior to delivery

310. TENDER POWER (1976-1985) Anchor Handling Tug

Tonnages: 461 gross, 186 net, 612 deadweight.
Dimensions: 40.47 (45.47 o.a.) x 13.01 x 6.65 m. 4.718 m draught.
Machinery: Two 12-cylinder 4 S.C.S.A. oil engines totalling 8,000 b.h.p. by MaK Maschinenbau G.m.b.H., Kiel, driving twin controllable pitch propellers. Service speed 15 knots.
7.11.1975: Launched by Hermann Sürken G.m.b.H. & Co. K.G., Papenburg (Yard No. 284) for Wilhelmsen Offshore Services, of which Wilh. Wilhelmsen were managers. *6.2.1976:* Completed. Price paid 22,300,000.00 kr. *19.12.1985:* Sold to Rimorchiatori Riuniti S.p.A., Italy and renamed A.H. CICLONE. *1987:* Sold to Finarge-Finanziaria Armamento Genovese S.p.A., Italy. *1990:* Sold to Boa Ltd. (Taubatkompaniet A/S, managers), Cayman Islands and renamed BOA POWER. Still in service.

TENDER COMMANDER

311. TENDER COMMANDER (1976-1982) Multi-purpose Supply Ship
Tonnages: 1,512 gross, 768 net, 2,599 deadweight.
Dimensions: 76.18 (81.08 o.a.) x 18.06 x 7.12 m. 4.026 m draught.
Machinery: Two 6-cylinder 4 S.C.S.A. oil engines totalling 4,000 b.h.p. by MaK
Maschinenbau G.m.b.H., Kiel, driving twin controllable pitch propellers.
Service speed 14 knots.
10.10.1975: Launched by by Ulstein Hatlo A/S, Ulsteinvik (Yard No. 137) for
Wilhelmsen Offshore Services, of which Wilh. Wilhelmsen were managers.
26.3.1976: Completed. Price paid 31,650,000.00 kr. *11.10.1982:* Sold to K/S
Saevik Supply II A/S, Aalesund and renamed NORTHERN COMMANDER.
1992: Transferred to K/S Northern Commander (Saevik Supply Management
A/S, managers), Aalesund. Still in service.

312. TITUS (II) (1976-1980) Tanker
Tonnages: 187,888 gross, 145,234 net, 379,999 deadweight.
Dimensions: 355.05 (373.54 o.a.) x 64.06 x 29.01 m. 22.886 m draught.
Machinery: Two steam turbines totalling 45,000 s.h.p. by Mitsubishi Heavy
Industries Ltd., Nagasaki, double reduction geared to a single screw shaft.
Service speed 16 knots.
8.11.1975: Launched by Nippon Kokan K.K., Tsu (Yard No. 34). *30.3.1976:*
Completed. Price paid 280,000,000.00 kr. *21.4.1980:* Sold to United

TITUS

Overseas Petroleum Carriers Inc. (Golden Peak Maritime Agencies Ltd., managers), Liberia and renamed ENERGY EXPLORER. *1983:* Managers became Island Navigation Corporation (Ship Management), Ltd. *1986:* Sold to Latin America Petroleum Carriers Inc. (Orient Overseas Management & Finance Ltd.), Liberia. *1987:* Managers became Island Navigation Corporation (Holdings) Inc., who in turn became Island Navigation Corporation International Ltd. *1988:* Sold to Great Beluga Shipping Inc. (same managers), Liberia. *1991:* Renamed NEW EXPLORER. Still in service.

Two sister ships, Yard Nos. 39 and 43, were cancelled. During these negotiations orders were placed for six multi-purpose carriers (Yard Numbers 47-52) and two bulk carriers (Yard Numbers 53 and 54).

313. TENDER PULL (1976-1981) Anchor Handling Tug
Tonnages: 460 gross, 136 net, 612 deadweight.
Dimensions: 40.44 (45.47 o.a.) x 13.82 x 6.86 m. 4.700 m draught.
Machinery: Two 12-cylinder 4 S.C.S.A. oil engines totalling 8,000 b.h.p. by MaK Maschinenbau G.m.b.H., Kiel, driving twin controllable pitch propellers. Service speed 15 knots.
7.11.1975: Launched by Hermann Sürken G.m.b.H. & Co. K.G., Papenburg (Yard No. 285) for Wilhelmsen Offshore Services, of which Wilh. Wilhelmsen were managers. *12.4.1976:* Completed. Price paid 22,000,000.00 kr. *6.3.1981:* Sold to P/R Frank Viking (K/S Viking Supply Ships A/S, later Bendt Rasmussen Rederi, managers), Kristiansund S and renamed FRANK VIKING. *1986:* Sold to Offshore Support Service Inc. (Reksten Management A/S, managers), Panama and renamed SCAN POWER. *1989:* Sold to Scan Power Inc. (Viking Supply Ships A/S, managers), Panama and renamed UTRECHT. *1990:* Sold to Boa Ltd. (Taubatkompaniet A/S, managers), Cayman Islands and renamed BOA PULL. *1992:* Renamed NAKARI TIDE. Still in service.

TENDER CONTEST

314. TENDER CONTEST (1976-1985) Multi-Purpose Supply Ship, later Diving Support Vessel
Tonnages: *1976-1977:* 1,363 gross, 667 net, 2,660 deadweight. *1977-on:* 1,539 gross, 607 net, 2,000 deadweight.
Dimensions: 76.21 (81.18 o.a.) x 18.04 x 7.32 m. 4.014 m draught.
Machinery: Two 6-cylinder 4 S.C.S.A. oil engines totalling 4,000 b.h.p. by MaK

Maschinenbau G.m.b.H., Kiel, driving twin controllable pitch propellers. *1977:* converted to diesel-electric propulsion. Service speed 14 knots. *16.1.1976:* Launched by Eid Verft A/S, Naustdal-Nordfjord (Yard No. 7) and *30.4.1976:* Completed by Smedvik Mekaniske Verksted, Tjørvag (Yard No.71) for Wilhelmsen Offshore Services, of which Wilh. Wilhelmsen were managers. Price paid 31,000,000.00 kr. *5.1977:* Converted by Nylands Verksted, Oslo, into a Diving Support Vessel with diesel-electric propulsion. *5.3.1985:* Sold to A/S Mosvolds Rederi, Farsund. *20.6.1985:* Sold to P/R Oceanfun, Farsund (Ugland Shipping Co. A/S, Grimstad, managers) and renamed HIGHLAND REEL. Converted into a Diving Support and Pipelaying Vessel with tonnages of 3,186 gross, 955 net and 2,206 deadweight and dimensions 90.82 x 18.04 x 4.32 m. *20.11.1985:* Transferred to British registry and registered at Inverness in the ownership of Reelmaster Ltd. (Ugland Shipping Co. A/S, managers). *1988:* A/S Mosvolds Rederi became managers. *1988:* Sold to Dover Strait Ltd. (A/S Mosvolds Rederi, managers), Liberia. *1992:* Sold to Bayonne Shipping Corporation (same managers), Liberia. Still in service.

TAMPA

315. TAMPA (IV) (1976-1982)
Tonnages: 11,519 gross, 6,919 net, 12,773 deadweight.
Dimensions: 163.76 (172.22 o.a.) x 20.78 x 12.60 m. 8.383 m draught.
Machinery: 9-cylinder 2 S.C.S.A. oil engine of 11,300 b.h.p. by the shipbuilders.
Service speed 19.25 knots.
753.06 cu. m. of refrigerated cargo space.
Container capacity: 227 TEU.
6.12.1960: Launched by Götaverken A/B, Gothenburg (Yard No. 757) as FERNLAKE for Fearnley & Eger, Oslo, and completed *8.4.1961* as a dry-cargo ship of 6,732 gross with a length of 155.51 m. o.a. In *1970* she was lengthened and converted into a part-container ship by Ishikawajima-Harima Heavy Industries Ltd. *6.12.1976:* Purchased by Wilh. Wilhelmsen and renamed TAMPA. Price paid 19,000,000.00 kr. *27.3.1982:* Sold to Blue Ocean Lines S.A., Panama and renamed BLUE ADVANCE. *1982:* Sold to Adventurer Navigation Ltd. S.A. (New World Ship Owners Pte. Ltd., managers), Panama and renamed SEA ADVENTURE. *16.11.1982:* Arrived at Chittagong to be broken up by Tranship Shipbreakers. *21.11.1982:* Demolition commenced at Bhatiary.

TAMESIS

316. TAMESIS (III) / TALABOT (V) (1977-1985) Bulk Carrier
Tonnages: 38,634 gross, 26,194 net, 70,610 deadweight.
Dimensions: 223.63 (233.61 o.a.) x 32.21 x 18.72 m. 13.640 m draught.
Machinery: 6-cylinder 2S.C.S.A. Sulzer oil engine of 17,400 b.h.p. by
Mitsubishi Heavy Industries Ltd., Kobe. Service speed 15.75 knots.
2.11.1976: Launched by Nippon Kokan K.K., Tsu (Yard No. 53). *4.2.1977:*
Completed. Price paid 110,300,000.00 kr. *19.7.1984:* Transferred to Arctic
Shipping Co. Ltd. (Barber Ship Management Ltd., managers), Hong Kong and
renamed TALABOT. *9.9.1985:* Sold to Peace Water Ltd. (Anglo-Eastern
Management Services Ltd., managers), Hong Kong and renamed WYWURRY.
1987: Sold to Shipping & Trading Inc., Philippine Islands and renamed RIZAL.
1990: Sold to Diadora Shipping Co. S.A. (Martontree Shipping Co. S.A.,
managers), Cyprus. Still in service.

TEXAS

317. TEXAS (III) (1977-1982)
Tonnages: 11,430 gross, 7,030 net, 12,788 deadweight.
Dimensions: 163.56 (172.22 o.a.) x 20.78 x 12.60 m. 8.560 m draught.
Machinery: 9-cylinder 2 S.C.S.A. oil engine of 11,300 b.h.p. by the shipbuilders.
Service speed 19.25 knots.
753.06 cu. m. of refrigerated cargo space.
Container capacity: 227 TEU.
8.10.1960: Launched by Götaverken A/B, Gothenburg (Yard No. 754) as
FERNVIEW for Fearnley & Eger, Oslo and *3.3.1961* completed as a dry-cargo
ship of 6,732 gross with a length of 155.51 m. o.a. In *1970* she was
lengthened and converted into a part-container ship by Ishikawajima-Harima
Heavy Industries Ltd. *18.3.1977:* Purchased by Wilh. Wilhelmsen and renamed
TEXAS. Price paid 19,000,000.00 kr. *19.1.1982:* Sold to Saudi Shipping Lines,
Saudi Arabia and renamed KHALED. *19.5.1986:* Arrived at Alang to be broken
up by Y.A. Investment. *6.1986:* Demolition commenced.

TAGUS

318. TAGUS (II) / TATRA (III) (1977-1986) Bulk Carrier
Tonnages: 38,634 gross, 26,194 net, 70,600 deadweight.
Dimensions: 223.63 (233.61 o.a.) x 32.21 x 18.72 m. 13.640 m draught.
Machinery: 6-cylinder 2 S.C.S.A. Sulzer oil engine of 17,333 b.h.p. by
Mitsubishi Heavy Industries Ltd., Kobe. Service speed 15.75 knots.
3.12.1976: Launched by Nippon Kokan K.K., Tsu (Yard No. 54). *20.4.1977:*
Completed. Price paid 112,479,000.00 kr. *23.8.1984:* Transferred to Arctic
Shipping Co. Ltd. (Barber Ship Management Ltd., managers), Hong Kong and
renamed TATRA. *5.2.1986:* Sold to Bulk Trade Investment Co. S.A. (Hanse
Bereederungs-Gesellschaft m.b.H. & Co. K.G., managers), Panama and
renamed NEW HOPE 1. *1986:* Sold to Crescent Shipping & Chartering
Corporation, Philippine Islands and renamed TERESITA. *1987:* Sold to San
Antonio Shipping Ltd., Hong Kong and renamed LUCKY BULKER. Still in
service.

TSU

319. TSU / BARBER TSU / TSU / HOEGH CAPE (1977-1986) Multi-purpose Carrier

Tonnages: 12,750 gross, 6,838 net, 21,713 deadweight.
Dimensions: 165.00 (171.02 o.a.) x 26.37 x 16.01 m. 9.983 m draught.
Machinery: 7-cylinder 2 S.C.S.A. Sulzer oil engine of 14,000 b.h.p. by Mitsubishi Heavy Industries Ltd., Kobe. Service speed 17.5 knots.
Container capacity: 668 TEU.
11.1.1977: Launched by Nippon Kokan K.K., Tsu (Yard No. 47). *25.4.1977:* Completed. Price paid 103,000,000.00 kr. *1981:* Renamed BARBER TSU. *1984:* Reverted to TSU. *1985:* Renamed HOEGH CAPE whilst on time charter. *16.10.1986:* Sold to Chinese-Polish Joint Stock Shipping Company, China and renamed DA YU. *1991:* Sold to Golden Route Shipping Co. Ltd. (Chinese-Polish Joint Stock Shipping Company, managers), Cyprus and renamed EVER HAPPY. Still in service.

320. TREASURE SEEKER (1977-1989) Semi-Submersible Oil Drilling Rig

Operating displacement 20,600 tonnes.
Dimensions: 108.20 x 36.58 m. Operating draught 21.30 m. Height of main deck above keel 36.60 m.
Diesel generator sets: Four x 2,200 h.p. Hedemora. Propulsion: Two 3,400 h.p. Kort nozzles. Transit speed 7 knots.
Maximum water depth capability 380 m.
Drilling depth to 7,620 m. BOP Stack: One 18¾" 10,000 psi and one 11" 15,000 psi. Riser 16" and 21" with buoyancy.
Tensioner: 6 x 80,000 lbs.
Operating deck load capacity 2,700 tonnes.

TREASURE SEEKER

Accommodation: 86 persons.
20.5.1977: Completed by Far East Levingston Shipbuilding Ltd., Singapore (Yard No. B 151) to Aker H-3 design. Price paid 220,000,000.00 kr. *1980:* Sponsons added to after columns. *1985:* Modified by Blohm + Voss A.G., Hamburg, transferred to British registry in the ownership of Treasure Seeker Ltd. and registered at Aberdeen. *1.6.1989:* Sold to Wilrig A/S, Oslo, with Aberdeen registry. Still in service.

321. TERRIER (IV) / BARBER TERRIER / HOEGH CARRIER / TERRIER (1977-1986) Multi-purpose Carrier
Tonnages: 12,751 gross, 6,838 net, 21,831 deadweight.
Dimensions: 165.00 (171.02 o.a.) x 26.37 x 16.01 m. 9.983 m draught.
Machinery: 7-cylinder 2 S.C.S.A. Sulzer oil engine of 14,000 b.h.p. by Mitsubishi Heavy Industries Ltd., Kobe. Service speed 17.5 knots.
Container capacity: 668 TEU.

TERRIER

18.2.1977: Launched by Nippon Kokan K.K., Tsu (Yard No. 48). *25.5.1977:* Completed. Price paid 97,000,000.00 kr. *1981:* Renamed BARBER TERRIER. *1985:* Renamed HOEGH CARRIER whilst on time charter. *1986:* Renamed TERRIER. *7.10.1986:* Sold to Chinsko-Polskie Towarzystwo Okretowe S.A., Poland and renamed POKOJ. Still in service.

TENNESSEE

322. TENNESSEE (IV) / BARBER TENNESSEE / TENNESSEE (1977-1985)
Multi-purpose Carrier
Tonnages: 12,755 gross, 6,841 net, 21,831 deadweight.
Dimensions: 165.00 (171.02 o.a.) x 26.37 x 16.01 m. 9.983 m draught.
Machinery: 7-cylinder 2 S.C.S.A. Sulzer oil engine of 14,000 i.h.p. by
Mitsubishi Heavy Industries Ltd., Kobe. Service speed 17.5 knots.
Container capacity: 668 TEU.
25.3.1977: Launched by Nippon Kokan K.K., Kobe (Yard No. 49). *24.6.1977:*
Completed. Price paid 97,000,000.00 kr. *1981:* Renamed BARBER
TENNESSEE. *1985:* Renamed TENNESSEE. *29.10.1985:* Sold to Chinsko-
Polskie Towarzystwo Okretowe S.A., Poland and renamed PRACA. Still in
service.

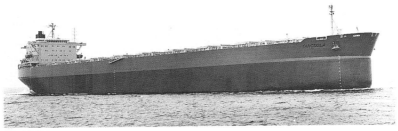

TARCOOLA

323. TARCOOLA / TROJA (IV) (1977-1986) Bulk Carrier
Tonnages: 64,692 gross, 50,881 net, 119,290 deadweight.
Dimensions: 259.01 (267.55 o.a.) x 39.07 x 22.03 m. 16.080 m draught.
Machinery: 7-cylinder 2 S.C.S.A. Burmeister & Wain oil engine of 23,900 b.h.p.
by Götaverken A/B, Gothenburg. Service speed 15.5 knots.
14.4.1977: Launched by Götaverken A/B (Øresundsvarvet Division),
Landskrona (Yard No. 258). *8.7.1977:* Completed. Price paid SEK
162,067,000. *20.1.1986:* Transferred to Arctic Shipping Co. Ltd. (Barber Ship
Management Ltd., managers), Hong Kong and renamed TROJA. *24.10.1986:*
Sold to Commodore Navigation Inc., Greece and renamed DESPINA. *1989:*
Sold to K/S Mega Brook (A/S Mosvolds Rederi, managers), Farsund and
renamed MEGA BROOK. *1991:* Sold to Brook Inc. (Farsund Ship Management
A/S, managers), Liberia. Still in service.

324. THERMOPYLÆ (III) / BARBER THERMOPYLÆ / ALS CONFIDENCE /
THERMOPYLÆ / TACNA II (1977-1988) Multi-purpose Carrier
Tonnages: 12,755 gross, 6,841 net, 21,466 deadweight.
Dimensions: 165.41 (171.02 o.a.) x 26.37 x 16.01 m. 9.983 m draught.
Machinery: 7-cylinder 2 S.C.S.A. Sulzer oil engine of 14,000 b.h.p. by
Mitsubishi Heavy Industries Ltd., Kobe. Service speed 17.5 knots.
Container capacity: 668 TEU.
27.4.1977: Launched by Nippon Kokan K.K., Tsu (Yard No. 50). *22.7.1977:*
Completed. Price paid 97,000,000.00 kr. *1981:* Renamed BARBER
THERMOPYLÆ. *1984:* Renamed ALS CONFIDENCE whilst on charter. *1984:*
Renamed THERMOPYLÆ. *27.3.1984:* Transferred to Wilship Inc. (Barber Ship
Management Ltd., managers), Liberia and renamed TACNA II. *7.10.1985:*
Reverted to Wilh. Wilhelmsen (Consorcio Naviera Peruano S.A., managers)
and placed under Vanuatu registry. *9.8.1988:* Sold to Advantage Shipholding

THERMOPYLÆ

Corporation (Red River Carriers Inc., managers), United States of America and renamed ADVANTAGE. *1993:* Sold to RR & VO Partnership, United States of America (same managers). Still in service.

325. TREASURE FINDER (1977-1991) Semi-Submersible Oil Drilling Rig, later Accommodation Vessel
1977-1979: Drilling Rig. *1979-on:* Accommodation Vessel.
Details as an Accommodation Vessel:
Operating displacement 19,640 tonnes.
Dimensions: 108.20 x 60.60 m.
Operating draught 21.40 m. Height of main deck above keel 36.60 m.
Diesel generator sets: Four x 2,200 h.p. Bergen. Propulsion: Two 3,400 h.p. Kort nozzles. Transit speed 7 knots.
Maximum water depth capability 300 m.
Operating deck load capacity 800 tonnes. Storage area 300 sq.m. Workshop area 50 sq.m.
Accommodation: 500 beds.
Cranes: One 40 tonnes capacity with 48 m boom, one 40 tonnes capacity with 36.5 m boom.
Heliport: Two separate helidecks with hangar for four helicopters. 30,000 U.S. gallons refuelling capability.
Gangway: One fixed gangway of 30 m length.
12.8.1977: Completed by Rauma-Repola Oy, Mantyluoto (Yard No. 9) to Aker H-3 design. Price paid 181,315,000.00 kr. *1979:* Converted by Framnæs Mekaniske Værksted, Sandefjord, into an Accommodation Vessel with living quarters for up to 500 persons and in *1980* sponsons added to after columns. *1983:* Transferred to British registry in the ownership of Treasure Offshore Ltd. and registered at Aberdeen. *28.5.1991:* Sold to K/S Rasmussen Offshore A/S, Kristiansand, renamed POLYCONCORD and transferred to Bahamas registry. Still in service.

TREASURE FINDER as an Accommodation Vessel

326. TYSLA (V) / WILLINE TYSLA (1977-1986) Multi-purpose Carrier
Tonnages: 12,755 gross, 6,841 net, 21,634 deadweight.
Dimensions: 165.00 (171.02 o.a.) x 26.37 x 16.01 m. 9.983 m draught.
Machinery: 7-cylinder 2 S.C.S.A. Sulzer oil engine of 14,000 b.h.p. by
Mitsubishi Heavy Industries Ltd., Kobe. Service speed 17.5 knots.
Container capacity: 668 TEU.

TYSLA

7.6.1977: Launched by Nippon Kokan K.K., Tsu (Yard No. 51). *20.9.1977:* Completed. Price paid 97,000,000.00 kr. *24.9.1982:* Transferred to Arctic Shipping Singapore (Pte.) Ltd. (Barber Ship Management Ltd., managers), Singapore and renamed WILLINE TYSLA. *4.2.1986:* Sold to Chinese-Polish Joint Stock Shipping Company, China and renamed CAI LUN. *1991:* Sold to Hawkson Ocean Shipping Co. Ltd. (Chinese-Polish Joint Stock Shipping Company, managers), Cyprus and renamed CARNIVAL. Still in service.

TONGALA

327. TONGALA (1977-1987) Bulk Carrier

Tonnages: 64,719 gross, 50,906 net, 119,290 deadweight.
Dimensions: 258.99 (267.55 o.a.) x 39.07 x 22.03 m. 16.001 m draught.
Machinery: 7-cylinder Burmeister & Wain oil engine of 23,900 i.h.p. by Götaverken A/B, Gothenburg. Service speed 15.5 knots.
17.6.1977: Launched by Götaverken A/B (Øresundsvarvet Division), Landskrona (Yard No. 260). *11.10.1977:* Completed. Price paid 200,000,000.00 kr. *5.2.1986:* Transferred to Arctic Shipping (Pte.) Ltd. (Barber Ship Management Ltd., managers), Singapore *1986:* Transferred to Arctic Shipping Hong Kong (Pte.) Ltd. (same managers), Hong Kong. *20.5.1987:* Sold to Bulkcarrier Schiffahrtsges. m.b.H & Co. K.G. (Osterreichischer Lloyd / Krohn Shipping Group, managers), Austria and renamed SALZBURG. *1989:* Sold to K/S Mega Dale (A/S Mosvolds Rederi, managers), Farsund and renamed MEGA DALE. *1991:* Sold to Dale Inc. (Farsund Ship Management A/S, managers), Liberia. Still in service.

328. TALISMAN (V) / BARBER TALISMAN (1977-1983) Multi-purpose Carrier

Tonnages: 12,755 gross, 6,841 net, 21,693 deadweight.
Dimensions: 165.00 (171.01 o.a.) x 26.37 x 16.01 m. 9.983 m draught.
Machinery: 7-cylinder 2 S.C.S.A. Sulzer oil engine of 14,000 b.h.p. by Mitsubishi Heavy Industries Ltd., Kobe. Service speed 17.5 knots.
Container capacity: 668 TEU.

TALISMAN

15.7.1977: Launched by Nippon Kokan K.K., Tsu (Yard No. 52). *20.10.1977:* Completed. Price paid 97,000,000.00 kr. *1981:* Renamed BARBER TALISMAN. *18.10.1983:* Sold to Saudi Livestock Transport & Trading Co., Saudi Arabia and renamed MAWASHI TABUK. *31.12.1984:* Arrived at Ulsan to be converted into a livestock carrier, tonnages then becoming 18,813 gross, 14,463 net, 23,438 deadweight. Still in service.

TOURCOING in ScanCarriers livery   *M. R. Dippy*

329. TOURCOING (III) (1978-   ) Ro-Ro Vessel
Tonnages: 22,434 gross, 12,220 net, 33,719 deadweight.
Dimensions: 210.01 (228.51 o.a.) x 32.26 x 20.22 m. 11.170 m draught.
Machinery: 9-cylinder 2.S.C.S.A. Sulzer oil engine of 30,150 b.h.p. by
Mitsubishi Heavy Industries Ltd., Kobe. Service speed 19.5 knots.
Container capacity: 1,707 TEU. Quarter stern door and ramp.

TOURCOING, 15.1.1991 *J. Y. Freeman*

14.5.1978: Launched by Mitsubishi Heavy Industries Ltd., Nagasaki (Yard No. 1832). *4.10.1978:* Completed. Price paid 132,000,000.00 kr. *3.2.1989:* Purchased by BHT Tourcoing Shipping Inc., Panama. *31.7.1989:* Owners became Wilhelmsen Lines A/S. Still in the service of Wilhelmsen Lines A/S.

BARBER TOBA

330. BARBER TOBA / TOBA (1979-   ) Ro-Ro Vessel
Tonnages: 22,008 gross, 11,867 net, 34,310 deadweight.
Dimensions: 210.01 (228.51 o.a.) x 32.31 x 20.22 m. 10.829 m draught.
Machinery: 9-cylinder 2 S.C.S.A. Sulzer oil engine of 30,150 b.h.p. by the shipbuilders. Service speed 19.5 knots.
Container capacity: 1,806 TEU. Quarter stern door and ramp.
19.9.1978: Launched by Mitsubishi Heavy Industries Ltd., Kobe (Yard No. 1094). *30.1.1979:* Completed. Price paid 152,500,000.00 kr. Still in the service of Wilhelmsen Lines A/S.

TOBA, 16.7.1990 *J. Y. Freeman*

BARBER TAIF

331. BARBER TAIF (1979-1986) Ro-Ro Vessel

Tonnages: 21,976 gross, 12,006 net, 31,930 deadweight.
Dimensions: 212.02 (228.51 o.a.) x 32.26 x 20.20 m. 10.802 m draught.
Machinery: 9-cylinder 2 S.C.S.A. Burmeister & Wain oil engine of 30,700 b.h.p.
by Nylands Verksted A/S, Oslo. Service speed 21 knots.
Container capacity: 1,774 TEU. Quarter stern door and ramp.
20.9.1978: Launched by Tangen Verft A/S, Kragero (Yard No. 785). *1.6.1979:*
Completed. Price paid 151,700,000.00 kr. *25.11.1986:* Sold to the United
States Department of Transportation for service with the Ready Reserve Force
of the U.S. Reserve Fleet. *19.6.1986:* Arrived at Hampton Roads for transfer
and later renamed CAPE HUDSON. Still in service.

BARBER TØNSBERG

332. BARBER TØNSBERG (1979-1986) Ro-Ro Vessel

Tonnages: 22,070 gross, 12,090 net, 31,800 deadweight.
Dimensions: 210.01 (228.51 o.a.) x 32.31 x 20.20 m. 10.823 m draught.
Machinery: 9-cylinder 2.S.C.S.A. Burmeister & Wain oil engine of 30,700 b.h.p.
by Nylands Verksted A/S, Oslo. Service speed 21 knots.
Container capacity: 1,772 TEU. Quarter stern door and ramp.
31.1.1979: Launched by Kaldnes Mekaniske Verksted A/S, Tønsberg (Yard No.
212). *4.7.1979:* Completed. Price paid 152,200,000.00 kr. *12.12.1986:* Sold
to the United States Department of Transportation for service with the Ready
Reserve Force of the U.S. Reserve Fleet and renamed CAPE HORN. Still in
service.

TENDER COMET

333. TENDER COMET (1979-1986) Diving Support Vessel

Tonnages: 1,728 gross, 695 net, 2,550 deadweight.
Dimensions: 76.23 (80.78 o.a.) x 18.01 x 7.35 m. 4.031 m draught.
Machinery: Two 6-cylinder 4 S.C.S.A. oil engines totalling 8,000 b.h.p. by MaK Maschinenbau G.m.b.H., Kiel driving twin controllable pitch propellers. Service speed 13.75 knots.

25.4.1979: Launched by Ulstein Hatlo A/S, Ulsteinvik (Yard No. 161) as a Multi-Purpose Supply Ship. *11.7.1979:* Completed as a Diving Support Vessel. Price paid 22,000,000.00 kr. *3.11.1986:* Sold to K/S Far Venture A/S (Sverre Farstad & Co., managers), Aalesund and renamed FAR COMET. *1988:* Sold to Alpha Marine Services Inc., Bahamas and renamed AMY CHOUEST. *1989:* Transferred to United States registry. *1993:* Reverted to Bahamas registry. Later in *1993:* Transferred to Vanuatu registry and renamed OCEAN EXPLORER. Still in service.

TENDER CHAMPION

Ken Turrell

334. TENDER CHAMPION (1979-1985) Special Pipe Carrier

Tonnages: 1,370 gross, 631 net, 2,571 deadweight.
Dimensions: 76.21 (81,08 o.a.) x 18.04 x 7.12 m 4,323m draught.

248

Machinery: Two 6-cylinder 4 S.C.S.A. oil engines by MaK Maschinenbau G.m.b.H., Kiel, totalling 4,800 b.h.p. driving twin controllable pitch propellers. Service speed 14 knots.
28.9.1979: Launched by Ulstein Hatlo A/S, Ulsteinvik (Yard No. 164). *5.11.1979:* Completed. Price paid 32,500,000.00 kr. *11.2.1985:* Sold to BP Shipping Ltd., registered in the ownership of Baltersan Offshore Ltd., Aberdeen and renamed BALBLAIR. *1993:* Sold, with the owning company, to GulfMark group, and registered in the name of Gulf Offshore North Sea Ltd., Aberdeen. Still in service.

TENDER CAPTAIN   *W. J. Harvey*

335. TENDER CAPTAIN (II) (1979-1985) Special Pipe Carrier, later Stand-by Safety Vessel
Tonnages: *1979 to 1981:* 1,375 gross, 631 net, 2,571 deadweight. *1981-on:* 1,757 gross, 877 net, 2,500 deadweight.
Dimensions: 76.21 (81.08 o.a.) x 18.04 x 7.12 m. 4.323 m draught.
Machinery: Two 6-cylinder 4 S.C.S.A. oil engines by MaK Maschinenbau G.m.b.H., Kiel, totalling 4,800 b.h.p. driving twin controllable propellers. Service speed 14 knots.
17.11.1979: Launched by Ulstein Hatlo A/S, Ulsteinvik (Yard No. 165). *13.12.1979:* Completed. Price paid 32,500,000.00 kr. *1981:* Converted by Tyne Shiprepair, South Shields into a Stand-by Safety Vessel. *19.12.1985:* Sold to Bukser og Bjergningsselskapet A/S (Wilhelmsen Offshore A/S, managers). *3.11.1986:* Sold to K/S Far Venture A/S (Sverre Farstad & Co., managers), Aalesund and renamed FAR CAPTAIN. *29.6.1988:* Transferred to Far Shipping A/S (same managers), Aalesund. *22.6.1989:* Sold to K/S District Supply III (Austevoll Management A/S, managers), Bergen and renamed SKANDI CAPTAIN. *4.1990:* Sold to K/S Brovig DOF Pipe Carriers (Brovig Offshore A/S, managers), Farsund. Still in service.

336. TIJUCA (III) (1980-1980)
Tonnages: 5,854 gross, 2,857 net, 7,651 deadweight.
Dimensions: 130.89 (142.86 o.a.) x 18.60 x 8.46 m. 7.830 m draught.
Machinery: 8-cylinder 2 S.C.S.A. Burmeister & Wain oil engine of 8,700 b.h.p. by the shipbuilders. Service speed 17 knots.
28.2.1963: Launched by Helsingor Skibsvaerft og Maskinbyggeri, Helsingor (Yard No. 365) as NORMA for A/S J. Ludwig Mowinckel's Rederi, Bergen. *28.6.1963:* Completed. *20.3.1980:* Purchased by Wilh. Wilhelmsen and

TIJUCA leaving Hamburg, 3.10.1980

Joachim Pein

renamed TIJUCA. Price paid 12,888,670.00 kr. *18.12.1980:* Sold to Montemar S.A. Comercial y Maritima, Uruguay and renamed LUCERO DEL MAR. *2.2.1987:* Arrived at Porto Alegre to be broken up by Estaleiro So S.A. *23.2.1987:* Demolition commenced.

TREASURE SUPPORTER alongside Amoco Valhalla A Production Platform

250

337. TREASURE SUPPORTER (1980-1986) Semi-Submersible Accommodation Vessel
Operating displacement 20,600 tonnes.
Dimensions: 93.80 x 63.50 m. Operating draught 18.30 m. Height of main deck above keel 33.8 m.
Diesel generator sets: Five x 2,550 h.p. Nohab. Propulsion: Four 3,260 h.p. azimuth thrusters. Transit speed 8 knots.
Maximum water depth capability 200 m.
Operating deck load capability 945 tonnes. Storage area: 1,220 m at 0.5-2.0 tonnes per sq.m. Workshop area 200 sq.m.
Accommodation: 600 beds.
Cranes: One 100 tonnes capacity with 61 m boom, one 40 tonnes capacity with 47 m boom.
Heliport: Helideck for Boeing Chinook 234.
Gangway: One telescopic gangway, hydraulically operated, with maximum length of 32m.
1980: Completed by Götaverken Arendal A/B, Gothenburg (Yard No. 912), to Friede and Goldman Pacesetter design, for Consafe Offshore A/B (subsequently Safe Offshore A/B), Sweden, and *9.6.1980* bareboat chartered by Wilh. Wilhelmsen for a period of eight years. *3.1986:* Re-delivered to Safe Offshore A/B and renamed SAFE SUPPORTER. *1990:* Owners became Safe Rig A/B (Safe Service A/B, managers), Sweden. Still in service.

TENDER TROUT

338. TENDER TROUT (II) (1980-1990) Anchor Handling Tug / Supply Ship
Tonnages: 1,116 gross, 406 net, 2,015 deadweight.
Dimensions: 59.42 (67.72 o.a.) x 14.56 x 6.91 m. 5.950 m draught.
Machinery: Four 12-cylinder 4 S.C.S.A. Normo oil engines totalling 10,560 b.h.p. by A/S Bergens Mekaniske Verksteder, Bergen driving twin controllable pitch propellers. Service speed 15.5 knots.
13.8.1980: Launched by Ulstein Hatlo A/S, Ulsteinvik (Yard No. 167). *26.9.1980:* Completed. Price paid 41,500,000.00 kr. *28.6.1990:* Sold to Far Shipping A/S (Sverre Farstad & Co. A/S, managers), Aalesund and renamed FAR TROUT. *1993:* Transferred to Farstad Shipping A/S, Aalesund. Still in service.

TENDER TURBOT

339. TENDER TURBOT (II) (1980-1990) Anchor Handling Tug / Supply Ship
Tonnages: 1,116 gross, 406 net, 2,015 deadweight.
Dimensions: 59.42 (67.72 o.a.) x 14.56 x 6.91 m. 5.950 m draught.
Machinery: Four 12-cylinder 4 S.C.S.A. Normo oil engines totalling 10,560
b.h.p. by A/S Bergens Mekaniske Verksteder, Bergen driving twin controllable
pitch propellers. Service speed 15.5 knots.
29.7.1980: Launched by Ulstein Hatlo A/S, Ulsteinvik (Yard No. 168).
3.10.1980: Completed. Price paid 41,500,000.00 kr. *28.6.1990:* Sold to Far
Shipping A/S (Sverre Farstad & Co. A/S, managers), Aalesund and renamed
FAR TURBOT. *1993:* Transferred to Far Shipping A/S, Aalesund. Still in service.

WILLINE TOYO

340. WILLINE TOYO (1981-1986) Container Ship

Tonnages: 17,631 gross, 10,257 net, 26,190 deadweight.
Dimensions: 167.65 (175.27 o.a.) x 26.60 x 13.72 m. 9.864 m draught.
Machinery: 7-cylinder 2 S.C.S.A. Sulzer oil engine of 11,380 b.h.p. by Barclay, Curle & Co. Ltd., Glasgow. Service speed 15.25 knots.
Container capacity: 1,000 TEU.
20.11.1968: Launched by Upper Clyde Shipbuilders Ltd. (Scotstoun Division), Scotstoun (Yard No. 513) as the bulk carrier CONON FOREST for Cottesbrooke Shipping Company (J. & J. Denholm (Management) Ltd., managers), Glasgow. *18.3.1969:* Completed. *1969:* Sold to J. Macdonald-Buchanan and others (same managers), Glasgow. *1972:* Managers re-styled Denholm Ship Management Ltd. *1977:* Sold to Scotstoun Shipping Co. Ltd. (same managers), Glasgow and converted into a container ship. *1980:* Renamed HAVRAIS. *1980:* Renamed WILLINE TOYO. *17.7.1981:* Purchased by Arctic Shipping Singapore (Pte.) Ltd., Singapore (Barber Ship Management Ltd., later Barber Ship Management Singapore (Pte.) Ltd., managers). *1986:* Sold for scrapping to China National Metals & Minerals Import & Export Corporation. *28.4.1986:* Arrived at Huangpu to be broken up.

TREASURE SWAN

341. TREASURE SWAN (1981-1987) Semi-Submersible Oil Drilling Rig

1978-1981: Support Platform, *1981-on:* Semi-Submersible Oil Drilling Rig.
Details as a Drilling Rig:
Operating displacement 20,670 tonnes.

Dimensions: 103.23 x 67.36 m. Operating draught 21.3 m. Height of main deck above keel 36.6 m.
Diesel generator sets: Four x 2,200 h.p. Bergen. Propulsion: Two 3,400 h.p. Kort nozzles. Transit speed 7 knots.
Maximum water depth capability 300m.
Drilling depth to 7,620 m. BOP Stack: 18¾", 10,000 psi. Riser: 21" with buoyancy. Tensioner: 6 x 80,000 lbs.
Operating deck load capacity 2,550 tonnes.
Accommodation: 86 persons.
5.1978: Completed by Rauma-Repola Oy, Mantyluoto (Yard No. 8) to Aker H-3 design (modified) as the Support Platform SEAWAY SWAN for K/S Seaway Offshore Work Platform A/S (Stolt-Nielsen Rederi A/S, managers), Haugesund. *31.10.1981:* Purchased by Wilh. Wilhelmsen, initially with a 25% interest which increased to 40% during the period of the charter, and renamed TREASURE SWAN. Price paid 215,246,000.00 kr. Later in *1981* converted by Framnæs Mekaniske Værksted, Sandefjord into a Semi-Submersible Oil Drilling Rig with sponsons on the aft columns. *5.1987:* Sold to Perforadora Mexico S.A., Mexico, renamed MEXICO and registered in Panama. Still in service.

TENDER BEHANZIN

342. TENDER BEHANZIN (1981-1988) Anchor Handling Tug / Supply Ship
Tonnages: 497 gross, 166 net, 981 deadweight.
Dimensions: 46.21 (52.79 o.a.) x 13.01 x 6.76 m. 4.519 m draught.
Machinery: Two 12-cylinder 4 S.C.S.A. Normo oil engines totalling 5,280 b.h.p. by A/S Bergens Mekaniske Verksteder, Bergen driving twin controllable pitch propellers. Service speed 14.5 knots.
9.1981: Launched by Langsten Slip & Batbyggeri A/S, Tomra i Romsdal (Yard No. 96), hull sections having been constructed by four other Norwegian shipbuilding yards. *15.12.1981:* Completed. Price paid 38,000,000.00 kr. *30.6.1988:* Sold to Li-Ship IV Inc., Panama. *1990:* Sold to The Great Eastern Shipping Co. Ltd., India and renamed MALAVIYA SIX. Still in service.

343. TENDER BANFF (1982-1987) Anchor Handling Tug / Supply Ship
Tonnages: 399 gross, 128 net, 900 deadweight.
Dimensions: 51.69 (53.29 o.a.) x 11.59 x 4.88 m. 4.180 m draught.
Machinery: Two 16-cylinder 2 S.C.S.A. oil engines totalling 4,000 b.h.p. by
General Motors Corporation Electro-Motive Division, La Grange driving twin
controllable pitch propellers. Service speed 12 knots.
18.8.1981: Launched by Mangone Swiftships Inc., Houston, Texas (Yard No.
131) for A/S Tudor, Tønsberg. *21.1.1982:* Completed for Tudor France A/S,
Panama. Price paid $5,500,000. *26.6.1987:* Sold to Crystal Star Inc., United
States of America, converted into a stern trawling fish factory ship of 1,389
gross with a length of 72.01 m. o.a. and renamed CRYSTAL CLIPPER. *1991:*
Sold to American Pacific Fisheries, United States of America and renamed
PACIFIC EXPLORER. *1993:* Sold to Pacific Explorer Ltd Partnership, United
States of America. Still in service.

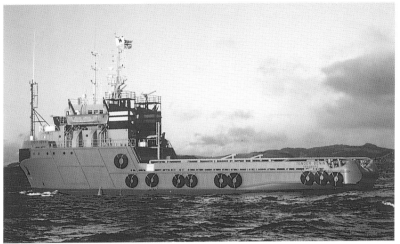

TENDER BENIN

344. TENDER BENIN (1982-1988) Anchor Handling Tug / Supply Ship
Tonnages: 497 gross, 166 net, 980 deadweight.
Dimensions: 47.25 (52.79 o.a.) x 13.01 x 6.76 m. 4.519 m draught.
Machinery: Two 12-cylinder 4 S.C.S.A. Normo oil engines totalling 5,280 b.h.p.
by A/S Bergens Mekaniske Verksteder, Bergen driving twin controllable pitch
propellers. Service speed 14.5 knots.
Passenger capacity: 12.
22.12.1981: Launched by Sigbjorn Iversen Mekaniske Verksted-Skipsbyggeri,
Flekkefjord (Yard No. 61). *29.1.1982:* Completed. Price paid: 38,0000,000.00
kr. *30.6.1988:* Sold to Li-Ship IV Inc., Panama. *1990:* Sold to The Great
Eastern Shipping Co., Ltd., India and renamed MALAVIYA FIVE. Still in service.

345. TROLL VIKING (1982-1986) Open Type Bulk Carrier
Tonnages: 24,102 gross, 18,188 net, 41,270 deadweight.
Dimensions: 183.32 (192.01 o.a.) x 29.67 x 16.77 m. 12.031 m draught.
Machinery: 7-cylinder 2 S.C.S.A. oil engine of 13,100 b.h.p. by A/S Burmeister
& Wain's Motor-og Maskinfabrik af 1971, Copenhagen. Service speed 14.5
knots.
9.1968: Ordered from A/S Burmeister & Wain's Maskin-og Skibsbyggeri,
Copenhagen as Yard No. 840 by Olsen Daughter A/S, Oslo. The contract

TROLL VIKING

was subsequently sold and she was launched *9.2.1971* as ROLAND BREMEN for Hapag-Lloyd A.G., West Germany. *6.1971:* Completed. *1974:* Renamed MANNHEIM. *1976:* Sold to Kosmos Bulkschiffahrt G.m.b.H., West Germany. *11.3.1982:* Purchased by Troll Ltd (Wilh. Wilhelmsen, managers), Liberia and renamed TROLL VIKING. Price paid 11,825,000.00 kr. *12.9.1986:* Sold to Grindale Ltd (Palm Navigation Trust S.A., managers), Gibraltar and renamed CITY OF PIRAEUS. *1988:* Transferred to Honduran registry and renamed MERIDIAN. *1990:* Sold to Equinox Shipping Co. Ltd., Malta and renamed AL TAIF. *13.5.1991:* Laid up at Ravenna and in *7.1993* reported to be for sale by auction by order of the local court.

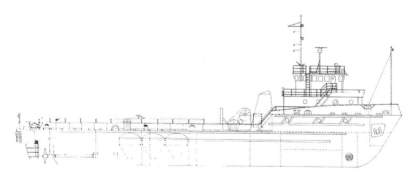

346. TENDER BALI (1982-1987) Anchor Handling Tug / Supply Ship
Tonnages: 399 gross, 128 net, 900 deadweight.
Dimensions: 51.69 (56.32 o.a.) x 11.59 x 4.88 m. 4.187 m draught.
Machinery: Two 16-cylinder 2 S.C.S.A. oil engines totalling 4,000 b.h.p. by General Motors Corporation Electro-Motive Division, La Grange driving twin controllable pitch propellers. Service speed 12 knots.
25.9.1981: Launched by Mangone Swiftships Inc., Houston, Texas (Yard No. 132). *17.3.1982:* Completed for A/S Tudor, Tønsberg. Price paid $5,500.000.

256

1982: Transferred to Tudor France A/S and to Panamanian registry. *26.6.1987:* Sold to Crystal Star Inc., United States of America, converted into a stern trawling fish factory ship of 1,389 gross with a length of 72.01 m. o.a. and renamed CRYSTAL VIKING. *1991:* Sold to American Pacific Fisheries, United States of America and renamed PACIFIC SCOUT. Still in service.

TROLL MAPLE

Fotoflite incorporating Skyfotos

347. TROLL MAPLE (1982-1986) Open Type Bulk Carrier

Tonnages: 24,102 gross, 18,188 net, 41,270 deadweight.
Dimensions: 183.32 (192.01 o.a.) x 29.67 x 16.77 m. 12.031 m draught.
Machinery: 7-cylinder 2 S.C.S.A. oil engine of 13,100 b.h.p. by the shipbuilders.
Service speed 14.5 knots.
9.1968: Ordered from A/S Burmeister & Wain's Maskin-og Skibsbyggeri, Copenhagen as Yard No. 833 by Olsen Daughter A/S, Oslo. *3.1970:* Contract sold to Unterweser Reederei G.m.b.H., West Germany and *31.7.1970* launched for them as KELKHEIM. *31.12.1970:* Completed as ROLAND KELKHEIM, having been renamed while fitting out. *1971:* Renamed KELKHEIM. *1975:* Sold to Hapag-Lloyd Lloyd A.G. (Unterweser Frachtschiffahrts G.m.b.H. & Co. K.G., managers), West Germany. *1976:* Managers became Kosmos Bulkschiffahrts G.m.b.H. *24.3.1982:* Purchased by Troll Ltd. (Wilh. Wilhelmsen, managers), Liberia and renamed TROLL MAPLE. Price paid 11,825,000.00 kr. *12.9.1986:* Sold to Tinsley Ltd. (Palm Navigation Trust S.A., managers), Gibraltar and renamed CITY OF SALONIKA. *1989:* Sold to Future Shipping Ltd., Malta and renamed AL TALUDI. *1990:* Renamed FLYING FALCON. *6.6.1992:* Went aground off the coast of Somalia in a position 10.58 N, 51.10 E during a voyage from Bangkok to Lisbon with a cargo of tapioca and rice and abandoned.

257

TREASURE SCOUT

348. TREASURE SCOUT (1982-1989) Semi-Submersible Oil Drilling Rig
Operating displacement 25,080 tonnes.
Dimensions: 79.25 x 59.50. Operating draught 19.8 m. Height of main deck above keel 33.5 m.
Diesel generator sets: Four 2,650 h.p. Nohab. Propulsion: Two 3,260 h.p. azimuth thrusters. Transit speed 7 knots.
Maximum water depth capability 460 m.
Drilling depth to 7,620 m. BOP Stack: $18\frac{3}{4}$", 15,000 psi. Riser: 21" with buoyancy. Tensioner: 6 x 80,000 lbs.
Operating deck load capacity 2,800 tonnes.
Accommodation: 92 persons.
1.4.1982: Completed by Götaverken Arendal A/B, Gothenburg (Yard No. 923) to Friede & Goldman Enhanced Pacesetter design. Price paid 591,600,000.00 kr. *2.5.1989:* Sold to China National Offshore Oil Corporation, China and renamed NAN HAI VI. Still in service.

TENDER BAY

349. TENDER BAY / TENDER GENOVA (1982-1992) Anchor Handling Tug / Supply Ship
Tonnages: *1982-1984:* 399 gross, 169 net, 900 deadweight. *1984-on:* 497 gross, 221 net, 900 deadweight.

258

Dimensions: *1982-1984:* 50.32 (56.42 o.a.) x 11.59 x 4.91 m. 3,963 m draught. *1984-on:* 51.03 (55.89 o.a.) x 11.59 x 4.88 m. 4.174 m draught.
Machinery: Two 16-cylinder 2 S.C.S.A. oil engines totalling 4,000 b.h.p. by General Motors Corporation Electro-Motive Division, La Grange driving twin controllable pitch propellers. Service speed 12 knots.
22.4.1982: Launched by Mangone Swiftships Inc., Houston, Texas (Yard No. 134) as TENDER BAY for A/S Tudor, Tønsberg. *3.8.1982:* Completed for Tudor France A/S, Panama. Price paid $6,200,000. *1984:* Transferred to Maritankers S.r.l., Italy (Wilhelmsen Offshore Services, managers) and renamed TENDER GENOVA. *1985:* Bareboat chartered to Zapata Marine Service Italia S.p.A., Italy (Wilhelmsen Offshore Services, managers). *1989:* Bareboat chartered to Castalia S.p.A., Italy and renamed CASTALIA VERDE. *29.4.1992:* Sold to Basileasing S.p.A., Italy. Still in service.

TENDER TARPON

350. TENDER TARPON (II) (1982-1986) Anchor Handling Tug / Supply Ship
Tonnages: 1,443 gross, 392 net, 1,400 deadweight.
Dimensions: 63.02 (72.01 o.a.) x 15.02 x 7.01 m. 4.909 m draught.
Four 12-cylinder 4 S.C.S.A. oil engines of 10,560 b.h.p. by Normo Gruppen A/S, Bergen driving twin controllable pitch propellers. Service speed 15.5 knots.
29.4.1982: Launched by Amels Holland B.V., Makkum (Yard No. 378). *6.8.1982:* Completed. Price paid 58,000,000.00 kr. *3.11.1986:* Sold to K/S Far Venture A/S (Sverre Farstad & Co., managers), Aalesund and renamed FAR TARPON. *29.6.1988:* Transferred to Far Shipping A/S (same managers), Aalesund. *1989:* Sold to Anapis Shipping Co. Ltd., Cyprus and renamed RED TERN. Still in service.

259

TUAREG as **NERVA**, laid up at Onarheim 28.8.1982, two days before her purchase by W.W.   *Joachim Pein*

351. TUAREG (III) (1982-1982) Tanker
Tonnages: 109,637 gross, 89,476 net, 215,551 deadweight.
Dimensions: 312.23 (327.72 o.a.) x 46.46 x 26.04 m. 20.422 m draught.
Machinery: Two steam turbines of GEC design totalling 30,400 s.h.p. by Kvaerner Brug, Oslo. Service speed 16 knots.
9.12.1970: Completed by Stord Verft A/S, Stord (Yard No. 667) as NERVA for R/A Diocletian (Hilmar Reksten, manager), Bergen. The hull had been constructed, in three sections, by Tangen Verft A/S, Kragero, Bergens Mekaniske Verksteder A/S, Bergen, and Stord Verft A/S, Stord (all companies in the Aker Group) and joined together by Stord Verft, whose section was launched *28.9.1970*. *1976:* Transferred to Rederi-A/S Trajan (Hilmar Reksten, manager), Bergen. *11.4.1976:* Laid up near Bergen. Following the collapse of the Reksten Group, taken over by Akers Mekaniske Verksted as creditor. *30.8.1982:* Purchased by Wilh. Wilhelmsen. Price paid 12,296,700.00 kr. Sailed in ballast from Bergen and *20.12.1982* arrived at Kaohsiung to be scrapped by First Copper & Iron Industrial Co. Ltd. *9.1.1983:* Demolition commenced.

352. TENDER BOUNTY / TENDER GELA (1982-1992) Tug / Supply Ship
Tonnages: *1982-1984:* 399 gross, 128 net, 900 deadweight. *1984-on:* 498 gross, 222 net, 900 deadweight.
Dimensions: *1982-1984:* 50.32 (56.42 o.a.) x 11.59 x 4.91 m. 3.963 m draught. *1984-on:* 51.03 (55.89 o.a.) x 11.59 x 4.88 m. 4.174 m draught.
Machinery: Two 16-cylinder 2 S.C.S.A. oil engines totalling 4,000 b.h.p. by General Motors Corporation Electro-Motive Division, La Grange driving twin controllable pitch propellers. Service speed 12 knots.
5.6.1982: Launched by Mangone Swiftships Inc, Houston, Texas (Yard No. 135) as TENDER BOUNTY for Tudor France A/S, Panama. *29.9.1982:* Completed. Price paid $6,200,000 *1984:* Transferred to Maritankers S.r.l.,

TENDER GELA, left, with **ADARA** and **TENDER GENOVA**, right, lying   *Michael Cassar*
at Messina in 8.1987

Italy (Wilhelmsen Offshore Services, managers) and renamed TENDER GELA. *1985:* Bareboat chartered to Zapata Marine Service Italia S.p.A., Italy (Wilhelmsen Offshore Services, managers). *1989:* Bareboat chartered to Castalia S.p.A., Italy and renamed CASTALIA AZZURRA. *29.4.1992:* Sold to Basileasing S.p.A., Italy. Still in service.

TREASURE SAGA

353. TREASURE SAGA (1983-1989) Semi-Submersible Oil Drilling Rig
Operating displacement 25,790 tonnes.
Dimensions: 80.60 x 73.10 m. Operating draught 20.5 m. Height of main deck above keel 41 m.

Diesel generator sets: Four 3,060 h.p. Nohab. Propulsion: Two 3,260 h.p. azimuth thrusters. Transit speed 6.5 knots.
Maximum water depth capability 460 m.
Drilling depth to 7,620 m. BOP Stack 18¾" 15,000 psi.
Riser: 21" with buoyancy. Tensioner: 8 x 80,000 lbs.
Operating deck load capacity 3,950 tonnes.
Accommodation: 100 persons.
28.1.1983: Completed by Götaverken Arendal A/B, Gothenburg (Yard No. 926) to GVA 4000 design. Price paid 839,300,000.00 kr. *1.6.1989:* Sold to Wilrig A/S, Oslo. Still in service.

TENDER TRACER

354. TENDER TRACER (1983-1986) Supply Ship
Tonnages: 1,472 gross, 461 net, 1,400 deadweight.
Dimensions: 63.02 (72.07 o.a.) x 15.02 x 7.01 m. 4.901 m draught.
Machinery: Four 12-cylinder 4 S.C.S.A. oil engines totalling 10,560 b.h.p. by Normo Gruppen A/S, Bergen, driving twin controllable pitch propellers. Service speed 15.5 knots.
11.11.1982: Bow and stern sections launched by Scheepswerf ''Friesland'' B.V., Lemmer for Amels Holland B.V., Makkum, who built the centre section and *28.1.1983* completed the ship (Yard No. 379) for Stanship Ltd., Aberdeen. Price paid 62,000,000.00 kr. *3.11.1986:* Sold to K/S Far Venture A/S (Sverre Farstad & Co., managers), Aalesund and renamed FAR TRACER. *1988:* Sold to Far Shipping A/S, Norway (NIS) (Australian Offshore Services Pty. Ltd., managers). *17.7.1989:* Sold to P & O Australia Ltd. (same managers), Australia and renamed LADY ELAINE. *1991:* Sold to The United Salvage Pty. Ltd. (same managers), Australia. *1991:* Sold to P & O Maritime Services Pty. Ltd. (same managers), Australia. Still in service.

355. TENDER BORDEAUX (1983-1987) Anchor Handling Tug / Supply Ship
Tonnages: 851 gross, 335 net, 1,000 deadweight.
Dimensions: 47.86 (53.57 o.a.) x 11.82 x 5.52 m. 4.552 m draught.
Machinery: Two 7-cylinder 2 S.C.S.A. oil engines totalling 4,000 b.h.p. by A/S Wichmann, Rubbestadneset, driving twin controllable pitch propellers. Service speed 12.5 knots.
1.2.1983: Launched by Ateliers et Chantiers du Sud-Ouest, Bordeaux (Yard

No. 1198) for A/S Tudor France II, Panama. *29.4.1983:* Completed. Price paid 36,000,000.00 kr. *18.3.1987:* Sold to Offshore de Remorquage Inc., Panama and renamed BORDEAUX. *1988:* Sold to O.I.L. Ltd., Panama and renamed OIL PRODUCER. *1991:* Sold to Eurofish Services Ltd. (Feronia International Shipping, managers), St. Vincent and renamed ANGEL FISH. *1993:* Sold to Compagnie Nationale de Navigation (same managers), Antarctic Territory (France). Still in service.

NOSAC TAKAYAMA

356. TAKAYAMA / NOSAC TAKAYAMA (1983-   ) Car Carrier
Tonnages: 9,958 gross, 6,033 net, 10,599 deadweight.
Dimensions: 157.08 (165.00 o.a.) x 27.64 x 11.56 m. 7.800 m draught.
Machinery: 12-cylinder 4 S.C.S.A. M.A.N. oil engine of 12,000 b.h.p. by Kawasaki Heavy Industries Ltd., Kobe. Service speed 18 knots.
Capacity: 3,200 cars.
20.2.1983: Launched by Kurushima Dock Co. Ltd., Onishi (Yard No. 2240) for Wilfram Shipping Ltd., Liberia. *18.5.1983:* Completed. Price paid 21,823,000.00 kr. *2.9.1986:* Renamed NOSAC TAKAYAMA. Still in Nosac service.

357. TORO HORTEN / TORO (III) / TORONTO (III) (1983-1990) Tanker
Tonnages: 30,050 gross, 17,624 net, 55,337 deadweight.
Dimensions: 198.69 (207.42 o.a.) x 32.26 x 16.77 m. 16.750 m draught.
Machinery: 6-cylinder 2 S.C.S.A. Sulzer oil engine of 13,800 b.h.p. by A/S Horten Verft, Horten. Service speed 15.25 knots.
19.11.1982: After section launched by A/S Horten Verft, Horten (Yard No. 205). Forward section launched by Tangen Verft A/S, Kragero. The two sections were joined and completed *30.6.1983* for K/S Toro Horten A/S (a subsidiary of Horten Verft A/S, in which Wilh. Wilhelmsen had a 15% interest). Price paid 202,900,000.00 kr. *20.12.1985:* Transferred to K/S Toro A/S and renamed TORO. *9.12.1986:* Transferred to Toronto Ltd., Bermuda, in which

TORO HORTEN

Wilh. Wilhelmsen had a 20% interest, and renamed TORONTO. *1.3.1989:* Transferred to Toronto K/S, Tønsberg, in which Wilh. Wilhelmsen had a 20% interest. *2.3.1990:* Sold to Tornado Shipping Pte. Ltd., Singapore and renamed ADVANCE. Still in service.

THALATTA leaving Bremen 14.7.1983, the day after her purchase   *Torsten Andreas*

358. THALATTA (III) / TOMAR (II) (1983-1989) Bulk Carrier
Tonnages: 65,885 gross, 40,419 net, 120,143 deadweight.
Dimensions: 247.00 (261.02 o.a.) x 40.67 x 22.51 m. 16.533 m draught.
Machinery: 9-cylinder 2 S.C.S.A. Sulzer oil engine of 26,100 b.h.p. by

Mitsubishi Heavy Industries Ltd., Kobe. Service speed 15 knots.
15.12.1972: Launched by Mitsubishi Heavy Industries Ltd., Hiroshima (Yard No. 226) as ERSKINE BRIDGE for H. Clarkson & Co. Ltd. (Denholm Ship Management Ltd., managers), London. *23.3.1973:* Completed. *1974:* Sold to Silver Line Ltd., London. *1981:* Sold to Erskine Bridge Shipping Ltd. (Dene Shipping Co. Ltd., managers), London. *1983:* Sold to Yu Sing Shipping Co. Ltd. (Shipping Management S.A.M., managers), Hong Kong and renamed YU SING. *1983:* Sold to Silvermerlin Shipping Ltd., London. *13.7.1983:* Purchased by K/S A/S Wilh. Wilhelmsen Shippinginvest I and renamed THALATTA. Price paid 67,454,000.00 kr. *1.9.1986:* Transferred to Tolten Shipping Ltd, Hong Kong and renamed TOMAR. *13.12.1989:* Sold to Coastalglory Shipping Ltd., Cyprus and renamed PYTHIA. *1992:* Sold to Reward Shipping, Cyprus and renamed ORFEAS. Still in service.

359. TENDER BOURGOGNE (1983-1987) Anchor Handling Tug / Supply Ship
Tonnages: 750 gross, 219 net, 1,000 deadweight.
Dimensions: 47.86 (53.57 o.a.) x 11.82 x 5.52 m. 4.552 m draught.
Machinery: Two 7-cylinder 2 S.C.S.A. oil engines totalling 4,000 b.h.p. by A/S Wichmann, Rubbestadneset, driving twin controllable pitch propellers. Service speed 12.5 knots.
19.6.1983: Launched by Ateliers et Chantiers du Sud-Ouest, Bordeaux (Yard No. 1199) for A/S Tudor France II, Panama. *29.9.1983:* Completed. Price paid 36,000,000.00 kr. *18.3.1987:* Sold to O.I.L. Ltd., Panama and renamed BOURGOGNE. *1987:* Transferred to O.I.L. Marine Ltd., Panama and renamed OIL PROWLER. *1991:* Sold to Eurofish Services Ltd. (Feronia International Shipping, managers), St. Vincent and renamed VALIANT FISH. Still in service.

THEMIS, when named YOU'RE MY SUNSHINE, at Europoort, 18.6.1982. *Joachim Pein*
She is being assisted by the tug SCHOUWENBANK

360. THEMIS (IV) (1983-1986) Bulk Carrier
Tonnages: 64,076 gross, 46,240 net, 122,974 deadweight.
Dimensions: 258.00 (272.32 o.a.) x 39.07 x 22.31 m. 16.079 m draught.
Machinery: 8-cylinder 2 S.C.S.A. oil engine of 23,200 b.h.p. by Sulzer Brothers Ltd., Winterthur. Service speed 16 knots.
24.4.1976: Launched by Rheinstahl Nordseewerke G.m.b.H., Emden (Yard No. 440) as FERNSEA for Fearnley & Eger A/S, Oslo. *3.9.1976:* Completed, *1978:* Transferred to P/R M/S Fernsea (Falcon Shipping A/S, managers), *1979:* Transferred to Skips A/S Kim and others (Fearnley & Eger A/S, managers). *1981:* Sold to Rising Sun Bulk Carriers Corporation (Kokusai Kisen K.K., managers), Liberia and renamed YOU'RE MY SUNSHINE. *9.11.1983:* Purchased by K/S A/S Wilh. Wilhelmsen Shippinginvest II (Wilh. Wilhelmsen, managers) and renamed THEMIS. Price paid 79,681,500.00 kr. *11.10.1986:*

Sold to Glenanil Ltd (Anglo-Eastern Management Services Ltd., managers), Hong Kong and renamed STABOR. *1987:* Sold to Cartlidge Ltd. (Unique Shipping Agencies Ltd., managers), Hong Kong and renamed UNIQUE CARRIER II. *1988:* Renamed NAVIOS UNIQUE. *1991:* Sold to Ropalo Shipping Co. Ltd (Nafsiploia Maritime Corporation, managers), Cyprus and renamed NAVIOS PROTECTOR 2. Still in service.

THEBEN

361. THEBEN (II) (1983-1988) Tanker
Tonnages: 17,880 gross, 12,432 net, 31,600 deadweight.
Dimensions: 161.88 (170.72 o.a.) x 26.09 x 14.91 m. 11.329 m draught.
Machinery: 7-cylinder 2 S.C.S.A. Burmeister & Wain oil engine of 14,600 b.h.p. by the shipbuilders. Service speed 16 knots.
9.10.1976: Launched by Eriksbergs Mekaniska Verkstads A/B, Gothenburg (Yard No. 703) as INLAND for Angfartygs-A/B Tirfing (Axel Brostrom & Son, managers), Sweden. *11.1.1977:* Completed. *1979:* Owners became Brostroms Rederi A/B. *1979:* Transferred to Rederi-A/B Ejdern & Brostroms Rederi A/B (Brostroms Rederi A/B, managers). *1982:* Sold to Brostroms Rederi A/B and Rederi A/B Zenith (same managers), Sweden and renamed CROWN INLAND. *10.11.1983:* Purchased by Wilinvest Inc., Liberia (Wilh. Wilhelmsen, managers) and renamed THEBEN. Price paid 84,024,225.00 kr. *6.1.1988:* Sold to the Government of the People's Republic of China (Bureau of Maritime Transport—Guangzhou Branch) and renamed LIAN CHI. Still in service.

BARBER TAMPA arriving at Rotterdam, 17.6.1986   *Joachim Pein*

362. BARBER TAMPA / TAMPA (V) (1984-   ) Ro-Ro Vessel
Tonnages: 28,287 gross, 16,244 net, 44,014 deadweight.
Dimensions: 246.41 (262.01 o.a.) x 32.26 x 21.01 m. 11.730 draught.

Machinery: 8-cylinder 2 S.C.S.A. Burmeister & Wain oil engine of 36,600 b.h.p. by Hyundai Shipbuilding & Heavy Industries Co. Ltd., Ulsan. Service speed 21 knots.
Container capacity: 2,451 TEU. Quarter stern door and ramp.
10.10.1983: Launched by Hyundai Heavy Industries Co. Ltd., Ulsan (Yard No. 248). *10.2.1984:* Completed. Price paid 532,300,000.00 kr. *10.2.1989:* Renamed TAMPA. Still in the service of Wilh. Wilhelmsen Lines A/S.

TAMPA *J. Krayenbosch*

363. BARBER TEXAS / TEXAS (IV) (1984-   ) Ro-Ro Vessel
Tonnages: 28,287 gross, 16,244 net, 44,081 deadweight.
Dimensions: 246.41 (262.08 o.a.) x 32.31 x 21.01 m. 11.729 m draught.
Machinery: 8-cylinder 2 S.C.S.A. Burmeister & Wain oil engine of 36,600 b.h.p. by Hyundai Shipbuilding & Heavy Industries Ltd., Ulsan. Service speed 21 knots.
Container capacity: 2,451 TEU. Quarter stern door and ramp.
4.11.1983: Launched by Hyundai Heavy Industries Co. Ltd., Ulsan (Yard No. 249). *14.3.1984:* Completed. Price paid 511,800,000.00kr. *10.2.1989:* Renamed TEXAS. Still in the service of Wilh. Wilhelmsen Lines A/S.

BARBER TEXAS

BIG ORANGE XVIII

364. BIG ORANGE XVIII (1984-   ) Offshore Well-Stimulation Vessel
Tonnages: 3,719 gross, 1,115 net, 3,424 deadweight.
Dimensions: 67.72 (76.10 o.a.) x 18.01 x 7.52 m. 6.512 m draught.
Machinery: Three 18-cylinder 4 S.C.S.A. Normo oil engines totalling 13,695
b.h.p. by A/S Bergens Mekaniske Verksteder, Bergen, connected to electric
motors and two directional propellers. Service speed 13 knots.
15.5.1984: Launched by Ulstein Hatlo A/S, Ulsteinvik (Yard No. 190).
30.7.1984: Completed. Price paid 96,645,500.00 kr. Still in Wilhelmsen
Offshore service.

NOSAC TASCO   *J. Krayenbosch*

268

365. NOSAC TASCO (1985-1988) Car Carrier
Tonnages: 48,393 gross, 29,137 net, 22,067 deadweight.
Dimensions: 182.40 (195.03 o.a.) x 32.26 x 30.97 m. 11.058 m draught.
Machinery: 6-cylinder 2 S.C.S.A. Burmeister & Wain oil engine of 19,250 b.h.p.
by Hyundai Shipbuilding & Heavy Industries Ltd., Ulsan. Service speed 19
knots.
Capacity: 5,550 cars.
30.9.1984: Launched by Daewoo Shipbuilding & Heavy Machinery Ltd., Okpo,
Koje (Yard No. 4401). *7.2.1985:* Completed. Price paid 310,837,000.00 kr.
16.1.1987: Transferred to Panamanian registry. *30.12.1988:* Sold to K/S
Fernboat (Norwegian Ship Management A/S, managers), Oslo. *1989:* Sold
to Hafslund Transport A/S (Den norske Amerikalinje A/S, managers), Oslo.
1990: Renamed NOSAC EXPLORER. *1993:* Sold to K/S Benargus & Co. A/S
(same managers), Oslo. Still in service.

ROSA TUCANO leaving Santos, Brazil, 14.6.1989   *Torsten Andreas*

366. ROSA TUCANO (1985-1989) Ro-Ro Vessel
Tonnages: 32,951 gross, 9,885 net, 27,577 deadweight.
Dimensions: 170.10 (185.02 o.a.) x 32.31 x 20.76 m. 11.251 m draught.
Machinery: 10-cylinder 4 S.C.S.A. Pielstick oil engine of 15,120 b.h.p. by
Nippon Kokan K.K., Tsurumi Works, Yokohama. Service speed 16 knots.
Container capacity: 1,446 TEU. Quarter stern door and ramp.
7.12.1984: Launched by Nippon Kokan K.K., Tsu (Yard No. 94). *30.4.1985:*
Completed. Price paid 304,848,000.00 kr. *1.7.1989:* Sold to Rosa Tucano
A/S (Barber International A/S, managers), Oslo. *1993:* Sold to Strait
Navigation Ltd. (Hamburg—Sudamerikanische Dampfschifffahrts-
Gesellschaft Eggert und Amsinck, managers), Liberia and renamed
CALAPOGGIO. Still in service.

269

TOLUMA

367. TOLUMA (III) (1985-1989) Tanker
Tonnages: 43,363 gross, 27,649 net, 73,000 deadweight.
Dimensions: 220.2 (228.61 o.a.) x 32.26 x 18.75 m. 15.017 m draught.
Machinery: 4-cylinder 2 S.C.S.A. Burmeister & Wain oil engine of 12,772 b.h.p.
by the shipbuilders. Service speed 15.75 knots.
18.1.1985: Launched by Uddevallavarvet A/B, Uddevalla (Yard No. 331). *28.5.1985:*
Completed. Price paid 250,590,800.00 kr. *30.3.1987:* Transferred to Panamanian
registry. *15.2.1989:* Sold to Forever Navigation S.A. (Fuyo Kaiun Co. Ltd., managers),
Panama and renamed A.C.ATOM. *1993:* Renamed LOYALTY. Still in service.

368. POLAR PIONEER (1985-1994) Semi-Submersible Oil Drilling Rig
Operating displacement 46,440 tonnes.
Dimensions: 122.00 x 71.00 m Operating draught 23.0 m. Height of main
deck above keel: 41.65 m.
Diesel generator sets: Five 2,750 h.p. Bergen. Propulsion: Four 3,220 h.p.
azimuth thrusters. Transit speed 6 knots.
Maximum water depth capability 450 m.
Drilling depth to 6,500 m. BOP Stack $18\frac{3}{4}''$ 15,000 psi.
Riser: 21" with buoyancy. Tensioner: 8 x 100,000 lbs.
Operating deck load capacity 4,460 tonnes.
Accommodation: 100 persons.
Of a design developed by her owners, her structure is designed to withstand
winds of 55 m per second, and wave heights of 32 m. Her structural
components have an atmospheric design temperature of -20°. The derrick
and pipe racks are completely enclosed and pipe handling is fully mechanised
and remotely controlled throughout. There is a data gathering system for
centralized and distributed monitoring of all major functions via CRT-screens.
There are de-icing devices on the open deck and underneath the deck box.
14.10.1985: Completed by Hitachi Zosen, Ariake Works, Nagasu (Yard No.
1050) for Polar Frontier Drilling A/S, Tromsø, in which Wilh. Wilhelmsen had
a 47.5% interest. Price paid 976,000,000.00 kr. *31.1.1994:* WW interest taken
over by the other partner and delivered to Sonat Offshore Inc., Houston, U.S.A.
Still in Polar Frontier Drilling A/S service.

POLAR PIONEER

NOSAC TAKARA at the vehicle berth at Drammen

369. NOSAC TAKARA (1986-　) Vehicles Carrier
Tonnages: 48,547 gross, 14,565 net, 15,546 deadweight.
Dimensions: 180.02 (190.05 o.a.) x 32.29 x 13.75 m. 8.921 m draught.
Machinery: 7-cylinder 2 S.C.S.A. Sulzer oil engine of 10,669 b.h.p. by
Sumitomo Heavy Industries Ltd., Tamashima. Service speed 18 knots.
Capacity: 5,930 cars. Two midship side ramps and quarter stern door.
15.6.1986: Launched by Sumitomo Heavy Industries Ltd., Oppama Shipyard,
Yokosuka (Yard No. 1138) for Astral Carriers Ltd., Liberia. *19.9.1986:*
Completed and bareboat chartered to Wilh. Wilhelmsen for the Nosac service.
30.8.1989: Owners became Sirius Carriers Ltd., Liberia. Still in Nosac service.

TENDER FIGHTER displaying her fire-fighting capabilities   *Ulstein*

370. TENDER FIGHTER (1986-1991) Supply and Search & Rescue Ship
Tonnages: 2,075 gross, 622 net, 1,900 deadweight.
Dimensions: 59.67 (69.32 o.a.) x 15.51 x 7.32 m. 5.712 m draught.
Machinery: Two 12-cylinder 4 S.C.S.A. Normo oil engines totalling 5,990 b.h.p.
by BMV Maskin A/S, Bergen, driving twin controllable pitch propellers. Service
speed 14 knots.
18.8.1986: Launched by Trosvik Verksted A/S, Brevik (Yard No. 141).
8.12.1986: Completed by Ulstein Hatlo as Yard No. 206. Price paid
82,000,000.00 kr. *4.1990:* Transferred to K/S A/S Sassaby, Haugesund.
3.12.1991: Sold to K/S Eidesvik & Co. A/S (Eidesvik & Co. A/S, managers),
Bomlo, and renamed VIKING FIGHTER. Still in service.

DOCEFJORD

371. DOCEFJORD (1986-   ) Ore / Oil Carrier
Tonnages: 159,534 gross, 107,933 net, 305,675 deadweight.
Dimensions: 316.01 (332.01 o.a.) x 57.26 x 30.92 m. 23.188 m draught.
Machinery: 8-cylinder 2 S.C.S.A. Sulzer oil engine of 22,340 b.h.p. by the
shipbuilders. Service speed 13.5 knots.
18.12.1985: Launched by Ishikawajima do Brasil S.A., Rio de Janeiro (Yard
No. 145) for Wilsea Shipping Inc., Liberia (a 50/50 joint venture with
Docenave, Rio de Janeiro). *15.12.1986:* Completed. Price paid $65,640,000.
Still in Wilsea Shipping Inc. service.

NOSAC TAI SHAN

372. NOSAC TAI SHAN (1986-   ) Car Carrier
Tonnages: 48,676 gross, 14,603 net, 15,577 deadweight.
Dimensions: 180.02 (190.05 o.a.) x 32.29 x 13.75 m. 8.921 m draught.
Machinery: 7-cylinder 2 S.C.S.A. Sulzer oil engine of 11,850 b.h.p. by
Sumitomo Heavy Industries Ltd., Tamashima. Service speed 18 knots.
Capacity: 5,930 cars. One side midship ramp and quarter stern ramp.
11.10.1986: Launched by Sumitomo Heavy Industries Ltd., Oppama Shipyard,
Yokosuka (Yard No. 1139) for Austral Carriers Ltd., Liberia. *15.12.1986:*
Completed and bareboat chartered to Wilh. Wilhelmsen for the Nosac service.
Still in Nosac service.

NOSAC TANCRED   *J. Krayenbosch*

373. NOSAC TANCRED (1987-1988) Car Carrier
Tonnages: 48,676 gross, 14,603 net, 15,577 deadweight.
Dimensions: 180.02 (190.05 o.a.) x 32.29 x 13.75 m. 8.921 m draught.
Machinery: 7-cylinder 2 S.C.S.A. Sulzer oil engine of 11,849 b.h.p. by
Sumitomo Heavy Industries Ltd., Tamashima. Service speed 18 knots.
Capacity: 5,930 cars. Side and quarter stern ramp.
18.2.1987: Launched by Sumitomo Heavy Industries Ltd., Oppama Shipyard,
Yokosuka (Yard No. 1142) for Astral Carriers Ltd., Liberia. *17.4.1987:*
Completed and bareboat chartered to Wilh. Wilhelmsen. *23.12.1988:* Bareboat
charter party and purchase option acquired by Procyon Carriers Ltd
(Norwegian Ship Management A/S, managers), Liberia and renamed NOSAC
SEA. *18.6.1991:* Sold to K/S Benargus A/S & Co. (Den norske Amerikalinje
A/S, managers), Oslo. Still in service.

TIJUCA

374. TIJUCA (IV) (1987-   ) Ore / Oil Carrier
Tonnages: 159,534 gross, 107,933 net, 305,675 deadweight.
Dimensions: 316.01 (332.01 o.a.) x 57.21 x 30.92 m. 23.032 m draught.
Machinery: 8-cylinder 2 S.C.S.A. Sulzer oil engine of 22,340 b.h.p. by the
shipbuilders. Service speed 13.5 knots.
15.12.1986: Launched by Ishikawajima do Brasil S.A., Rio de Janeiro (Yard
No. 146) for Wilsea Shipping Inc., Liberia (a 50/50 joint venture with
Docenave, Rio de Janeiro). *29.5.1987:* Completed. Price paid $65,840,000.
Still in Wilsea Shipping Inc. service.

TARIM RIVER

375. TARIM RIVER (1988-1989) Tanker
Tonnages: 54,055 gross, 32,505 net, 87,464 deadweight.
Dimensions: 236.81 (246.87 o.a.) x 39.91 x 19.03 m. 13.020 m draught.
Machinery: 10-cylinder 4 S.C.S.A. Pielstick oil engine of 17,400 b.h.p. by the
shipbuilders. Service speed 14 knots.
31.3.1979: Launched by Ishikawajima Harima Heavy Industries, Ltd., Aioi (Yard
No. 2716) as NARNIAN SEA for Globtik Tankers Ltd. (Globtik Management,
Ltd., managers), London. *30.6.1979:* Completed. *1983:* Transferred to
Bahamas registry. *1988:* Sold to Nargic Shipping Co. Inc., Bahamas.
21.4.1988: Purchased by Wiltank K/S, in which Wilh. Wilhelmsen had a 20%
interest. Price paid 84,994,000.00 kr. *29.12.1989:* Sold to K/S Stavanger
Prince (Barber International A/S, managers), Stavanger and renamed
STAVANGER PRINCE. *1990:* Det Stavangerske D/S became managers. Still
in service.

PEONIA, which later became TALISMAN, at Europoort 1.6.1988   *Joachim Pein*

376. TALISMAN (VI) (1988-1991) Bulk Carrier
Tonnages: 14,267 gross, 8,689 net, 23,757 deadweight.
Dimensions: 150.02 (159.82 o.a.) x 24.64 x 13.62 m. 9.932 m draught.
Machinery: 8-cylinder 2 S.C.S.A. Mitsubishi oil engine of 10,650 b.h.p. by
Kobe Hatsudoki K.K., Tarami. Service speed 14.5 knots.
16.1.1977: Launched by Imabari Zosen K.K., Marugame (Yard No. 1039) as
GARZA STAR for Yamato Kisen K.K., Japan. *28.3.1977:* Completed. *1984:*
Sold to Garza Star Naviera S.A., Panama. *23.4.1985:* Abandoned by her crew

in a position 49.50 N, 141.30 W after developing a list during a voyage from Tacoma to Japan and subsequently towed back to Seattle. *1987:* Sold to Peonia Maritime S.A., Panama and renamed PEONIA. *1988:* Sold to Gibson Shipping Ltd., Philippine Islands and renamed PACIFIC DREAMER. *8.9.1988:* Purchased by Wilbulk I K/S, Tønsberg, in which Wilh. Wilhelmsen had a 20% interest, renamed TALISMAN and Wilship became managers. Price paid $6,800,000. *2.4.1991:* Sold to Chun Wah Marine (Panama) S.A., Panama and renamed CHUN WAH I. *1992:* Sold to Precious Lakes Ltd. (Great Circle Shipping Agency Ltd., managers), Thailand and renamed NIRA NAREE. Still in service.

TAIKO in Barber Blue Sea livery 25.4.1989, whilst registered at Gothenburg   *G. Prosser*

377. TAIKO (II) (1988-   ) Ro-Ro Vessel
Tonnages: 27,902 gross, 16,243 net, 43,986 deadweight.
Dimensions: 246.41 (262.08 o.a.) x 32.31 x 21.01 m. 11.729 m draught.
Machinery: 8-cylinder 2 S.C.S.A. Burmeister & Wain oil engine of 36,600 b.h.p. by Hyundai Shipbuilding & Heavy Industries Ltd., Ulsan. Service speed 21 knots.
Container capacity: 2,451 TEU. Quarter stern door and ramp.
16.11.1983: Launched by Hyundai Heavy Industries Co. Ltd., Ulsan (Yard No. 250) as BARBER HECTOR for Ocean Transport & Trading plc (Ocean Fleets Ltd, later Ocean Marine Ltd., managers), Liverpool. *17.4.1984:* Completed. *1987:* Transferred to Douglas, Isle of Man, registry. *20.12.1988:* Purchased by Swedish Liners KB, Gothenburg. On charter to Rederi AB Transatlantic,

TAIKO, re-registered at Tønsberg, in Wilhelmsen Lines livery   *J. Y. Freeman*

Gothenburg, with further charter to Wilhelmsen Lines A/S (Transatlantic Ship Management AB, Gothenburg, managers) and renamed TAIKO. *21.12.1989:* On charter to Wilhelmsen Lines Services A/S, with further charter to Wilhelmsen Lines A/S (same managers). *24.2.1993:* Purchased by Wilhelmsen Lines A/S and·registered at Tønsberg. Price paid $37,000,000. Still in the service of Wilhelmsen Lines A/S.

TALABOT   *J. Krayenbosch*

378. TALABOT (VI) (1988-   ) Ro-Ro Vessel
Tonnages: 21,816 gross, 11,942 net, 34,605 deadweight.
Dimensions: 210.50 (228.51 o.a.) x 32.31 x 20.22 m. 11.170 m draught.
Machinery: 9-cylinder 2 S.C.S.A. Sulzer oil engine of 30,150 b.h.p. by Mitsubishi Heavy Industries Ltd., Kobe. Service speed 19.5 knots.
Container capacity: 1,806 TEU. Quarter stern door and ramp.
7.2.1979: Launched by Mitsubishi Heavy Industries Ltd, Nagasaki (Yard No. 1841) as BARBER PERSEUS for Perseus Shipping Ltd. (Ocean Fleets Ltd., managers), Liverpool. *11.6.1979:* Completed. *1983:* Transferred to Barber Menelaus Shipping Corporation (same managers), Panama. *1984:* Reverted to Perseus Shipping Ltd (Ocean Fleets Ltd, later Ocean Marine Ltd., managers), Liverpool, *1987:* Transferred to Douglas, Isle of Man, registry. *21.12.1988:* Purchased by Swedish Liners KB, Gothenburg. On charter to Rederi AB Transatlantic, Gothenburg, with further charter to Wilhelmsen Lines A/S (Transatlantic Ship Management AB, Gothenburg, managers) and renamed TALABOT. *21.12.1989:* On charter to Wilhelmsen Lines Services A/S, with further charter to Wilhelmsen Lines A/S (same managers). *29.1.1993:* Purchased by Wilhelmsen Lines A/S and registered at Tønsberg. Price paid $15,000,000. Still in the service of Wilhelmsen Lines A/S.

379. TAMPERE (1989-   ) Ro-Ro Vessel
Tonnages: 22,087 gross, 12,120 net, 35,098 deadweight.
Dimensions: 212.02 (228.53 o.a.) x 32.29 x 20.15 m. 11.170 m draught.
Machinery: 9-cylinder 2 S.C.S.A. Burmeister & Wain oil engine of 30,700 b.h.p. by the shipbuilders. Service speed 19.5 knots.
Container capacity: 1,814 TEU. Quarter stern door and ramp.
17.1.1979: Launched by Mitsui Engineering & Shipbuilding Co. Ltd., Tamano (Yard No. 1187) as BARBER NARA for Brostroms Rederi A/B, Sweden. *25.5.1979:* Completed. *1984:* Transferred to Rederi-A/B Transocean (Transatlantic Ship Management AB, managers), Sweden. *1987:* Transferred to Swedish Liners AB (same managers), Sweden. *31.1.1989:* Purchased by Tampere Shipping Inc., Tønsberg and renamed TAMPERE. Price paid $15,000,000. *31.7.1989:* Owners became Wilhelmsen Lines A/S. Still in the service of Wilhelmsen Lines A/S.

TAMPERE   *J. Krayenbosch*

380. TAPIOLA (1989-   ) Ro-Ro Vessel

Tonnages: 22,325 gross, 12,190 net, 33,702 deadweight.
Dimensions: 210.01 (228.51 o.a.) x 32.26 x 20.22 m. 11.170 m draught.
Machinery: 9-cylinder 2 S.C.S.A. Sulzer oil engine of 30,150 b.h.p. by
Mitsubishi Heavy Industries Ltd., Kobe. Service speed 19.5 knots.
Container capacity: 1,707 TEU. Quarter stern door and ramp.
10.3.1978: Launched by Mitsubishi Heavy Industries Ltd., Nagasaki (Yard
No.1831) as BOOGABILLA for Rederiaktiebolaget Transatlantic, Sweden.
25.8.1978: Completed. *3.2.1989:* Purchased by BHT Tapiola Shipping Inc.,
Panama and renamed TAPIOLA. Price paid $15,000,000. *31.7.1989:* Owners
became Wilhelmsen Lines A/S, and re-registered at Tønsberg Still in the
service of Wilhelmsen Lines A/S.

TAPIOLA   *J. Krayenbosch*

TENNESSEE RIVER

381. TENNESSEE RIVER (1989-1991) Tanker

Tonnages: 40,570 gross, 32,127 net, 84,814 deadweight.
Dimensions: 235.01 (246.90 o.a.) x 42.04 x 19.11 m. 12.202 m draught.
Machinery: 14-cylinder 4 S.C.S.A. M.A.N. oil engine of 14,670 b.h.p by
Kawasaki Heavy Industries Ltd., Kobe. Service speed 15 knots.

31.5.1978: Launched by Kawasaki Heavy Industries Ltd., Sakaide (Yard No.
1286) as INTERMAR CLARION for Compton Shipping Ltd., Liberia.
27.10.1978: Completed. *1984:* Sold to Camelia Transport Co. Ltd., Liberia
and renamed COMPTON CAMELIA. *1986:* Sold to Tokyo Specialised Tankers
Co. Ltd., Panama and renamed SOARING EAGLE. *1987:* Sold to Sea Eagle
Shipping Ltd., St.Kitts Nevis, Bahamas flag, and renamed SEA EAGLE.
16.5.1989: Purchased by Tenn River K/S, Tønsberg, in which Wilh. Wilhelmsen
had a 20% interest, renamed TENNESSEE RIVER and Wilship became
managers. Price paid $18,475,000. *2.10.1991:* Sold to Nissos Delos Naftiki
Eteria (Kyklades Naftiki Eteria, managers). Greece and renamed NISSOS
DELOS. Still in service.

TORRENS, 1.5.1991   *J. Y. Freeman*

382. TORRENS (III) (1989-   ) Ro-Ro Vessel
Tonnages: 18,755 gross, 9,748 net, 23,716 deadweight.
Dimensions: 182.00 (199.50 o.a.) x 32.20 x 19.99 m. 10.020 m draught.
Machinery: 7-cylinder 2 S.C.S.A Sulzer oil engine of 23,450 b.h.p. by Astilleros
Espanoles S.A., Manises Works, Valencia. Service speed 18.5 knots.
Container capacity: 1,430 TEU. Angled stern door and ramp.
31.10.1981: Launched by Astilleros Espanoles S.A., Factoria de Puerto Real,
Cadiz (Yard No. 30) as KATOWICE II for Hiszpanska-Polskie Towarzstwo
Zeglugowe, Poland. *22.12.1982:* Completed. *23.8.1989:* Purchased by
Wilhelmsen Lines A/S and renamed TORRENS. Price paid 154,632,000.00
kr. It had originally been intended to name her TOPAZ, but the name was
changed because of the air tragedy. Still in the service of Wilhelmsen Lines A/S.

ESSI FLORA   *Fotoflite incorporating Skyfotos*

383. ESSI FLORA (1990-   ) Chemical Tanker
Tonnages: 11,977 gross, 6,020 net, 15,704 deadweight.
Dimensions: 148.75 (157.69 o.a.) x 20.28 x 12.76 m. 9.341m draught.
Machinery: 6-cylinder 2 S.C.S.A. oil engine of 5,400 b.h.p. by Maschinenbau
Augsburg-Nurnberg, Augsburg. Service speed 13.75 knots.
19.3.1959: Launched by Rheinstahl Nordseewerke, Emden (Yard No. 311) as
the bulk carrier ESSIFLORA for Skips A/S Ruped & Co. (later K/S Skips A/S
Ruped & Co.) (Bj. Ruud-Pedersen, manager), Oslo. *7.7.1959:* Completed.
Tonnages at that time 12,056 gross, 7,009 net, 16,819 deadweight. *1963:*
Renamed ESSI FLORA. *1964:* Converted by Stord Verft (Akers Mekaniske
Verksted A/S, Oslo) into a chemical tanker. *16.5.1974:* Managers became
Ruud-Pedersen Shipping A/S, renamed *22.4.1977* Bj. Ruud-Pedersen A/S.
1.1.1990: Wilh. Wilhelmsen acquired the managers and the ship became
58.17% Wilhelmsen owned. Still in Wilship service.

384. ESSI SILJE (1990-1992) Chemical Tanker
Tonnages: 11,023 gross, 3,395 net, 16,700 deadweight.
Dimensions: 143.15 (153.02 o.a.) x 20.64 x 12.70 m. 9.802 m draught.
Machinery: 6-cylinder 2 S.C.S.A. M.A.N. oil engine of 8,400 b.h.p. by Bremer
Vulkan, Vegesack. Service speed 15 knots.
The stern section, including the machinery, originally formed part of the bulk
carrier ESCAPE and was joined to the forepart of ESSI SILJE in 1983 after
the latter ship had suffered major fire damage aft. The constructional data
above refers to the period since her reconstruction and the details given below
are the histories, first of ESSI SILJE, then ESCAPE, and then of ESSI SILJE
as reconstructed.

281

ESSI SILJE

(ESSI SILJE). *15.5.1968:* Launched by Chantiers Navals de la Ciotat, Le Trait (Yard No. 189) as the bulk carrier SABINIA for Union Navale & Société Navale Caennaise, France. *15.8.1968:* Completed. She had tonnages of 11,397 gross, 7,798 net and 18,112 deadweight and dimensions 158.79 (166.77 o.a) x 21.39 x 12.19 m. 9.258 m draught. She was propelled by two 10-cylinder 4 S.C.S.A. Pielstick oil engines totalling 9,040 b.h.p. Her service speed was 15.5 knots. *1970:* Sold to Johs. Presthus Rederi (Johs. Presthus, manager), Bergen and renamed HELENE PRESTHUS. *4.9.1972:* Purchased by Bj. Ruud-Pedersen, Oslo and renamed ESSI SILJE. *1973:* Transferred to I/S Essi Silje (Bj. Ruud-Pedersen, manager) and converted by Akers Mekaniske Verksted A/S, Oslo into a chemical tanker with tonnages 11,370 gross, 6,649 net and 16,677 deadweight and dimensions 142.75 (154.51 o.a.) x 20.63 x 12.70 m. 9.576 m draught. *22.9.1973:* Conversion completed. *16.5.1974:* Managers became Ruud-Pedersen Shipping A/S, renamed *22.4.1977* Bj. Ruud-Pedersen A/S. *12.6.1982:* Abandoned by her crew in a position 44.40 N, 20.40 W after fire had broken out in her engine room during a voyage from Stanlow to Curacao. *5.7.1982:* Arrived in tow at Barry and subsequently discharged. *2.12.1982:* Arrived in tow at Bremerhaven, where the damaged stern section was cut off by Seebeckwerft and was later scrapped by Hansa Rohstoffe G.m.b.H. The forepart was then joined by Seebeckwerft to the stern section of ESCAPE.

(ESCAPE). *27.2.1968:* Launched by Bremer Vulkan A.G., Schiffbau und Maschinenfabrik, Vegesack (Yard No. 935), as the bulk carrier BELBLUE for Belships Co. Ltd. Skibs A/S (Christen Smith Shipping Co., managers), Oslo. *11.5.1968:* Completed. She had tonnages of 11,362 gross, 6,677 net and 18,420 deadweight and dimensions 152.53 (161.55 o.a.) x 20.63 x 12.20 m. 9.354 m draught. *1975:* Sold to Efniki Compania Naviera S.A., Greece and renamed DIMITRIS E. *1981:* Sold to Universal Shipping Enterprises Inc. S.A., Panama and renamed UNIVERSE GLORY. *21.12.1982:* Arrived at Bremerhaven for auxiliary boiler repairs. *31.1.1983:* Purchased by Skips A/S

Ruped & Co. (Bj. Ruud-Pedersen A/S, managers), Oslo and renamed ESCAPE. Her forepart was removed and sold and the afterpart, with the M.A.N. propelling machinery, was joined to the forepart of ESSI SILJE. *27.6.1983:* The rebuilt ESSI SILJE left Bremerhaven on trials prior to returning to service. *25.7.1983:* Transferred to K/S Skips A/S Essi Silje. *1.1.1990:* Wilh. Wilhelmsen acquired the managers. *14.1.1992:* Sold to Endeavour Navigation S.A., Panama and renamed AEGEAN MARINER. Still in service.

ESSI ANNE   *J. Prentice*

385. ESSI ANNE (1990-1992) Bulk Carrier
Tonnages: 15,920 gross, 11,149 net, 27,300 deadweight.
Dimensions: 156.65 (163.20 o.a.) x 25.94 x 15.22 m. 10.990 m draught.
Machinery: 6-cylinder 2 S.C.S.A. Sulzer oil engine of 10,200 b.h.p. by H. Cegielski, Poznan. Service speed 15 knots.
15.12.1971: Launched by Stocznia im "Komuny Paryskiej", Gdynia (Yard No. B523/05) as TRYM for H. Roed & Co., Tønsberg. *10.4.1972:* Completed for I/S Trym (Peter Thorvildsen, manager), Tønsberg. *1986:* Sold to Trym Shipping (S.) Pte. Ltd. (same manager), Singapore. *1987:* Sold to Havlom Shipping Pte. Ltd. (A/S Havtor Management, managers), Singapore and renamed HAVLOM. *28.12.1988:* Purchased by K/S Essi Anne (Bj. Ruud-Pedersen A/S, managers), Oslo and renamed ESSI ANNE. *1.1.1990:* Wilh. Wilhelmsen acquired the managers. *17.6.1992:* Sold to Sea Faith Maritime S.A., Panama and renamed IONIAN MASTER. Still in service.

ESSI GINA, 15.4.1987   *J. Y. Freeman*

386. ESSI GINA (1990-   ) Chemical Tanker
Tonnages: 11,721 gross, 6,342 net, 16,529 deadweight.
Dimensions: 149.00 (156.00 o.a.) x 21.26 x 12.35 m. 9.590 m draught.
Machinery: 6-cylinder 2 S.C.S.A. Burmeister & Wain oil engine of 11,200 b.h.p.

by Mitsui Engineering & Shipbuilding Co. Ltd., Tamano. Service speed 16.75 knots.
10.5.1979: Launched by Nippon Kokan K.K., Tsu (Yard No. 64) for Skips A/S Essi Gina (Bj. Ruud-Pedersen A/S, managers), Oslo. *28.9.1979:* Completed. *1.1.1990:* Wilh. Wilhelmsen acquired the managers. Still in Wilship service.

TORINO *J. Krayenbosch*

387. TORINO (II) (1990-   ) Tanker
Tonnages: 134,140 gross, 117,917 net, 280,108 deadweight.
Dimensions: 330.69 (342.98 o.a.) x 51.80 x 27.34 m. 21.351 m draught.
Machinery: Two steam turbines totalling 32,400 s.h.p. by the shipbuilders geared to a single screw shaft. Service speed 15 knots.
8.11.1974: Launched by Chantiers de l'Atlantique, St. Nazaire (Yard No. Y25) as OPALE for Compagnie Navale des Petroles, France. *17.1.1975:* Completed and initially laid up at Cherbourg. *1980:* Owners became Total Compagnie Française de Navigation. *27.10.1983:* Laid up at Agnefest. *1986:* Transferred to Total Compagnie Française de Navigation and Yucca Shipping Ltd., Bahamas. *1987:* Sold to K/S Finans Invest IV A/S, Oslo, renamed HAPPY PILOT and returned to service. *1988:* Sold to K/S Happy Pilot (Norman International A/S, managers), Oslo. *25.5.1990:* Purchased by Brudevold & Wilhelmsen Tankers I K/S, Oslo, in which Wilh. Wilhelmsen have a 30% interest, renamed TORINO and Wilship became managers. Price paid $34,100,000. *16.11.1992:* Wilh. Wilhelmsen ownership increased to 50%. Still in Wilship service.

TOSCANA *Fotoflite*

388. TOSCANA (II) (1990-1993) Tanker

Tonnages: 60,337 gross, 46,963 net, 130,529 deadweight.
Dimensions: 255.02 (265.62 o.a.) x 41.41 x 22.23 m. 16.838 m draught.
Machinery: 7-cylinder 2 S.C.S.A. Burmeister & Wain oil engine of 23,900 b.h.p.
by Hitachi Zosen, Sakurajima Works, Osaka. Service speed 14.7 knots.
15.9.1976: Launched by Hitachi Zosen, Sakai (Yard No. 4459) as ARIELA
G for Capricorn Tankers Inc., Liberia. *31.1.1977:* Completed. *1989:* Sold to
K/S Happy Sitani (Norman International A/S, managers), Oslo and renamed
HAPPY SITANI. *25.5.1990:* Purchased by Brudevold & Wilhelmsen Tankers
II K/S, Oslo, in which Wilh. Wilhelmsen had a 30% interest, renamed
TOSCANA and Wilship became managers. Price paid $23,550,000.
27.1.1993: Sold to Countess Shipping Ltd., Malta and renamed SEADANCER.
Still in service.

TARKWA at Cape Town in 4.92   *Table Bay Underway Shipping*

389. TARKWA (1990-) Ro-Ro Vessel

Tonnages: 15,075 gross, 4,581 net, 12,169 deadweight.
Dimensions: 140.01 (152.03 o.a.) x 26.31 x 17.28 m. 9,199 m draught.
Machinery: 16-cylinder 4 S.C.S.A. Pielstick oil engine of 10,400 b.h.p. by
Ishikawajima Harima Heavy Industries Ltd., Aioi. Service speed 17 knots.
Container capacity: 643 TEU. Quarter stern door and ramp.
1.2.1979: Launched by Tsuneishi Zosen K.K., Numakuma (Yard No. 435) as
SEKI ROKAKO for Sekihyo Seibaku K.K., Japan. *12.5.1979:* Completed. *1984:*
Sold to Pelly Shipping Ltd., Panama and renamed EASTERN UNICORN. *1988:*
Sold to Malcolm Shipping Ltd., Panama. *25.9.1990:* Purchased by Wilhelmsen
Lines A/S, registered at Tønsberg and renamed TARKWA. Price paid
$10,000,000. Still in the service of Wilhelmsen Lines A/S.

TARN at Cape Town, 7.3.1992   *Table Bay Underway Shipping*

390. TARN (III) (1991-   ) Ro-Ro Vessel

Tonnages: 15,075 gross, 4,581 net, 12,169 deadweight.
Dimensions: 140.01 (152.00 o.a.) x 26.31 x 17.28 m. 9.102 m draught.
Machinery: 16-cylinder 4 S.C.S.A. Pielstick oil engine of 10,400 b.h.p. by
Ishikawajima Harima Heavy Industries, Ltd., Aioi. Service speed 17 knots.
Container capacity: 643 TEU. Quarter stern door and ramp.

16.3.1979: Launched by Tsuneishi Zosen K.K., Numakuma (Yard No. 436)
as SEKI ROKEL for Sekihyo Seibaku K.K., Japan. *3.7.1979:* Completed. *1984:*
Sold to Cassiar Shipping Ltd., Liberia, Panama flag, and renamed EASTERN
PHOENIX. *1987:* Sold to Newcastle Shipping Ltd., Panama, and renamed
CANMAR SPIRIT. *28.1.1991:* Purchased by Wilhelmsen Lines A/S, registered
at Tønsberg and renamed TARN. Price paid $9,800,000. Still in the service
of Wilhelmsen Lines A/S.

TROLL FOREST   *Dietmar Hasenpusch*

391. TROLL FOREST (II) / NOSAC FOREST (1991-   ) Ro-Ro Vessel

Tonnages: 28,134 gross, 20,126 net, 42,525 deadweight.
Dimensions: 173.21 (182.51 o.a.) x 32.31 x 25.81 m. 12.020 m draught.
Machinery: 8-cylinder 2 S.C.S.A. Burmeister & Wain oil engine of 14,945 b.h.p.
by A/S Nye Fredriksstad Mekaniske Verksted, Fredrikstad. Service speed 15
knots.
Container capacity: 895 TEU. Quarter stern door and ramps.
30.6.1979: Launched by A/S Fredriksstad Mekaniske Verksted, Fredrikstad
(Yard No. 436) as SKAUBORD for K/S Woodbulk and A/S Eikland (I.M.Skaugen
Management Co. A/S, managers), Oslo. *25.9.1979:* Completed. *1986:*
Norwegian Ship Management A/S became managers. *1987:* Transferred to
Skaubord Ltd. (same managers), Liberia. *1988:* Reverted to K/S Woodbulk
and A/S Eikland (same managers), Oslo. *1990:* Skaugen Marine A/S became
managers. *6.11.1991:* Purchased by Wilhelmsen Lines A/S, registered at
Tønsberg and renamed TROLL FOREST. Price paid $23,000,000. *21.12.1992:*
Renamed NOSAC FOREST. Currently on charter to Wilship and sub-let to
Nosac.

TARTAR

392. TARTAR (IV) (1993—   ) Tanker

Tonnages: 155,359 gross, 97,869 net, 306,902 deadweight.
Dimensions: 317.00 (330.00 o.a.) x 60.04 x 30.60 m. 22.030 m draught.
Machinery: 7-cylinder 2 S.C.S.A. Sulzer oil engine of 24,660 b.h.p. by Diesel
United Ltd., Aioi. Service speed 15.7 knots.
11.7.1992: Launched by Sumitomo Heavy Industries, Ltd., Oppama (Yard No.
1179) *12.1.1993:* Completed. Price paid $89,000,000. Still in Wilship service.

287

393. TARIM (IV) (1993-   ) Tanker
Tonnages: 156,837 gross, 95,350 net, 280,954 deadweight.
Dimensions: 315.00 (328.00 o.a.) x 57.00 x 30.80 m. 22.150 m draught.
Machinery: 7-cylinder 2 S.C.S.A. Burmeister & Wain oil engine of 26,000 b.h.p.
by Hitachi Zosen, Osaka. Service speed 15.75 knots.
16.8.1993: Launched by Hitachi Zosen, Ariake (Yard No. 4864). *30.9.1993:*
Completed. Price paid 14,400,000,000 yen. Still in Wilship service.

TARIM fitting out

394. NOSAC TANABATA (For delivery in 1994) Car Carrier
Tonnages: About 49,500 gross, about 17,600 deadweight.
Dimensions: About 180.00 (190.00 o.a.) x 32.26 x 31.40 m. 9.880 m draught.
Machinery: 6-cylinder 2 S.C.S.A. Sulzer oil engine of 15,660 b.h.p. by Diesel
United Ltd., Aioi. Service speed 19.4 knots, 20.4 knots anticipated on trials.
Capacity: 5,830 cars.
1993: Ordered from Sumitomo Heavy Industries Ltd., Oppama (Yard No. 1198)
for delivery about *1.11.1994* to Taurus Carriers Ltd., Liberia, for bareboat
charter—with purchase option—to Wilh. Wilhelmsen for Nosac service.

288

ABEER MARINE SERVICES

Abeer Marine Services Limited, with headquarters in Hong Kong, and regional offices in Indonesia, Malaysia, Saudi Arabia and Singapore, operate a fleet of Crew Utility Vessels, the first of which came into service in 1981 in the MIDDLE EAST. In November 1993 the fleet numbered 26 vessels of varying types, ranging in length from 78 to 135 feet.

A "fleet list" follows, with photographs of representative types. Except for two craft sold in 1989, all the Abeer vessels have been built in the U.S.A.

1. 65 feet length. All built in the U.S.A. by Camcraft.

ABEER 1	Delivered 2.1981	Sold 1.1990
ABEER 2	Delivered 9.1982	Sold 1.1991
ABEER 5	Delivered 12.1983	Sold 9.1989

ABEER 13

2. 110 feet length, 25 feet beam, 12 feet depth, 6 feet draught.

Four Detroit oil engines totalling 2,080 b.h.p., giving a maximum speed of 24 knots. Deck load 40 tons. Passenger capacity: 18 as a Security Vessel, 100 as a crew boat.

ABEER 10	Built by Camcraft	Delivered 7.1983	In the present fleet
ABEER 11	Built by Camcraft Aluminium	Delivered 4.1984	In the present fleet
ABEER 12	Built by Camcraft Aluminium	Delivered 4.1984	In the present fleet
ABEER 13	Built by Aluminium Boats	Delivered 1.1986	In the present fleet
ABEER 14	Built by Aluminium Boats	Delivered 8.1987	In the present fleet
ABEER 18	Built by Aluminium Boats	Delivered 7.1990	In the present fleet

3. 78 feet length, 20 feet beam.

Two Detroit oil engines totalling 1,040 b.h.p., giving a maximum speed of 24 knots. Passenger capacity: 85.

ABEER 6	Built by Camcraft Aluminium	Delivered 8.1984	Sold 2.1989
ABEER 17	Built by Camcraft	Delivered 5.1988	In the present fleet

4. 85 feet length, 20 feet beam, 9 feet depth, 5 feet draught.

Two Detroit old engines totalling 1,040 b.h.p., giving a maximum speed of 23 knots. Deck load 18 tons. Passenger capacity: 60.

ABEER 7	Built by Camcraft	Delivered 2.1985	In the present fleet
ABEER 8	Built by Camcraft	Delivered 2.1985	In the present fleet
ABEER 9	Built by Camcraft	Delivered 2.1985	In the present fleet
ABEER 16	Built by Breaux Baycraft	Delivered 6.1988	Sold 8.1989
ABEER 19	Built by Aluminium Boats	Delivered 7.1990	In the present fleet
ABEER 22	Built by Aluminium Boats	Delivered 9.1990	In the present fleet
ABEER 23	Built by Aluminium Boats	Delivered 3.1991	In the present fleet
ABEER 24	Built by Aluminium Boats	Delivered 4.1991	In the present fleet
ABEER 26	Built by Aluminium Boats	Delivered 4.1991	In the present fleet
ABEER 27	Built by Aluminium Boats	Delivered 7.1991	In the present fleet
ABEER 28	Built by Aluminium Boats	Delivered 8.1991	In the present fleet
ABEER 29	Built by Aluminium Boats	Delivered 11.1991	In the present fleet
ABEER 30	Built by Aluminium Boats	Delivered 8.1990	In the present fleet
ABEER 5	Built by Aluminium Boats	Delivered 1.1990	In the present fleet

ABEER 2

5. 91 feet length, 23 feet beam.

Three Detroit oil engines totalling 1,560 b.h.p. giving a maximum speed of 24 knots. Deck load 20 tons. Passenger capacity: 100.

ABEER 2	Built by Camcraft	Delivered 7.1985	In the present fleet

6. 100 feet length. Built in Norway by Marinteknik

AMAL	Delivered 6.1988	Sold 1.1989
ZAKAT	Delivered 6.1988	Sold 1.1989

7. 120 feet length, 25 feet beam.
Four Detroit oil engines totalling 2,080 b.h.p. giving a maximum speed of 24 knots. Deck load 70 tons. Passenger capacity: 120.

ABEER 20   Built by Aluminium Boats   Delivered 7.1988   In the present fleet

ABEER 25

8. 135 feet length, 28 feet beam, 13 feet depth, 7 feet draught.
Four Detroit oil engines totalling 4,400 b.h.p. giving a maximum speed of 30 knots. Deck load 120 tons. Passengers: 125 as a crew boat, 20 when serbing as a Contingency Diving Support Craft.

ABEER 25   Built by Aluminium Boats   Delivered 11.1990   In the present fleet
ABEER 35   Built by Aluminium Boats   Delivered 6.1993   In the present fleet

ABEER 1

9. 85 feet length, 20 feet beam, 9 feet depth, 5 feet draught.
Two Detroit oil engines totalling 2,800 b.h.p. giving a maximum speed of 32 knots.

ABEER 1   Built by Aluminium Boats   Delivered 1.1992   In the present fleet
ABEER 3   Built by Aluminium Boats   Delivered 5.1992   In the present fleet

Aksel	2	Derived from the Hebrew "Absa Ion" = "Father of Peace". Male Christian name (Norway). "A man of power and authority"
Alabama	22	Name of a State in the Southern U.S.A., the 22nd in the Union. Also a river flowing into Mobile Bay. The name derived from a tribe of Indians named "Alibamos", which literally means "here we rest".
Alderney	58	One of the Channel Islands, 4 miles long and divided from the mainland of France by the Race of Alderney. The capital is St Anne, the only town.
Als Confidence	324	
Amerika	I 15	From Americus Vespucius, latinized form of
America	II 98	Amerigo Vespucci, the Italian seafarer who
	III 124	made several voyages to the continent, which he described in his book "Quattuor Navigationes". The German Waldseemüller suggested in "Cosmographiae Introductio" in 1507 that the new continent should be named after Americus Vespucius.
Artemis	102	In Greek mythology the daughter of Zeus and Leto, and twin sister of Apollo. She was the goddess of the Moon and wild nature, especially animals.
Atna	87	A river in the county of Hedmark Fylke, a tributary of the river Glomma, Norway's largest river.
Barber Taif	331	"Barber" derives from the name of the United States company Barber Steamship Co. Inc., a firm with which Wilh. Wilhelmsen has close relations. In 1927 the two companies reached an agreement to put ships on the "Barber Line" between New York and the Far East. See "Taif"
Barber Talisman	328	See "Talisman"
Barber Tampa	362	See "Tampa"
Barber Tennessee	322	See "Tennessee"
Barber Terrier	321	See "Terrier"
Barber Texas	363	See "Texas"
Barber Thermopylæ	324	See "Thermopylæ"
Barber Toba	330	See "Toba"
Barber Tønsberg	332	See "Tønsberg"
Barber Tsu	319	See "Tsu"
Belridge	97	Bel = beautiful + ridge.
Bernadotte	19	Jean Baptiste Jules Bernadotte, former French Marshal, chosen as Crown Prince of Sweden in 1810 and from 1818 to 1844 King of Sweden and Norway. The ancestor of the present Swedish Royal family.

| Bessa | 107 | A tributary of the Norwegian river Sjoa, starting from Lake Bessvatn, which is divided from the Lake Gjendin by the mountain Besseggen, in Ibsen's "Peer Gynt" called Gjenineggen, where Peer Gynt made his famous "Bukkeritt" (Norwegian "He-goat-ride"). See "Sjoa" and "Vinstra". |

BIG ORANGE XVIII

Big Orange XVIII	364	Dowell, the charterers of the ship, have the colour orange on all of their equipment, both onshore and offshore. The biggest item of equipment is the vessel—hence the name.
Bonna	101	In ancient Norwegian, a place where charcoal burning was carried on. The name of a place in Nordmarka (a large recreation area surrounding Oslo) now famous for ski-ing.
Caledonia	23	In historical times the area of north Britain, roughly equivalent to Scotland today, inhabited by the Calidones tribe.
Chapman	25	Frederik Henrik af Chapman (1721-1808), Swedish Admiral and shipbuilder.
Chipman	34	Small place in Canada. Also an American family name.
Christina	16	Female Christian name (Norway) = Christian.
Coringa	37	Town in Madras province, India, and formerly an important port.
Coromandel	41	A name given to the coast of S.E. India between Point Calimere and the mouth of the Kistna river.
Cosmo	31	"Cosma" (Latin), "Kosmos" (Greek) = the Universe.

Cubano	I	100	An inhabitant of Cuba (Spanish).
	II	119	
Cuzco		83	City of Peru, once the capital of the great Inca empire. Also a peak in Potosi province, Bolivia. "Cuzco" in the primitive language of Quichua means a woollen garment without collar or sleeves used by the Indians.
Delaware		118	Atlantic state of the U.S.A., west of Delaware Bay, and one of the original 13 states. Named after the river, which was in turn named after Thomas West, Lord Delaware (Baron de la Warr), colonial administrator in America in the 17th century.
Docefjord		371	"Doce" is the prefix to the names of all vessels belonging to Docenave, Wilhelmsen's Brazilian partner, and "fjord" is a gesture to the Norwegian partner — WW — representing the land of the fjords.
Dunmore		56	Dunmore Head, the most westerly point of the Irish mainland. "Dun" (Gaelic) = fortified place.
Dunnet		52	Dunnet Head, the northernmost Cape on the Scottish mainland.
Dunrae		57	Probably the Scottish place now rendered Dounray.
Elsa		78	Female Christian name (Norway). Derived from Elizabeth (Hebrew): "Dedicated to God".
Enrique		43	Male Christian name (Italy and Spain): "The great protector".
Enterprise		24	An undertaking, especially a bold or difficult one; courage, readiness. From the French "entreprendre" (entre = between + prendre = take).
Essi Anne		385	"Essi" is a "short-form" for Elsie (Ruud-Pedersen). Elsie was married to Bjarne Ruud-Pedersen, the former owner of the shipping company Bj. Ruud-Pedersen A/S. Bj.Ruud-Pedersen A/S was sold to Wilh. Wilhelmsen Limited A/S in 1990. Anne, Flora, Gina and Silje are all Christian names within the Ruud-Pedersen family.
Essi Flora		383	
Essi Gina		386	
Essi Silje		384	
Fin		4	"Finn", the usual form today. Male Christian name (Norway). "Wise, judicious, inventive". Also, a wanderer (globetrotter).
Foldin	I	10	The former name of the coastal areas around the Oslofjord, Norway. Today two counties — Østfold (Øst = East) and Vestfold (the county where Tønsberg is situated) have names derived from Foldin.
	II	28	

294

| Guernsey | I | 38 | The second largest of the Channel Islands. |
| | II | 51 | Guernsey, together with Herm and Sark, has its own government. The capital is St. Peter Port. Guernsey is also the name of a county in Ohio State, U.S.A. |

GUERNSEY (II) *W.S.P.L.*

Haabet	5	"Hope" (Norwegian).
Haabets Anker	21	"Anchor of Hope" (Norwegian).
Heimdal	79	The god of pure fire in Scandinavian mythology. The watchman of the rainbow — a bridge made by the gods between heaven and earth. Also a place south of the city of Trondheim
Helios	11	The ancient Greek sun god. "Helio" (Greek) = sun.
Hercules	108	In Greek "Herakles"—the greatest hero of Greek mythology, a son of Zeus and Alcmene, and renowned for his strength. Young Greek athletes regarded him, together with Hermes, as the ideal of strength and fair play and he is said to have instituted the Olympic games. Immensely popular among the Romans, in the beginning probably as their god for commerce and peaceful intercourse, which he was believed to have made possible through his great works. In the later Roman Empire known as "Hercules the Invincible".
Herm	68	One of the Channel Islands. See "Guernsey".
Hermes	9	The messenger of the gods, and the god of merchants and seafarers. A son of Zeus in Greek mythology. (Roman: Mercurius.) See "Hercules".

JETHOU   *W.S.P.L.*

Hoegh Cape	319	
Hoegh Carrier	321	
Ida	3	Female Christian name (Germany). "Ardent, persevering".
Jarlsberg	17	Norwegian. "Jarl" = earl, "berg" = mountain. The old county of Tønsberg was established in 1673 as Jarlsberg county and, together with the original Larvik county, today forms Vestfold. Nobility was abolished in Norway by the Constitution of 1814, but living peers kept their titles until their death. The last Count of Jarlsberg, Peder Anker Wedel Jarlsberg, died in 1893. Jarlsberg is now a family estate for the Norwegian line of the Wedel family.
Jethou	67	One of the Channel Islands.
La Habra	95	A city in S.W. California, U.S.A.

LOUISIANA   *Norsk Sjøfartsmuseum*

Lindsay	27	Australian (also English and American) family name. The ship was probably named after the Australian family as the first owner, A. B. Bull, was the leading Norwegian shipowner engaged in the Australian trade. David Lindsay (1856-1922) was a famous Australian explorer.
Losna	90	A lake in the Øyer and Ringebu districts of Norway. Also an island (Losneøy) in Gulen district, Sognefjord.
Louisiana	120	Originally the entire territory along the Mississippi River valley, so named in honour of the French King Louis XIV. Today a state in the U.S.A. bordered by the Gulf of Mexico.
Madrono	109	From the Latin "Memeclion", a strawberry plant common in Spain. Also, an inhabitant of Madronera in Caceres province, Spain.

MESNA

W.S.P.L.

Maersk Senior	307	
Mantilla	105	Typical Spanish head-dress worn at religious and other festivities. The word is probably of Moorish origin and in Arabic is "Mandila". Mantilla may also be a diminutive of the Spanish "manta".
Maricopa	96	A town, and range of mountains, in Arizona, U.S.A. Also, a town in California. Originally, the name of an Indian people of the Gita River valley.
Mathilde	1	Female Christian name (Germany): "The gigantic Valkyrie".
Mendocino	113	A county and cape in California, U.S.A. Also (Spanish) a citizen of Mendoza, Argentina.
Mesna	111	A district in Faaberg, Norway. Also a river of eastern Norway which empties into the Mjøsa Lake and is famous for its waterfalls.

Mexicano		93	Originally ''Mejicano'', a Mexican word derived from one of its leaders, Metxitlo, whose followers worshipped the god Vizilipuzli. Now, an inhabitant of Mexico.
Mexpetro		105	
Michigan		40	The 26th State of the U.S.A. Two peninsulas between Lakes Superior, Michigan and Huron. Area: 96,720 square miles, including 39,700 square miles of inland water.
Mirita		103	The opening, or ''peep-hole'', in the upper part of a door (Spanish). Probably associated with the look-out on board ship.
Mirlo	I	112	From the Latin ''Merula''—a black bird with yellow beak, common in Spain.
	II	126	
Montana		115	N.W. State of the U.S.A., on the Canadian border. Latin ''Montana'': a mountainous region.
Nora		7	Female Christian name (Norway), derived from the Greek Eleonora = ''the Merciful''. Also from ''Nord'' (Norway) = North. The principal female character in the drama ''A Doll's House'' by Henrik Ibsen (1828-1906).
Norman Isles		48	The Channel Islands. Formerly part of the Duchy of Normandy, they have been attached to England since the Conquest in 1066.
Noruega		94	''Norway'' (Spanish); in Norwegian ''Norge''. The oldest forms of the name are to be found in foreign hand-written descriptions from the 9th Century—for example ''Nordweg'' in Old English, latinized from Nort(h)wegia. The oldest written Nordic form (980) is Nuruiak, i.e. Norwægh. The last syllable is no doubt the same as the old word vegr = way. The first syllable is usually interpreted as noror = north, and according to this the name should mean ''Land of (or towards) the North''.
Nosac Forest		391	NOSAC = NOrwegian Specialised Auto Carriers.
Nosac Tai Shan		372	See ''Tai Shan''
Nosac Takara		369	See ''Takara''
Nosac Takayama		356	See ''Takayama''
Nosac Tanabata		394	See ''Tanabata''
Nosac Tancred		373	See ''Tancred''
Nosac Tasco		365	See ''Tasco''
Nystad		18	Swedish name for Uusikaupunki (= New Town), a port in S.W. Finland.
Ohio		106	A State in the Northern U.S.A.—the 17th in the Union. Also, an American river which is a tributary of the Mississippi.

| Polar Pioneer | | 368 | The first semi-submersible drilling rig specially designed and built for operation in Arctic waters. |
| Rena | | 89 | A tributary of the river Glomma, Norway, and itself formed of the combined waters of the rivers Finstada and Tysla (q.v.) |

RINDA (II) *Norsk Sjøfartsmuseum*

Rinda	I	104	A minor river which runs through the Saksum
	II	114	valley into the Mjøsa Lake, Norway.
Rosa Tucano		366	"Rosa" = ROll-on/roll-off South America. Tucano: The famous South American bird with the very large beak (toucan).
St. Andrews	I	39	Seaport in Scotland and seat of the oldest
	II	72	Scottish university. Named after Saint Andrew, one of the apostles, and patron saint of Scotland.
Salerno		59	Province and seaport of Campania, Italy, south-east of Naples. Salerno was the beach-head of the Allied landings in Italy in World War II.
San Joaquin		92	= Holy Joseph, father of the Virgin Mary. The name of a river and county in California, and of mountains in Colorado, U.S.A. Also, a town in Paraguay and a town in the Philippine Islands.
Sark		63	One of the Channel Islands, six miles from Guernsey. The chief harbour is Masseline, on the east coast. See also "Guernsey".
Simla		110	A district and town in the Punjab, India. Also, a female reindeer (Norway).
Sjoa		114	A tributary river of the Gudbrandsdalslågen, starting from Gjende, a green lake in the mountainous centre of Southern Norway, Jotunheimen. This is the fairy land of Ibsen's "Peer Gynt". See also "Bessa" and "Vinstra".

Snefrid	6	Female Christian name (Norway). "Beautiful as the snow", or "Friend of the Snow".
Stein	123	Male Christian name (Norway). "Stone" or "Rock". Also the name of a historical Norwegian manor-house near Hønefoss.
T.H.Aschehoug	12	Norwegian politician, professor and author of books on law and political economy (1822-1909).

TABOR (III)

Tabor	I II III	69 169 201	A small drum resembling a tambourine (Medieval English from the Old French "tabour"). Also a mountain in Israel, called the "Mountain of Revelation". Also a town in Bohemia, and a city in North Carolina, U.S.A.
Tabriz	I II	211 283	City of North-east Iran, capital of Azerbaidjan province. A trading centre, famous for its carpets. Etymological origin uncertain, but probably derived from the Armenian word "Dervij" = Revenge. Historians believe that the city was given this name when built by King Khosrow (590-628) on his triumphant return after conquering King Ardeshir and forcing him to flee to India. "Dervij" in course of time gradually changed into "Tavirz", and finally into "Tabriz".
Tachibana		304	A type of tree of South Chinese origin and in Chinese history regarded as symbolic of ambition. Also a wild orange, or the month of May in the old calendar.
Tacna II		324	

Tagaytay		225	A tourist town in the province of Cavite, Philippine Islands, which, according to popular legend, got that name because of a Spaniard, who in the 17th century came to the then little town and when asking a boy for its name, got the answer "Taga Itay!" — meaning "Father, cut him down with a knife" — the father and son were at the time hunting for an escaped hog. Captain Wilhelmsen and his daughters visited the beautiful town and decided that the next new ship should be called Tagaytay.
Tagus	I	206	The English and Latin name of the Ingesto river on the Iberian peninsula, rising in Montes Universales, east of Madrid, and flowing into the sea at Lisbon. The river is called "Tejo" in Portuguese and "Tajo" in Spanish.
	II	318	
Tai Ping	I	155	"Great peace and/or happiness" (Chinese)
	II	226	
Tai Ping Yang		156	"The great Pacific Ocean" (Chinese)
Tai Shan		157	One of the five sacred mountains of China,
(Nosac) Tai Shan		372	situated in West Shantung province.
Tai Yang		152	"The Sun" (Chinese)

TAI YIN   *W.S.P.L.*

Tai Yin		154	"The Moon" (Chinese)
(Barber) Taif		331	A city close to Mecca in Saudi Arabia.
Taiko	I	267	Pet name of the great Toyotomi Hideyoshi (1537-1598). The son of a poor farmer, he rose to be the greatest Japanese warrior and built the magnificent Osaka Castle, which still stands. He is known to every Japanese as Napoleon is to the French and his biography has been written in many languages.
	II	377	

Taimyr		275	A peninsula in Siberia whose northern point, Cape Tsjeljuskin, is the northernmost point of the Asian mainland. In the middle of the peninsula, which is sheer tundra, lies Lake Taimyr, from which the River Taimyr flows into the Arctic Ocean.
Taiwan	I II	135 202	The Chinese name of the island of Formosa = ''Pretty''.
Takachiho	I II	299 268	A very famous name in Japanese mythology for mountain Kyushu. According to the myth, the founders of Japan descended to this place from Heaven.
Takamine		294	''High mountain peak'' (Japanese)

NOSAC TAKARA   *J. Krayenbosch*

Takara (Nosac) Takara	271 369	Derived from ''Takarabune'' (Takara = treasure, bune = ship), which is the mythical Japanese ''Treasure Ship of the Seven Gods of Luck''. Pictures of this mythical ship are bought on New Year's Day and placed under pillows to ensure lucky dreams. The Seven Gods of Luck are supposed to be aboard the ship, guarding a cargo of precious symbolic objects.
Takasago	288	The name of a city on the Inland Sea of Japan. Also the name of a Japanese folk-song, sung at celebrations such as weddings.
Takayama	356	A town in Japan, north of Nagoya, in the high mountains. The town is famous for its old Japanese architecture and festivals.

TALABOT (IV), 24.5.1969　　　　　　　　　　　　　　　　*J. Y. Freeman*

Talabot	I	26	The name of the French engineer
	II	167	(1799-1885) who built the first railway in
	III	180	France and in 1847 made plans for a canal
	IV	266	between Alexandria and Suez. TALABOT (I)
	V	316	was the first steamship in the Wilhelmsen
	VI	378	fleet and originated the "T" nomenclature.
Talisman	I	47	Spanish, from the late Greek "Télesma" =
	II	132	consecrated object. A small object endowed
	III	173	with magical powers, especially to bring good
	IV	204	luck to the bearer and guard him against evil.
	V	328	
	VI	376	
Talleyrand	I	149	Charles Maurice de Talleyrand-Perigord
	II	193	(1754-1838), a French statesman and one of
			the greatest diplomats of world history.
Tamano	I	270	Seaport in Japan, near Okayama, Southern
	II	274	Honshu.
Tambo River		288	River in East Grippland. Also a State in
			Victoria, Australia.
Tamerlane	I	168	= Timur Leng (Timur the Lame), Mongol
	II	264	conqueror (1336-1405). In 1358 he began a
			series of conquests which took him from his
			kingdom in Turkestan as far as the Caspian
			Sea, the Urals, the Volga, though Persia, to
			Egypt and India.

TALISMAN (III) in war time, 13.5.1942　　　　　　　　　　　*W.S.P.L.*

TAMESIS (II) at No. 1 Circular Quay, Sydney (the site today of the Opera House), 29.8.1950   *David Finch*

Tamesis	I	177	Ancient name (Latin) for the River Thames in
	II	198	England. Akin to the Sanskrit ''Tamasas''.
	III	316	
Tampa	I	133	Probably from the Caloosa Indian word
	II	235	''Tampania'', meaning a meeting place or
	III	277	village. The Caloosas later shortened the
	IV	315	name of their village to ''Tanpa'', but an early
	V	362	map-maker mis-spelt the name ''Tampa'', and
			it has so remained. In today's Florida, a tourist
			resort and university city.
Tampere		379	University city in Finland, north of Helsinki.
Tana	I	125	A river in N.E. Norway which forms the border
	II	219	between Finland and Norway for some
			distance and empties into Tanafjord. Famous
			for salmon fishing. Also, a river and lake in
			East Africa.
Tanabata		269	= a Weaver, but the word is most familiar in
(Nosac) Tanabata		394	relation to the Japanese Tanabata Festival, a
			festival which is also widely celebrated in
			China and Buddhist countries by all women
			engaged in weaving, sewing, dress-making,

TAMPA (III), 1.11.1969   *J. Y. Freeman*

etc., music, poetry and other gentle arts. Farmers celebrate it to pray for a good harvest. The mythical origin refers to a herdsman (represented by a star in the constellation of Aquila) and a pretty weaver (represented by the star Vega) who fell so deeply in love that they neglected their work. Finally the Emperor separated them (the stars are on either side of the Milky Way, or ''River of Heaven''), and allowed them to come together only once a year (on the 7th day of the 7th month of the Lunar Calendar).

Tancred	I	30	Tancred of Brindisi (d. 1112), Norman
	II	60	crusader, famous for conquering Jerusalem
	III	139	in 1099. Became a prince of Tiberias and
	IV	188	Galilea, Antiochia and Edessa.
(Nosac) Tancred		373	
Tapiola		380	A suburb of Helsinki, the capital of Finland, and known for its famous garden. Also a name from Finnish mythology as described in the national legend ''Kalevala'', the name of the God of the Forest.

TARAGO in Scanmel (Scandinavian Middle East Line) livery, 18.6.1980   *W.S.P.L. Slide collection*

Tarago		295	Name of a place in New South Wales, Australia.
Tarantel		233	= Tarantella, a South Italian dance. The name derives from the Tarantula spider, whose bite was supposed to cause dancing-mania.
Tarcoola		323	A former gold mining town, about 310 miles west of Port Pirie, South Australia.
Tarifa	I	170	From the Arabic, ''a making known'',
	II	186	''information''. The southernmost point of Spain, about 25 miles W.S.W. of Gibraltar. Named after the Arab leader Tarik-Ben-Zeiad, who lived in the 8th Century and gave names to the villages of Tarifa and Gibraltar (Djeb-Al-Tarik = the mountains of Tarik).
Tarim	I	215	The largest river in Sinkiang province, China
	II	246	(over 1,300 miles long).
	III	281	
	IV	393	

TARN (II) at Hamburg, 29.5.1972

Joachim Pein

Tarim River		375	
Tarkwa		389	A city in Ghana, West Africa.
Tarn	I	163	A small mountain lake (Norwegian ''Tjern'',
	II	238	Old Norse ''Tjorn'' = a tear drop). Also, a river
	III	390	in France which is a tributary to the River Garonne.
(Willine) Taro		282	''Willine'' — see below.
			''Taro''. A boy's name (Japan), often given to the first-born son, particularly in former times.
Taronga	I	148	The name of the zoological garden in Sydney,
	II	165	N.S.W., Australia.
	III	263	
Tartar	I	199	Or ''Tatar'' — originally used to describe Asian
	II	251	Mongol tribesmen. Later used about all Asian
	III	289	races, and then for people whose language
	IV	392	was Turkish. Today, Tartar-or Tatar-indicates a native of Tartary, Krim-Tatar (which group of people is now deported) and some small groups of people in Siberia. Colloquially, the word ''tartar'' is used to describe a savage, intractable person, or a person of irritable temper.

TARONGA (II) at anchor in Sydney harbour with her bows pointing towards the Zoological Garden

David Finch

306

TAURUS (IV) *W.S.P.L.*

Tasco		195	The English rendering of Taxco, a town in
(Nosac) Tasco		365	south Mexico.
Tatra	I	171	The Tatras are a mountain range on the Polish-
	II	257	Slovakian border, the Slovakian part being
	III	318	known as the High Tatra (Vysoké Tatry).
			Always used in the plural form "Tatry", in
			both Polish and Slovakian.
Taurus	I	36	= The Bull, the name given to the second
	II	70	sign in the Zodiacal Constellation in the
	III	166	heavens. Also, the name of a mountain range
	IV	184	in Southern Turkey with many peaks above
	V	260	10,000 feet.
Teheran	I	224	The capital of Iran, situated south of the
	II	273	Elburz Mountains, seventy miles from the
			Caspian Sea. Founded in the 12th Century,
			it has been the capital city since 1788. The
			Teheran Conference between Churchill,
			Roosevelt and Stalin, held in 1943,
			represented the climax in military and political
			co-operation in World War II.
Tellus	I	35	"The world" (Latin). The Goddess of the
	II	85	Earth in Roman Mythology.
Tema	I	249	Seaport in Ghana, 27 miles east of Accra.
	II	230	Brought into use in 1962, it is today a major
			port.
Temeraire	I	144	A daredevil (French). The name of the second
	II	150	ship in Nelson's fleet at the Battle of Trafalgar.
	III	221	

TEHERAN (II) *W.S.P.L.*

Templar	I	14
	II	153
	III	244
	IV	262

A member of a religious military order (the Knights Templars) for the protection of pilgrims to the Holy Land, suppressed in 1312. Also a Lawyer with chambers in the Temple (City of London). The Good Templars = a temperance society. From the Latin ''templarius'' — of the temple.

TEMPLAR (II)

Tender Bali		346
Tender Banff		343
Tender Bay		349
Tender Behanzin		342
Tender Benin		344
Tender Bordeaux		355
Tender Bounty		352
Tender Bourgogne		359
Tender Captain	I	306
	II	335
Tender Carrier		301
Tender Champion		334
Tender Clipper		303
Tender Comet		333
Tender Commander		311
Tender Contest		314
Tender Fighter		370
Tender Gela		352
Tender Genova		349
Tender Power		310
Tender Pull		313
Tender Searcher		308
Tender Senior		307
Tender Tarpon	I	298
	II	350
Tender Tracer		354

Ships named ''Tender'' were support craft for the oil industry

TENDER TUNA *Ken Turrell*

Tender Trigger		302
Tender Trout	I	291
	II	338
Tender Trumpet		305
Tender Tuna		293
Tender Turbot	I	296
	II	339
Teneriffa	I	127
	II	203
Tennessee	I	130
	II	190
	III	280
	IV	322

Teneriffa — The largest of the Canary Islands. The highest peak in Spain, Pico del Teide, 12,200 feet, is located on this island.

Tennessee — From Cherokee ''Tenasi'' (the name of a village). The 16th state in the United States of America.

TENNESSEE (III) at Mombasa

309

Tennessee River		381	A navigable river in the U.S.A.
Terje Viken		61	The title of a famous poem by Henrik Ibsen (1828-1906).
Terrier	I	42	A breed of small dogs notable for their
	II	84	determination—A French word meaning
	III	218	"Earth Dog"—hunters of quarry
	IV	321	underground.
Texas	I	191	Name of a State and seaport of the U.S.A.,
	II	279	derived from the original Indian word "Tejas"
	III	317	= friend.
	IV	363	

THALATTA (I)

Thalatta	I	128	"The Ocean" (Greek)
	II	200	
	III	358	
Theben	I	209	Thebe, or Theba, a famous city in Ancient
	II	361	Greece described by Homer as the town of the seven gates, crowned with a profusion of flowers. In Greek mythology the town was named after Thebe, daughter of the River Asopos, which runs through the plain of Thessaly. Also, a city in Upper Egypt.
Thelma		77	Female Christian name (Northern Europe)
Themis	I	49	Goddess of law and justice in Greek
	II	86	mythology; married to Zeus.
	III	208	
	IV	360	
Thermopylæ	I	159	A mountain pass in Eastern Greece famous
	II	196	for the battle in 480 B.C. when the Persian
	III	324	invaders were defeated. The name is derived from the nearby warm sulphurous springs (= "Therme" in Greek) and "Pylæ", the Greek word for gates. In ancient times there were probably iron gates shutting the entrance to the narrow defile.
Thetis		8	An ocean nymphe, the wife of Peleus and mother of Achilles in Greek mythology. To make Achilles invulnerable she put him into the fire and the River Styx—but she held him by the heel, thus making that part of him vulnerable ("Achilles' heel").

Thode Fagelund	I	66	Thode Fagelund, born on 3rd March 1844,
	II	116	was a prominent Norwegian shipping man
			and a partner in the British firm H. Clarkson
			& Co. from 1880 to 1918. He was also a
			noteworthy public benefactor.
Thor		80	Tor: The Thunder God, in Nordic mythology
			the son of Odin. His weapon was the magic
			hammer Mjølner which, when thrown, always
			returned to him.
Thordis	I	55	Female Christian name (Norway). Formed
	II	76	from "Tor" = the Thunder God, and the old
			Norwegian "dis" = Goddess.

THYRA aground in Duncansbay   *K. J. O'Donoghue collection*

Thyra		54	Female Christian name (Norway and Denmark) = the Sanctuary of Tor, the Thunder God. Also female form of "Tyr". Queen of the Norwegian King Olav Trygvesson (968-1000), who in 994 attacked London with 94 ships and forced King Ethelred II to pay £16,000 to achieve peace. Became the Norwegian king in 995, and brought Christianity to Norway.
Tiber		212	The Latin name for Tevere, the river upon which Rome was founded in 753 B.C. and the longest river in Central Italy.
Tiberius		255	Claudius Nero Tiberius (42 B.C.-37 A.D.), Roman Emperor. Adopted son of Emperor Augustus, whom he succeeded in 14 A.D. His reign was prosperous for the Empire.
Tibetan	I	214	An inhabitant of Tibet, a country in Central Asia.
	II	250	
	III	284	
Tiger		44	An Asian animal, the largest of the cats. "Tigerstaden" (Norwegian) = Tiger-town", a common nick-name for Oslo, the dangerous and merciless big city (!), first used by Bjørnstjerne Bjørnson in a poem in 1870.

TIGRE (I) in the Nylands Verksted floating dock   *W.S.P.L. Slide collection*

Tigre	I	146	A river in Ecuador and Peru. Also, a former
	II	248	kingdom in Northern Ethiopia. Also, the nick-
	III	300	name of the French politician Georges
			Clemenceau (1841-1929). See also ''Tiger''.
Tijuca	I	145	Mountain, south-west of Rio de Janeiro.
	II	229	Tijuca Bay is an inlet in Southern Brazil. The
	III	336	name is derived from the Indian word ''Tuiuca
	IV	374	= a swamp or marsh.
Times		74	''The Times'', the London newspaper,
			regarded by many as Britain's premier journal.
			It was founded in 1785 by John Walker and
			was called ''The Daily Universal Register''
			until 1788.
Tiradentes		129	Joaquim Jose da Silva Xavier Tiradentes
			(1748-1790), a Brazilian patriot and national
			hero.
Tirranna	I	175	= ''Running waters''. The capital of Albania
	II	202	(Tirané). Also the name of a place in Australia.
	III	265	
Titania	I	50	The Queen of the Fairies, and wife of Oberon.
	II	131	From the medieval French poem ''Huon de
	III	172	Bordaux''. The theme was used by
	IV	242	Shakespeare in ''A Midsummer Night's
			Dream'', and by v. Weber in ''Oberon''.
Titus	I	227	(A.D. 40-81), Roman Emperor, son of
	II	312	Vespasian. The terrible eruption of Vesuvius
			occurred during the first year of his reign. He
			completed the Colosseum in Rome and in 70
			A.D. conquered Jerusalem.

TIRRANNA (II)

TOBA in the River Elbe, 17.10.1993   *Torsten Andreas*

Toba		330	A town in Japan, south-east of Tsu, and south of Nagoya.
Tobruk		258	A small seaport on the coast of Libya. During World War II it was taken by the Allies in 1941, besieged for a year and taken back by Axis forces in June 1942. It was finally captured by the South Africans in November 1942.
Toledo	I	147	Name of a province, town and mountain range
	II	232	in Central Spain. Also, the name of a city in Ohio State, U.S.A."Toledo" is probably derived either from the Latin "Toletum" ("Thol" = elevated + "Etum" = city) or from the Hebrew "Toledoth", meaning "Mother of the peoples". Juan de Toledo was a famous Spanish architect in the 16th Century.
Tolga		268	"The river running through the pine trees". (Norwegian)
Toluma	I	121	A mountain peak in Bolivia.
	II	228	
	III	367	
Tomar	I	187	The name of one of the oldest towns in
	II	358	Portugal, famous for the Castle of Templars and Convent of the Order of Christ, built in the 13th Century."Tomar" comes from the Greek "Ktoma" = to take possession of.
Tombarra		297	A mountain trout.

TOMBARRA in ScanCarriers livery, 23.8.1980   *W.S.P.L. Slide collection*

313

Tonga		268	An independent Polynesian Kingdom, consisting of about 150 islands called the Tonga, or Friendly, Islands. The country is governed by a Legislative Assembly, elected triennially, and a hereditary monarch. The climate is mild and healthy. Also the name of a light two-wheeled carriage—"Tanga" in Hindustani.
Tongala		327	The name of a stretch of the Murray River, about 150 miles from Melbourne, Victoria, Australia.
Tønsberg	I	32	"Tunsberg" in Old Norwegian, from "Tun" =
	II	234	fenced place, settlement, and "Berg" =
(Barber) Tønsberg		332	"mountain. The oldest town in Norway, and probably in all the Nordic countries, celebrating its 1100th anniversary in 1971. Many early Norwegian kings lived in Tønsberg Castle (Tunsberghus) for shorter or longer periods. Tønsberg again became a thriving town in the 19th Century as a centre for shipping and pelagic whaling (Svend Foyn). Today it is a busy and prosperous town, an Episcopal residence and centre for the County administration (Vestfold County). Tønsberg was the cradle of the firm Wilh. Wilhelmsen, and is still the port of registry of their ships.
Topeka	I	138	The capital of Kansas State, U.S.A.
	II	192	
Toreador		217	From the Latin "Taurus", Spanish "Toro" = Bull. The word "toreador" is not at all correct Spanish, but is probably an Italian "barbarism" from the opera "Carmen". The correct Spanish word for a bull fighter is "torero".
Tordenskjold	I	33	Peder Wessel Tordenskjold (1691-1720). A
	II	64	famous Norwegian naval officer, he was knighted in 1716 under the name Tordenskjold: "Torden" = thunder,"skjold" = shield.
Torino	I	243	= Turin, the ancient capital of the Italian
	II	387	kingdom, and now a major industrial city in the north of the country.
Toro	I	239	= A bull (Spanish). See also "Taurus".
	II	276	
	III	357	
Toro Horten		357	A city in Norway, south of Oslo. This ship was built by Horten Verft A/S, previously Marinens Hovedverft. The city is well-known for its naval activities and for the Naval Museum.
Toronto	I	151	The capital of Ontario province, Canada. Also
	II	220	the name of cities in Australia, Mexico and
	III	357	the U.S.A.
Torrens	I	176	A lake in South Australia, named after the
	II	261	Australian statesman Sir Robert Richard Torrens
	III	382	(1814-1884), who, as premier, introduced the public registration of land in Australia.

TORONTO (III) in American waters   *Rüdiger von Ancken*

Torsdal		81	Tor's dal (Norwegian) = The Thunder God's valley. See also ''Thor''.
Tortugas	I	134	The Dry Tortugas are a group of low coral
	II	179	islands about sixty miles west of Key West,
	III	278	Florida, U.S.A. and called Tortugas because of the many turtles in nearby waters.
Toscana	I	236	= Tuscany, a region and former kingdom in
	II	388	the centre of Italy, of which Florence is the main city.
Toulouse	I	164	A city in Southern France and an important
	II	245	political and intellectual centre from Roman times onwards.
Touraine		140	An ancient province of France, today part of the departement Indre-et-Loire. Because of its fertile soil, Touraine has been called ''The Garden of France'' and is famous for its good wines. The principal town is Tours.
Tourcoing	I	137	A French town on the border of Belgium, and
	II	181	one of the country's main textile centres.
	III	329	
Tournai		182	A commercial and manufacturing centre in south-west Belgium and former capital of the Merovingian-Frankish Kingdom. It was a Roman settlement under the Latin name ''Tornacum'' and in the 17th and 18th centuries was an important border fortress town.
Towada		206	A lake in Honshu, Japan.
Toyama		292	Town on Honshu Island, Japan, about 110 miles N.N.E. of Nagoya.
Toyo		208	= Far East (Japanese)
(Willine) Toyo		340	
Trafalgar	I	73	A cape on the south-west coast of Spain,
	II	174	famous for the battle on the 21st October
	III	194	1805, when Nelson defeated the Franco-Spanish fleet.
Transit	I	29	Moving from one place to another, passage.
	II	71	From the Latin word ''Transire'' = to go
	III	142	across.
Traviata		230	''La Traviata'', an opera by Verdi (1813-1901). ''La Traviata'' means ''The one who is led astray'' and the text for the famous opera is an adaptation from the novel ''La Dame aux Camélias'' by Alexandre Dumas fils.

TREASURE FINDER alongside the Shell/Esso Brent D platform

Treasure Finder		325	The prefix ''Treasure'' was given to the drilling rigs—the treasure being, of course, oil.
Treasure Hunter		309	
Treasure Saga		353	''Saga'' was the name of the Norwegian oil company—Saga Petroleum—which had the rig on charter from 1983 to 1993.
Treasure Scout		348	
Treasure Seeker		320	
Treasure Supporter		337	
Treasure Swan		341	
Treport		20	A seaport on the north-west coast of France.
Trianon	I	143	The French royal palaces—Grand Trianon and Petit Trianon—built in 1687 and 1755 in the great park of Versailles.
	II	237	
Tricolor	I	65	''Three colours''. The French national flag— blue, white and red—adopted during the French Revolution in 1789.
	II	75	
	III	141	
	IV	162	
	V	231	
	VI	290	
Trinidad	I	185	An island in the West Indies discovered by Columbus in 1498. The capital and chief port is Port of Spain. Also the name of several towns in Central and Southern America.
	II	274	

TRIPOLI as **KIMON**   *W.S.P.L.*

Tripoli		259	City and seaport of Libya, North Africa. The name derives from ''Three Cities'' (= Tri + poli) which included the old Roman cities of Oea (the site of Tripoli today), Sabratha and Leptis Magna.
Triton	I II	160 183	In Greek mythology the son of the sea-god Poseidon and Amphitrite, each of a race of minor sea-gods usually represented as men with fishes' tails and occasionally with horses' fore-feet, and carrying shell-trumpets.
Troja	I II III IV	161 247 231 323	= English ''Troy''. An ancient city in Asia Minor, the scene of the Trojan War. The Greeks finally captured the city by the stratagem of the wooden horse (''Trojan Horse'').
Trold		53	In modern Norwegian ''Troll''. A figure in Norwegian folklore—a gnome or monster— and plays an important part in most Norwegian fairy tales.
			See ''Trold'', above
Troll Forest	I II	282 391	
Troll Lake		287	
Troll Maple		347	
Troll Park		285	
Troll Viking		345	
Troms		241	A county of Norway whose name comes from the island on which Tromsø is situated. The name derives from the old Norwegian word ''Straume'' = stream or current because the island lies in a narrow strait with strong tides.
Troubadour	I II	117 213	A lyric poet of a class originating in Provence in the 11th Century, also a strolling singer of the same period. The name derives from the Provençal ''trobar'' = French ''trouver'' (to find) and the late Latin ''tropare'' = make poetry.
Tsu		319	= ''port'' (Japanese). Tsu city is the site of the Nippon Kokan shipbuilding yard, where this ship was built.

TUAREG (II)   *Alex Duncan*

Tuareg	I	207	The Arab name for Saharan Berber peoples,
	II	253	nomadic tribesmen of the Central and
	III	351	Western Sahara Desert, with the unusual
			habit that the men wear the veil day and
			night, and the women never.
(Rosa) Tucano		366	= Toucan, the famous South American bird
			with the very large beak.
Tuddal		82	A district in Hjartdal, Telemark county,
			Norway.
Tudor	I	158	An English dynasty from 1485 (Henry VII) to
	II	189	1603 (death of Elizabeth I); previously Welsh
			nobility. "Tudor" is probably the Welsh form
			of Theodore (Latin "Theodorus") = God's
			Gift.
Tugela	I	122	A river in Natal, rising in Mont aux Sources
	II	216	and flowing east into the Indian Ocean, north
			of Durban. The name Tugela comes from the
			Zulu word "Tukela" = startling—the Zulu
			description of the river when in full flood.
Tulane	I	178	A privately endowed, non-sectarian,
	II	256	university in Louisiana, U.S.A., established in
			1834, but named after Paul Tulane, its great
			benefactor in the 1880s.
Tungsha	I	136	A lightship and shoal off Shanghai. Also, a
	II	205	town in Kiangsu province, China.
Tungus	I	62	Derived from Tunguska, three rivers in central
	II	197	Siberia.

TUGELA (II)   *J. Y. Freeman*

TULANE (I), post war *W.S.P.L.*

Turandot		223	An oriental fantasy in verse by Carlo Gozzi, transformed into an opera (''Turandotte'') by Puccini. The story — which is to be found among all Indo-European peoples — originates from a Persian legend about a Princess Turandocht, who gives her suitors riddles to guess and when they cannot find the right answers, kills them.
Turcoman	I	210	Turkomen, Turkmen — a Turkish people living
	II	252	in the Republic of Turkmenistan. Some also
	III	286	live in Turkistan, in Afghanistan and in Persia.
Tyr	I	45	The ancient German god of war. Also a
	II	222	Norwegian word for ''bull''. See ''Taurus''.
	III	272	
Tysla	I	88	A river in Upper Rendal, Hedmark county,
	II	99	Norway, which joins the Finstada and
	III	240	becomes the river Rena (q.v.).
	IV	254	
	V	326	
Vinstra		91	A tributary of the Gudbrandsdalslågen, one of Norway's largest rivers. It has its source in lake Vinsteren, not far from lake Gjende. See also ''Sjoa'' and ''Bessa''.

VINSTRA *Norsk Sjøfartsmuseum*

Waterloo	46	A town in Belgium, the scene of the battle on 18th June 1815 in which Napoleon was defeated by the British and Prussian armies. Later used as a place-name in several Anglo-Saxon parts of the world (cf. Waterloo Station in London and Waterloo, suburb of Liverpool, etc.).
Willine Taro	282	''Willine'' is the trade name of the Line between the Far East and the Middle East established by Wilh. Wilhelmsen in 1971.
Willine Toyo	340	
Willine Tysla	326	
Yarra	102	A river in Victoria, Australia. Also, an Australian tree.
Zippora	13	Female Christian name (Hebrew)
Zurita	103	Jeronimo de Zurita, Spanish scholar and writer of the 16th century.

The Ro-Ro Vessels **TAMPA** and **TOBA** pass in the Panama Canal

D.NO. QR-6970-00

5,800 UNITS CAR CARRIER
OUTLINE ARRANGEMENT